Revenue and reform offers a reappraisal of Britist
third quarter of the eighteenth century. It is t:
1760s as a time when British politicians were pre
which eventually led to the outbreak of the American War of
Independence in 1775. Here, for the first time, a different imperial
problem – the Indian problem – is examined in detail. Politicians
struggled to come to terms with the East India Company's unexpected
acquisition of territory and great wealth in Bengal, and they endeavoured
to formulate policy related to many new and unfamiliar issues. New light
is shed on debate about revenue collection, territorial rights, diplomacy,
justice and administrative reform in order to illustrate the central theme
of the book: the gradual and reluctant assumption of responsibility by
ministers for the Indian empire. Firm guidelines for the development of
the Anglo-Indian imperial connexion were eventually laid down by
Lord North's Regulating Act of 1773, and the background to, and
principles underpinning, this important legislative landmark are fully
explored in the concluding chapters.

Revenue and reform: the Indian problem in British politics 1757–1773

Revenue and reform: the Indian problem in British politics 1757–1773

H. V. Bowen

Rugby School

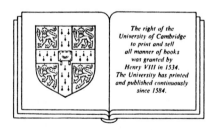

The right of the
University of Cambridge
to print and sell
all manner of books
was granted by
Henry VIII in 1534.
The University has printed
and published continuously
since 1584.

Cambridge University Press

Cambridge
New York *Port Chester*
Melbourne *Sydney*

PUBLISHED BY THE PRESS SYNDICATE OF THE UNIVERSITY OF CAMBRIDGE
The Pitt Building, Trumpington Street, Cambridge, United Kingdom

CAMBRIDGE UNIVERSITY PRESS
The Edinburgh Building, Cambridge CB2 2RU, UK
40 West 20th Street, New York NY 10011-4211, USA
477 Williamstown Road, Port Melbourne, VIC 3207, Australia
Ruiz de Alarcón 13, 28014 Madrid, Spain
Dock House, The Waterfront, Cape Town 8001, South Africa

http://www.cambridge.org

First published 1991
First paperback edition 2002

A catalogue record for this book is available from the British Library

Library of Congress Cataloguing in Publication data
Bowen, H. V.
Revenue and reform: the Indian problem in British politics,
1757-1773/H. V. Bowen.
      p.   cm.
Includes bibliographical references and index.
ISBN 0 521 40316 2 (hardback)
1. India – History – 18th century.   2. East India Company –
History – 18th century.   3. Great Britain – Politics and
government – 1760-1789.   I. Title.
DS471.B68   1991
954.02'9–dc20   90-22178   CIP

ISBN 0 521 40316 2 hardback
ISBN 0 521 89081 0 paperback

Contents

Tables

Preface

This book explores a neglected dimension of the British imperial experience: it seeks to examine how metropolitan decision-makers came to terms with the many problems stemming from the East India Company's unexpected acquisition of territory and wealth in Bengal during the 1760s. The book began its life as a doctoral thesis which was intended to up-date and revise Dame Lucy Sutherland's magisterial work on East India Company issues in eighteenth-century British politics. However, as I read contemporary newspapers, pamphlets, committee papers, and Henry Cavendish's reports of parliamentary debates, it became clear to me that historians, perhaps partly because of a preoccupation with the events leading up to the American War of Independence, have failed to address a number of important questions related to the response of British politicians to imperial activity in South Asia. The domestic trials and tribulations of the East India Company received a thorough examination from Sutherland, but the place of Indian issues in British politics has still not been studied in detail. This, therefore, is not simply a thesis dressed up for publication. Since completion of my thesis in 1986, I have refocused my sights, looked beyond the East India Company, and tried instead to place Indian issues in their proper political context. In doing so I hope to have presented here a fuller picture of what Sir Lewis Namier once described as the 'imperial problem' in British politics during the third quarter of the eighteenth century.

During the course of my research I visited a number of libraries and record offices around the country. I would like to express my gratitude to all those who made my task such a pleasant one, but it would be churlish not to single out the staff at the India Office Library and Records for special thanks: they provide a first-class service for historians of India. Part of the research was undertaken during my tenure of a Sir James Knott Fellowship at the University of Newcastle upon Tyne, and I must record my thanks to the Department of History for providing me with a safe and pleasant haven between 1985 and 1987.

I have to thank Olive, Countess Fitzwilliam's Wentworth Settlement Trustees and the Director of Sheffield City Libraries for permission to quote from the Wentworth Woodhouse Muniments, and the William L. Clements Library for allowing me to use material in the Lansdowne MSS. Mr Galen Wilson, the Curator of Manuscripts at the Clements Library, and Mr Alexander Hunter, the Archivist at Mount Stuart, provided invaluable help by answering detailed questions about the material in their care.

My thesis was supervised by Professor P.D.G. Thomas who guided, criticized, and encouraged with unfailing good humour. He has subsequently provided assistance far beyond the call of duty by reading the whole text several times in typescript. My debt to him is a very large one. Early drafts were also read by Professor P.J. Marshall, and I owe him thanks for his comments and many helpful suggestions. Philip Lawson first pointed me in the general direction of the East, while more recently Robin Barlow subjected the typescript to careful scrutiny: I am grateful to them both for their help. Needless to say, my greatest debts are those incurred close to home. My parents have unfailingly provided every form of support and assistance over the years. Similarly, my wife and children have made numerous sacrifices, and without their encouragement and patience I could never have completed my task. It is for these and many other reasons that I dedicate the book to Eileen, Emma, and Tom.

Abbreviations

Add. MSS:	Additional Manuscripts
BL:	British Library
Bodl.:	Bodleian Library
CJ:	*Commons Journals*
CO:	Colonial Office
Eg. MSS:	Egerton Manuscripts
FWIHC:	*Fort William – India House Correspondence and Other Contemporary Papers Relating Thereto* (21 vols., New Delhi, 1949–85)
HMC:	Historical Manuscripts Commission
HMS:	Home Miscellaneous Series
IOL:	India Office Library
IOR:	India Office Records
LJ:	*Lords Journals*
NLW:	National Library of Wales
PRO:	Public Record Office
RCHC:	*Reports from Committees of the House of Commons, 1715–1801* (15 vols., 1803)
WO:	War Office
WWM:	Wentworth Woodhouse Muniments

Unless otherwise stated, the place of publication of all works cited is London.

Introduction

Lord North's appointment as Prime Minister in January 1770 following the Duke of Grafton's resignation brought to an end a decade of political turmoil. Since George III's accession in 1760 there had been six administrations, and most of the leading political figures had played their part in a seemingly endless game of ministerial musical chairs. North, a most underrated Prime Minister, established a ministry which eventually lasted for twelve years, although at first it seemed unlikely that he would remain in office for twelve weeks. He needed all his good humour, political acumen, and debating skills (which were put to effective use in the lower House) to overcome the combined threat posed by the followers of former First Ministers Lord Chatham, George Grenville, and the Marquess of Rockingham. This talented opposition failed to press home its attack, and North found that the ministerial majority in the Commons grew steadily to almost a hundred. By February he was safe, much to the King's relief.[1]

Stability was much needed, and not only in the world of high politics. The ending of the Seven Years War in 1763 created a whole host of new economic, imperial, and political problems, many of which contributed, directly or indirectly, to the eventual outbreak of the War of American Independence in 1775. Economic recovery after the war was hampered by damaging credit crises in 1763 and 1772, and the national debt continued to spiral upwards, rising from £98 million in 1760 to £131 million in 1767.[2] Food shortages led to serious public disorder in 1766, while in the extra-parliamentary political sphere the rapid growth of metropolitan radicalism was based upon the extraordinary figure of John Wilkes. In a wider context there were difficulties related to British activity in Ireland, India and, above all, North America. Contemporary observers spilled a great deal of ink analyzing these problems and, while the historian must take care not to overstate the seriousness of the

---

[1] P.D.G. Thomas, *Lord North* (1976), pp. 33–51.
[2] *Parliamentary Papers*, LII (1898), 'History of the earlier years of the funded debt from 1694 to 1786', p. 301.

various crises, many believed that Britain was on the point of ruin and bankruptcy.

It was against this background that the affairs of the East India Company entered the political arena as an important and enduring issue. Problems related to the Company had held the attention of politicians before, but now, for a variety of reasons, Indian issues became a permanent feature in British politics. Between 1766 and 1773 the Company, its relationship with the state, its activities in India, and the behaviour of its servants, were subjected to the scrutiny of politicians and public alike. Full-scale parliamentary inquiries into British activities in India were carried out in 1767 and 1772–3, and they helped to pave the way for Lord North's fundamental reorganization of the way in which the East India Company conducted its political, administrative, and judicial functions on the subcontinent. The *Annual Register* was quite correct when it summed up this new preoccupation with British India by remarking in 1768 that 'The affairs of the East India Company were now become as much an object of annual consideration as the raising of the supplies.'[3]

While historians of Britain have recently been subjecting the eighteenth century to detailed examination and reinterpretation, historians of India have been undertaking an important revisionist task of their own. The past twenty years or so have seen a great deal of work devoted to a reassessment of modern Indian history and, as part of that process, there has been a significant reappraisal of the part played by British imperialism and expansion in the development of Indian society. In particular, it now seems quite clear that European forces or impulses were not, as was once thought by older generations of historians, the only, or even the most important, motors of change on the Indian subcontinent during the eighteenth and nineteenth centuries. Far more significance is now attached to factors such as climate, geography, trade, and local politics; factors which were ignored or given scant attention by those who sought to trace the seemingly inevitable and inexorable rise of British India.[4]

In spite of these great advances in our understanding of the relationship between British imperialism and indigenous change in South Asia, we still know very little about the way in which the tides of

---

[3] *Annual Register* (1768), p. 76*.
[4] C.A. Bayly, *Indian Society and the Making of the British Empire* (Cambridge, 1988) and P.J. Marshall, *Bengal: The British Bridgehead. Eastern India 1740–1828* (Cambridge, 1987). Both of these works are part of the *New Cambridge History of India* and present modern overviews of the subject, but of course countless other authors have contributed to the debate over the last two or three decades.

political and economic fortunes in India affected opinions, perceptions, and decision-making in Britain, particularly during the 1760s when the foundations of a large territorial empire were being laid in Bengal by the East India Company. In fact, the student has no choice but to rely on the study written by Dame Lucy Sutherland almost fifty years ago.[5] This is far from satisfactory for, although most of Sutherland's work has stood the test of time, her aim was not to consider Indian issues at length, but instead to analyze the position of the East India Company in its domestic political context. Sutherland herself noted that the problem (as defined by Sir Lewis Namier) to which she addressed herself was not that of 'the significance in the history of British imperialism of the territorial expansion [in India] in and after the Seven Years War'. On the contrary, she was concerned with an altogether different problem: an examination of 'the way in which a large financial, trading, and territorial corporation, itself undergoing great administrative and political strain, could be affected by, and itself affect, the intricate workings of politics at Westminster, and the unending struggle of the governments of the day to maintain the "connexion" on which their survival depended'.[6]

Sutherland observed that it is possible to discuss the East India Company 'with scarcely a reference to India'.[7] This is not my intention and hence I have attempted to avoid being drawn into an examination of the complexities of the Company's many internal political crises. Instead, I have focused upon the position in British politics of issues related to India and the Company's activities there. Of course one cannot entirely discount East India Company politics for, as I shall argue, what happened in the Company's General Court or Court of Directors was always of the greatest significance for national politics and the development of government policy towards India. But, even so, internal Company politics with all its related factional in-fighting and conflict is not granted the same indulgence as the central issues of this study: how did the British – Company servants, politicians, the press, and public – come to terms with the rapid and unexpected acquisition of a vast territorial empire in north-east India? What was the real and perceived value of the new acquisitions, and what were the benefits, if any, derived from them? How were British activities and relations with the indigenous population to be shaped and regulated in the future? Above all, was the Company able to fulfil its new role as a territorial proprietor in Bengal, and was it able to meet its new financial obligations to the British government?

[5] L.S. Sutherland, *The East India Company in Eighteenth-Century Politics* (Oxford, 1952). Much of the book was completed before the outbreak of war in 1939.
[6] *Ibid.*, p. v.   [7] *Ibid.*, p. 44.

Given this framework and these lines of enquiry, it is necessary to explore both ends of the imperial connexion. Hence, in the chapters that follow almost as much space has been devoted to the British in India as to Indian issues in British politics: one cannot be understood without the other.

1   Traders into sovereigns: the East India Company, 1757–1765

Between 1757 and 1765 the East India Company acquired a vast territorial empire in north-east India. Accordingly, the nature, direction, and purpose of British activity in India underwent a dramatic and lasting transformation. The Company, the sole legal vehicle of that activity on the subcontinent, ceased to be what it had been for more than a century and a half. It was no longer simply one of a number of European trading companies competing for Indian markets and goods but, instead, it found that it had evolved into a near-sovereign power in its own right. The British had become, rather to their surprise, the dominant military and political agents in Bengal and the surrounding area.

The general long-term process which prompted this transformation of the East India Company's position and status was unplanned, unforeseen, and extremely complex.[1] However, in the short term and within a strictly political context, British success and expansion was founded upon the overthrow of the Nawab of Bengal, Siraj-ud-daula, following the battle of Plassey in June 1757. This event and the establishment of a new political regime, the 'revolution' of 1757, elevated the Company to the status of influential powerbroker and kingmaker in Bengal, and this position was reinforced in 1760 when Mir Jafar was in turn deposed as Nawab in order to be replaced by his son-in-law Mir Kasim. The whole process of expansion culminated between 1763 and 1765 in the Company's successful military struggle against the combined forces of a disaffected Mir Kasim, the Mughal Emperor Shah Alam II, and the Wazir of Awadh Shuja-ud-daula, and a decisive victory at the battle of Buxar in October 1764 left the British as undisputed masters of Bengal.[2] In the meantime Mir Jafar had been reinstated as

---

[1] The literature on the dynamics of British expansion in Bengal is vast. The most recent, accessible, and authoritative study is that provided by Marshall, *Bengal*, esp. chs. 3 and 4.

[2] Detailed accounts of the Company's campaigns between 1763 and 1765 are to be found in H. Dodwell, *Dupleix and Clive: The Beginning of Empire* (1920, reprinted 1967), pp.

Nawab, but upon his death in February 1765 the Company installed his son, the entirely dependent Najm-ud-daula, in his place, thus confirming their position as the *de facto* if not *de jure* sovereign power in the province.[3] In short, the Company had become the power behind the throne, and this was spelt out in unequivocal terms when the new sixteen-year-old Nawab was informed by the Bengal Council that 'he receives and must hold the government by the influence and authority of the Company'.[4] However, the greatest prize of all was not forthcoming until August 1765, when the Mughal Emperor, recognizing the realities of the new political and military order, bestowed upon the Company the office of *Diwan* and the right to collect the territorial and customs revenues of Bengal, Bihar, and Orissa. Above all else, it was this particular development which served to focus political attention in Britain upon India and the East India Company.

Following its initial direct involvement in the politics of Bengal in 1757, the Company had been drawn further and further into problems related to the minutiae of local political, economic, and administrative life. As some contemporaries recognized, this process had developed a considerable momentum of its own which proved almost impossible to control or regulate, especially after 1760.[5] Whereas previously the Company had attempted to stand aside from direct involvement in such affairs, it now found itself in the decisive and lucrative role of supporting Indian individuals and factions against their political opponents. In effect this elevated the Company to a position of unrivalled influence, but it also served further to destabilize Indian politics by focusing the attention of the dethroned, dispossessed, and dissatisfied upon the Company. Consequently, the perpetual forming and re-forming of alliances that occurred after 1757 offered the region little prospect of any long-term stability. It caused much friction and tension; it disrupted trade; and ultimately it caused warfare on a massive and expensive scale.

The bankruptcy of the prevailing political situation became apparent to the more perceptive first-hand observers of the unfolding drama in Bengal. To men such as Harry Verelst, a member of the Bengal Council and later Governor of the Presidency, there was only one path that the

213–37; Sir J. Fortescue, *A History of the British Army* (13 vols., 1899–1930), III, 64–108.

[3] Dodwell, *Dupleix and Clive*, pp. 238–51; A.M. Khan, *The Transition in Bengal, 1756–1775: A Study of Saiyid Muhammed Reza Khan* (Cambridge, 1969), pp. 69–78.

[4] *Fort William – India House Correspondence and Other Contemporary Papers Relating Thereto.* XIV: (*Secret and Select Committee*) *1752–1781*, ed. A. Prasad (New Delhi, 1985), 162.

[5] H. Verelst, *A View of the Rise, Progress, and Present State of the English Government in Bengal: Including a Reply to the Misrepresentations of Mr. Bolts and Others* (1772), pp. 55–6. For a later expression of this view see D. Macpherson, *The History of the European Commerce with India* (1818), p. 190.

Company could now follow, and he later recalled that 'a decided superiority became the only means of safety.'[6] It was this as much as anything else that led to the Company's war against Mir Kasim and his allies being fought to the bitter end in 1765. For not only did this result in the temporary elimination of a significant military threat to the Company,[7] but it also led to the stabilization of the internal political situation in Bengal. The Company was now in a position of supremacy, and it was this that was recognized and codified in the treaties and *firmans* signed by Lord Clive on the Company's behalf at Allahabad in August 1765. Whereas the Company had refused the offer of the office of *Diwan* from the Mughal Emperor in 1758, 1761, and 1763, they were more than willing and able to accept it in 1765, for it confirmed and consolidated all the political and military advances that had been made during the previous decade.[8]

The political and administrative settlement established in Bengal in 1765 vested considerable power and influence in the East India Company. The Nawab was allowed to maintain only a small number of troops for ceremonial purposes, and the Company itself assumed responsibility for the defence of his former territories. The Company also now sanctioned the appointment of government officials. Most important of all, however, as *Diwan* the Company had been granted a key position in the loose administrative framework that made up the Mughal empire. In return for these privileges the Company had acknowledged the Emperor's *de jure* sovereignty over the provinces it now controlled and defended, and it had undertaken to guarantee the annual payment of a tribute of twenty-six *lakhs* of rupees from the Nawab to the Emperor.

Nevertheless, despite its considerable political success, the Company assumed few primary administrative responsibilities itself. Such a development was neither practicable nor prudent in the circumstances, and Clive had taken great care to distance the Company from involvement in the routine affairs of government and administration.[9] The Nawab continued to supervise the civil administration of Bengal, although in effect authority was devolved upon his deputy or *Naib*, Muhammed Reza Khan, who administered all policing and judicial affairs.[10] Moreover, the existing means and methods of revenue administration and collection were maintained, and they too were placed under the management of Reza Khan. The *Khalsa*, or office of revenue,

---

[6] Verelst, *A View of the Rise*, p. 56.
[7] The reduction of Shuja-ud-daula's strength was by no means considered final: *FWIHC*, IV: (*Public Series*), ed. C.S. Srinivasachari (New Delhi, 1962), 145.
[8] *Ibid.*, IV, xxxiv.   [9] *Ibid.*, IV, 337–8.
[10] Khan, *Transition in Bengal*, ch. 6.

acted as the focal point of the entire operation, with its offices at Murshidabad being entirely staffed by native officials. In effect, however, leading officials such as Reza Khan, Rai Durlabh, and Shitab Rai, 'who hold in their hands the most important employments of the government', were placed on the Company's payroll in 1767 when they were granted twelve *lakhs* of rupees a year between them in place of their 'traditional emoluments and perquisites which have always by the custom of the country been annexed to their station and offices'.[11] The actual collection of revenues continued to be farmed out to *zamindars*, who held hereditary privileges in such matters. Their payments to the central administration were settled each year at the *punyah* ceremony, and they paid their dues into the treasury on a monthly basis.[12] The Company's point of contact with the whole operation came only at the highest of levels. For this purpose Francis Sykes was appointed as Resident at the Nawab's Durbar at Murshidabad to oversee the revenue administration of Bengal, his brief being to eliminate all unnecessary expense and to identify and correct abuses. Similarly, although his position was considered to be subordinate to that of Sykes, the Company's chief at Patna supervised, with the assistance of Shitab Rai, the collection of revenue in the province of Bihar.

These arrangements were wholeheartedly endorsed by the Company's directors in London, and they asked only in addition that the Resident's activities be closely monitored and audited by the Select Committee at Fort William (Calcutta). Previous attempts by the Company to collect revenue in Burdwan province had not been particularly successful, and significantly less revenue had been forthcoming than when the system had been administered by the local authorities during the 1740s and 1750s.[13] Indeed, the lessons learned from this experience led the directors to assert that they were convinced as to 'how unfit an Englishman is to conduct the collection of revenues and follow the subtle native through all his arts to conceal the real value of his country to perplex and to elude payments'.[14] For this reason they were at first quite content to allow the onerous task of revenue collection to remain in native hands. In the short term, at least, the 'ancient form of government' was quite deliberately preserved.[15]

---

[11] *FWIHC*, V: (*Select and Secret*), ed. N.K. Sinha (New Delhi, 1949), 280.

[12] For a full description of the *zamindari* see Marshall, *Bengal*, pp. 53–8; and for a detailed account of the Company's initial attempts to administer revenue collection see *ibid.*, pp. 103–20.

[13] In 1764 the Company collected five *lakhs* of rupees less in Burdwan province than the Nawab Alivardi Khan had collected in 1752: *FWIHC*, IV, 186.

[14] *Ibid.*, IV, 184.

[15] Marshall examines in detail how these assumptions changed during the late 1760s. In particular, assessments of the Burdwan revenue-collection experience underwent a

In 1773 the Secret Committee of the House of Commons identified four main types of revenue from which the Company had benefited following the assumption of the *Diwani* in 1765: land rents, farms of exclusive privileges, fines and forfeits, and customs duties. The last item, they observed, was levied upon 'almost every article of life' at the discretion of the Nawab and *Diwan*.[16] Because of this, Clive was confident that after all the expenses had been met a large surplus would accrue to the Company from these revenues, and he predicted to the directors in September 1765 that in the forthcoming year there would be a 'clear gain' to the Company of £1,650,900 which would serve to 'defray all the expense of the investment [in goods for export], furnish the whole of the China treasure, answer the demands of all your other settlements in India, and leave a considerable balance in your treasury besides'.[17]

Clive was even more optimistic in the financial estimates he made to his friends and acquaintances. He told his close political ally George Grenville, for example, that the revenues, if properly managed, 'cannot fall far short of four millions per annum',[18] and he expressed similar sentiments in all of the fourteen letters he wrote on 29 and 30 September 1765, reporting the Company's assumption of the *Diwani*. While it remained to be seen whether such optimism could be justified in practice, Clive nevertheless had good reason to be satisfied with the progress that had been made since his arrival in India five months earlier. 'Revolutions', he informed the directors, 'are no longer to be apprehended'.[19]

For the sake of appearances, and not wanting to alarm her European rivals, the Company had left the Nawab in nominal control of his province, and there was little outward sign of the Company's accession to power. But informed contemporaries entertained little doubt as to where the source of real influence in Bengal now lay. The Company might not have procured *de jure* sovereignty over its new territory and possessions, for that still theoretically lay with the Mughal Emperor, but it did now exercise *de facto* sovereignty. This was the position as perceived and acknowledged by those within the Company itself. Indeed the prevailing balance of power and division of responsibility in Bengal allowed the Select Committee at Fort William to declare in January 1767 that 'the armies they maintained, the alliances they formed and the

significant revision as the shortcomings in Clive's settlement were gradually exposed: Marshall, *Bengal*, pp. 117–20.

[16] *Reports from Committees of the House of Commons, 1715–1801* (15 vols., 1803), IV (Nine reports from the Secret Committee on East India Company affairs, 1772–3), 95–6.

[17] *FWIHC*, IV, 338–9.   [18] NLW, Clive MSS 236, p. 13.

[19] *FWIHC*, IV, 337.

revenues they possessed procured them consideration as a sovereign and politic, as well as a commercial body'.[20]

Moreover, those in Britain outside the Company with an interest in Indian affairs were soon made aware of the realities of the new situation in Bengal. When Clive made his maiden speech in the House of Commons in February 1769 he paid particular attention to the Company's unrivalled position of power and influence. He spelt this out in simple terms: 'the great Mogul (*de jure* Mogul, *de facto* nobody at all)... The Nabob (*de jure* Nabob, *de facto* the East India Company's most obedient humble servant).'[21] As the imperial theorist Thomas Pownall concluded when he analyzed Indian affairs in 1773, 'The merchant is become the sovereign',[22] and this is perhaps the most appropriate brief summary of what had happened to the Company since 1757.

In spite of the fact that great advances were made in 1765, the general form and structure of the Company's presence in India remained largely undisturbed. Apart from Fort William, the Company possessed two other Presidencies, Fort St George (Madras) and Bombay. In theory these three centres of British activity were independent, self-governing trading settlements, and there was no central authority for the supervision of the Company's affairs in South Asia. To some observers, especially after the assumption of the *Diwani*, this situation was increasingly unsatisfactory. They argued that the needs and requirements of Madras and Bombay should be made subordinate to those of Calcutta, and that strategic and commercial planning for the Company's operations throughout India should be directed by those in control of affairs in Bengal. These arguments soon developed into calls for the appointment of a Governor-General for India to be based in Calcutta, for only then, it was argued, could a satisfactory overview of the Company's activities be obtained.[23]

The Company's affairs in Bengal were directed by a President and a Council which varied in size between nine and twelve members. In addition to this, a small Select Committee of four councillors, first

[20] *Ibid.*, V, 278. This letter contains a detailed elaboration of the workings of the political and revenue systems established in Bengal after the Company's assumption of the *Diwani*.   [21] BL, Eg. MSS 218, ff. 151–2.
[22] T. Pownall, *The Right, Interest, and Duty of Government, as Concerned in the Affairs of the East Indies* (1773), p. 3. Thomas Pownall (1722–1805), MP for Tregony 1767–74 and Minehead 1774–80, had begun his career as an administrator in North America, and had served as Governor of Massachusetts Bay between 1757 and 1759. Although regarded in some quarters as being rather tiresome and self-important, Pownall had established a reputation for himself as an influential expert on colonial affairs following the publication of *The Administration of the Colonies: Wherein Their Rights and Constitution are Discussed and Stated* (six editions, 1764–77).
[23] See Clive's speech of 27 Feb. 1769, BL, Eg. MSS 218, f. 157.

established in 1756 and then recreated by Clive in 1765, attended to matters which demanded secrecy. But those who served on the Council or Select Committee were not professional administrators in the true sense of the term. They were employed in the first instance to fulfil commercial functions and to make business decisions, and the structure of the Company's operation at Fort William continued to reflect this after the acquisition of the *Diwani*.[24] Yet individuals who had begun their careers as writers in the Company's service increasingly found that their roles demanded a knowledge of far more than just trade and commerce. In particular, after 1768 they needed to come to terms with the intricacies of revenue collection and administration.[25] The directors were thus keen to encourage their servants to learn Persian and Hindi so as to enable them to understand better the social and economic life of the territories they now governed.[26] But, even so, those in London frowned upon any attempts at full integration into the Indian way of life. This was made clear when they declared to the Bengal Council in 1769 that 'In your public system you seem to entertain the idea that the Company are to adopt the eastern parade and dignity, but we are of the opinion that European simplicity is much more likely to engage the respect of the natives than an imitation of their manners.'[27] The ultimate objective was to free Company servants from a dependence on Indian officials and intermediaries, thereby allowing them to develop and implement Company policy without recourse to what those in London saw as being corrupt 'asiatic' principles and practices of government. For the time being, however, this policy was undermined, if not contradicted, by the Company's reluctance to adopt primary administrative responsibilities itself: the system established in 1765 could not function at all without the active support and cooperation of thousands of natives throughout Bengal, Bihar, and Orissa.

The directors responded to news of the assumption of the *Diwani* on 17 May 1766 when they wrote to the Bengal Council and, separately, to Clive. In doing this they sought not only to congratulate their servants on their recent success, but also to establish guidelines for the future management of the Company's affairs in India which would serve to 'bring the great work to perfection'.[28] But while the directors introduced a wide range of new orders, rules, and regulations, they did not seek fundamentally to reshape the settlement of the Company's affairs already implemented by Clive. Indeed, they had no alternative course of action open to them. Having been presented with a *fait accompli* by

---

[24] There is much interesting information on the British way of life in eighteenth-century India in P. Spear, *The Nabobs: A Study of the Life of the English in Eighteenth-Century India* (Oxford, 1932). [25] See below pp. 112–15.
[26] *FWIHC*, V, 232, 237.   [27] *Ibid.*, V, 189.   [28] *Ibid.*, IV, 182.

Clive, they could do little else other than apply a seal of approval to a political and administrative order which, after all, had been in operation for nearly nine months.[29] They realized that it could well be dangerous to seek major alterations to the settlement and, in particular, the flow of revenues into the Company's treasury might be interrupted by the implementation of new policies or strategies. Effectively, therefore, it was Clive and not those in London who determined the general course and direction of the Company's activities during the next few years and, indeed, the directors were quite happy for a time to bask in Clive's reflected glory. However, when the 'dual system' began to fall into disrepute and disrepair the Company's unity of purpose began to disintegrate, and those in Bengal increasingly began to move out of step with those in control of the Company's affairs in London. As part of this process, Clive, who returned to Britain in 1767, found that his own relationship with the Company's directors deteriorated quite rapidly during the late 1760s and early 1770s as the limitations of his achievements, as well as his personal shortcomings, were gradually exposed by the press to the British public.

The Company's political and military successes brought into question the very nature of the British presence in India, for trade for trade's sake very rapidly became a thing of the past. From the mid-1760s the Company's primary objective was to secure as large a revenue surplus as possible and then to effect the transfer of that surplus to Britain. This posed innumerable practical problems, for it transpired that the only way in which the revenue surplus could be remitted to London was by investing that surplus in goods for export and subsequent sale at India House. As the Bengal Council noted to the directors in 1769, 'Your trade from hence may be considered more as a channel for conveying your revenues to Britain than as only a mercantile system.'[30] The Company was forced to reshape its commercial activities in order to serve the wider purpose of transferring a tribute, but in the short term it remained to be seen whether or not a revenue surplus could be realized at all.

One particular and immediate problem was that by 1765 the size of the Company's armed forces had far outstripped the ability to pay for them: the number of troops had risen from 3,000 in 1756 to 26,000 a decade later, and military expenditure in Bengal alone had soared from £377,002 in 1761/2 to £886,909 in 1765/6.[31] Because of this, the assumption of the *Diwani* was something akin to a gift from heaven to

---

[29] *Ibid.*, IV, 183–5.   [30] *Ibid.*, V, 11.

[31] G.J. Bryant, 'Officers of the East India Company's army in the days of Clive and Hastings', *Journal of Imperial and Commonwealth History*, VI (1978), 203; *RCHC*, IV, 60–1.

the directors. As they (if no one else) realized, the territorial revenues would not provide an immediate surplus, but would instead help to offset the huge military expenditure undertaken during the previous decade.[32] Indeed, the directors calculated that without this new source of income the Company would have been 'considerable sufferers' in 1766 and 1767.[33] Even so, while the *Diwani* revenues served the immediate short-term purpose of balancing the Company's books and underwriting the cost of recent expansion, there were few, even among the directors, who doubted that the Company would derive considerable financial benefit from its new role in Bengal. In the words of one director, Clive's success could well provide 'the salvation of the Company'.[34]

The Chairman of the directors in 1766, George Dudley, was more aware than most of the realities of the Company's new economic situation. In particular he was distressed at the manner in which the assumption of the *Diwani* had been represented in some quarters, most notably the City of London's money markets, as the acquisition of instant wealth by the Company. His opinion was that if the Company did not at once tackle the many new problems at hand it could well find itself 'in great affluence abroad and bankrupt at home'.[35] He therefore carefully defined the broad outline of the measures that the Company should adopt when he wrote to Clive in May 1766, following the arrival in Britain of news of the assumption of the *Diwani*:

[I] also induce…you to take every measure in your power to put them [the revenues] into a flow of cash, by sending home large quantities of goods, supplying the China supercargoes with great sums of money and providing Bombay with what ever treasure they may want, and lastly by drawing upon the Court of Directors for as little money as possible. These are the two grand points to be now attended to, for if we do not find ways and means to bring our great acquisitions to centre in England neither the Company nor the nation will reap the expected benefit from them. To send home gold and silver I apprehend would exhaust the country of its necessary specie in a few years.[36]

Such sentiments found consistent and repeated expression in the orders sent by the directors to the Bengal Council over the next few years. In particular they requested that special attention be paid to the trade in raw silk and fine goods, so that the Company 'through this channel may have the benefit of receiving as large a proportion of the Bengal revenues as circumstances will possibly admit of'.[37] All available finance was to be used to invest in these goods, and experimentation with

---

[32] For evidence that the territorial revenues were intended in the first instance to support 'the burden of war' see *FWIHC*, IV, 184.   [33] *Ibid.*, V, 10.
[34] NLW, Clive MSS 52, p. 179.   [35] *Ibid.*   [36] *Ibid.*
[37] *FWIHC*, V, 43.

new primary production techniques was encouraged. Each Company ship bound for Britain was to be loaded with as much 'surplus tonnage as she can carry consistent with her safety',[38] and specie left unused in the Bengal treasury was regarded as a wasted resource. Clive impressed this upon his successor as Governor of Bengal, Harry Verelst, when he told him in February 1768 that it was for the benefit of the nation as well as the Company that he should 'lay out the whole of your [revenue] receipts in goods'.[39] If surplus revenues could not be invested then they should be 'thrown into the Ganges'. The need to maximize investment of the surplus revenues in Indian and Chinese goods thus became the Company's primary concern after 1765, for without such investment the *Diwani* would remain little more than an unrealized asset.

Yet from the beginning of the Company's time as *Diwan* there were very well-defined theoretical bounds beyond which the directors in London would not permit their servants in Bengal to cross in search of further commercial, military, or political influence. Firstly, the 'dignity' of the Nawab was to be upheld at all times, and government was to be administered in his name and not the Company's. Secondly, the efforts to maximize revenue collection were in no way to 'oppress' the population, whose happiness and prosperity were held to be of paramount importance to the directors. For, as the directors reminded the Bengal Select Committee, 'it is upon their affections and confidence the permanency of our possessions will depend'. Finally, under no circumstances was there to be any further extension of the Company's territory: the only justification for offensive military action was that it would help the Company in the fulfilment of its treaty obligation to assist the Emperor and Shuja-ud-daula in the defence of their territories.[40]

Such was the scope of the Company's activities as defined by those in London in 1767 but, as ever, the directors could only hope that their instructions would still be relevant when they arrived in India after a six-month sea journey. Furthermore, as recent history illustrated, there was no guarantee that the Bengal servants would take the slightest notice of decisions made in London. Herein, perhaps, lay the real crux of what was shortly to become known in British political circles as the East Indian problem, because geographical factors alone provided the single greatest obstacle to those who were attempting to regulate and control the development of British activity in Bengal. A way had to be found of applying decisions made in London with some degree of consistency in India. If this could not be done then the pace and direction of British

---

[38] *Ibid.*   [39] NLW, Clive MSS 57 (no foliation).   [40] *FWIHC*, XIV, 15.

expansion would continue to be determined by those in the field, who might well be motivated by personal rather than corporate or national interest.

Few of those who had witnessed at first hand the events of 1757–65 would have dissented from Clive's opinion, advanced in February 1769, that 'the British nation there [in India] have been attended with a series of success almost unparalleled in any age'.[41] For the benefit of those in the House of Commons Clive contrasted the Company's position in 1769 with that of 1744 when he first stepped ashore at Madras. 'I was in India', he told the House, 'when the Company was established for the purposes of trade only, when their fortifications scarce deserved that name, when their possessions were within very narrow bounds, when under a despotic prince they had as many tyrants over them as they had settlements.' While he declared that 'it would be presumption in me' to claim responsibility for all the Company's success, he nevertheless painted a vivid sketch of how things now stood for the British in Bengal a quarter of a century later:

The East India Company are at this time sovereigns of a rich, populous, fruitful country in extent beyond France and Spain united; they are in possession of the labour, industry, and manufactures of twenty million of subjects; they are in actual receipt of between five and six millions a year. They have an army of fifty thousand men. The revenues of Bengal are little short of four million sterling a year. Out of this revenue the East India Company, clear of all expenses receives £1,600,000 a year.

Not all of those with an intimate knowledge of the Company's affairs endorsed this rosy picture,[42] but few would have questioned the basic fact that unprecedented political, military, and economic advances had been made in Bengal in recent years. The central issue now was that of how best to consolidate those advances and then apply the related economic benefits to the British nation as a whole.

[41] This and the following quotations are taken from BL, Eg. MSS 218, ff. 149–51.
[42] See for example the speech of one of the leading Company politicians, George Johnstone, *ibid.*, ff. 169–71.

2   Perceptions of empire

News of the Company's assumption of the *Diwani* arrived in London on
19 April 1766, and the stockmarket, always a sensitive barometer on
such occasions, responded in positive fashion at once. The price of
Company stock rose from 165 in mid-April to 186 by mid-June, and by
September it had reached 200. 'More money', commented *Lloyd's
Evening Post* on 28 April, 'was made on the buying and selling of India
stock following the late good news from Lord Clive than at any time
during the late war.' That was a fair assessment of the situation, but this
episode was in fact only the prelude to a bout of sustained speculation
in India stock which was to last for three years until it was abruptly
halted in 1769. Over a quarter of the Company's nominal share capital
changed hands during May 1766 alone, as investors and speculators
bought up stock in the hope that the financial fruits of Clive's success
would be made available to them in the form of increased dividend
payments. They were to be disappointed, however, because the
following month the Court of Directors refused to bow to pressure and
argued, quite correctly, that the *Diwani* revenues were as yet a potential
and not a realized Company asset. Accordingly, despite loud protests
from some of the Company's new stockholders, the dividend remained
at 6 per cent.[1]

Even so, the frenzied activity in Exchange Alley underlined the extent
to which informed sections of society were aware of the significance of
events in Bengal. This stands in marked contrast to the situation during
the Seven Years War, when even successful military operations in India
had passed almost unnoticed in the press.[2] Now the Company's
achievements were perceived as a cause for celebration. The news of the
Bengal settlement received full coverage in the provincial press,[3] and in

---

[1] H.V. Bowen, 'Lord Clive and speculation in East India Company stock, 1766',
Historical Journal, 30, 4 (1987), 905–20.
[2] M. Peters, *Pitt and Popularity: The Patriotic Minister and London Opinion During the
Seven Years War* (Oxford, 1980), p. 24.
[3] See, for example, *Newcastle Chronicle*, 26 Apr. 1766.

16

some towns there were enthusiastic public celebrations. The citizens of Bishop's Castle, Shropshire (the parliamentary seat of Clive's cousin, George) 'erected a canopy, under which was represented by fireworks in an elegant manner, Britannia supported by trade, with an Indian crown at her feet'.[4] For them, the Company's achievement was a matter of national pride: conquest and commerce had elevated the British to a position of unrivalled supremacy in north-east India.

Although the assumption of the *Diwani* had set the seal on a decade of spectacular political and military advances by the East India Company, steady commercial expansion in India had in fact been taking place over a much longer timescale. This was fully recognized by those with a particular interest in trade and commerce, and it was seen as part of a broad restructuring of British overseas activity which had begun in the early years of the century. Indeed, during the course of the eighteenth century Europe was gradually replaced as the major source and destination of British imports and exports. But such a decline was relative not absolute, and it resulted to a large extent from a marked increase in trade with the empire.[5] Within the context of this general pattern the contribution of India and the East Indies was important, but it was no greater than that from other parts of the empire. In 1770, for example, the volume of the Indian trade did not compare with the trade with the Caribbean, and its rate of growth was no greater than the trade with other parts of the globe. In short, British overseas trade continued to be dominated by the West Indies and North America.[6]

Some contemporary observers were well aware of these important developments in British commercial activity. The political economist Thomas Mortimer noted in 1772, for example, that 'a kind of revolution highly advantageous to Great Britain has taken place within the last twenty years in several branches of commerce which makes their different plans and states of her commerce with the four corners of the globe quite erroneous, and their theories founded thereon quite obsolete'.[7] In this scheme of things the East Indian trade played an important part, and Mortimer observed that 'on its present footing' it

---

[4] *Lloyd's Evening Post*, 25 May 1766.
[5] R.P. Thomas and D.N. McCloskey, 'Overseas trade and empire, 1700–1860' in R. Floud and D.N. McCloskey (eds.), *The Economic History of Britain Since 1700. 1: 1700–1860* (1981).
[6] K.N. Chaudhuri, *The Trading World of Asia and the English East India Company 1660–1760* (Cambridge, 1978), pp. 13–14.
[7] T. Mortimer, *The Elements of Commerce, Politics and Finance in Three Treatises on Those Important Subjects* (1780, reprinted from the 1772 edition), p. 131. Thomas Mortimer (1730–1810) was also the author of the best-selling guide to the stockmarket, *Every Man His Own Broker* (13 editions, 1761–1801).

was 'one of the chief sources of the power and commercial prosperity of Great Britain'. However, this was a view that did not win universal approval, for there were fundamental differences of opinion within the mercantile community over the true worth and value to the nation of Britain's Indian trade and possessions. These differences were based in the main on theoretical interpretations of how best the Indian trade should be organized, conducted, and regulated.

Few would have denied that, in theory at least, India was a great potential asset to Britain, but many were deeply committed to the view that the prevailing system of trade placed a heavy financial burden upon the mother country. As the Seven Years War had recently demonstrated, the cost to the nation of supporting the Company in military and naval terms alone could at times offset any of the benefits that the India trade might bring to the domestic economy. However, more important to many in the mercantile and nascent industrial community was the fact that the organization of the India trade was such that the balance was very much weighted in favour of goods imported into London: comparatively few British products and manufactures found their way to Asia.[8]

Critics of the Anglo-Indian economic relationship included anti-monopolists and free traders who had campaigned long and hard against the East India Company's privileged commercial position. They argued that only by releasing India from the Company's monopolistic grip would it become a source of sustained profit and wealth for the nation as a whole. They thus sought repeatedly to depict the India trade as a 'losing trade', and one of them wrote in 1767 that it caused 'more hurt to this nation than most people are capable of conceiving'.[9] The general position of the anti-monopolists was best summed up in 1772 when it was observed that they always castigated the Company as 'a pernicious establishment because...they exported our bullion, and very little of our natural products or manufactures, while they brought home great quantities of commodities perfectly manufactured, which hindered the consumption of our own'.[10] When, therefore, Adam Smith wrote in the *Wealth of Nations* in 1776 that he considered monopolistic companies 'nuisances in every respect' he was giving expression to a belief that was widely held in British business circles.[11]

[8] See below, pp. 110–11.

[9] Anonymous author of *An Attempt to Pay Off the National Debt by Abolishing the East India Company of Merchants and Other Monopolies With Other Interesting Measures* (1767), p. 20.

[10] Mortimer (not himself an anti-monopolist), *Elements of Commerce, Politics and Finance*, p. 130.

[11] Adam Smith, *An Inquiry into the Nature and Causes of the Wealth of Nations* (1776) eds. R.H. Campbell, A.S. Skinner, and W.B. Todd (2 vols., Oxford, 1976), p. 641.

Of course, many of the Company's critics and enemies were motivated by animus founded upon commercial self-interest. They were traders and merchants in London and the provinces who were denied access to markets east of the Cape of Good Hope. Accordingly, throughout the period there was a steady stream of petitions from outlying ports such as Aberdeen, Bristol, Dublin, Exeter, Glasgow, Hull, and Liverpool calling for the revocation of the Company's charter.[12] But there was also a significant, long-standing, political motive within the campaign against the Company's privileged position. The radicals of the 1760s, like the 'country' opposition earlier in the century,[13] entertained deep suspicions of the Company and its close financial links with the government: payment by the Company for the periodic renewal of its charter was held to promote an unhealthy alliance based upon the interdependence of the two parties. A torrent of unrelenting criticism poured forth from the pages of the *Middlesex Journal* and the *London Evening Post*, and this served to reinforce these suspicions: corruption, patronage, and ministerial interference in the Company's affairs were identified as the main, debilitating, characteristics of the state–Company relationship. Finally, the Company's critics added a new dimension to their attack during the 1760s, when news of crimes perpetrated by the Company's servants in Bengal became known in Britain. The Company was no longer simply a representative of the metropolitan monied interest; to some it had become an active and uncontrollable agent of corruption and repression within the empire.

The anti-monopolists found a staunch ally in William Beckford, MP for, and Lord Mayor in 1770 of, the City of London. Throughout the 1750s he had taken advantage of every opportunity to attack the Company, and he made his sentiments known in no uncertain terms during the course of debates in the House of Commons.[14] This continued into the 1760s, and when, in November 1766, Lord Chatham initiated the first parliamentary inquiry into the Company's affairs and entrusted the conduct of the business in the Commons to Beckford, it struck fear into the hearts of all those closely connected with the Company. As recently as February 1766 Beckford had used a debate in the Commons as

an opportunity to abuse the Company as an unconstitutional monopoly, and [he declared] that their conduct merited the enquiry of Parliament; that they had a revenue of two millions in India, acquired God knows how, by unjust wars with

---

[12] *Gazetteer*, 3 Mar. 1768, 8 Jan. 1773; 'Letter from Liverpool', *London Evening Post*, 26 Mar. 1767; letter from 'Hampden', *ibid.*, 18 May 1773; *Gentleman's Magazine*, 1768, p. 91.
[13] H.T. Dickinson, *Liberty and Property: Political Ideology in Eighteenth-Century Britain* (1977), pp. 171–3.   [14] Sutherland, *East India Company*, pp. 30–1.

the natives. That their servants came home with immense fortunes obtained by rapine and oppression, yet the proprietors received no increase of dividend; that it was necessary to know how those revenues were consumed and whence these oppressions so loudly talked of.[15]

Beckford's anti-monopolist sentiments were thus woven into a patchwork of criticisms of the Company, and this undoubtedly struck a chord outside Parliament as well as in it. This was illustrated quite clearly when Beckford chose to make opposition to the Company a central theme in his successful campaign in London during the general election of 1768.[16]

In spite of the vociferous condemnations of the Company by critics like Beckford, the attacks of the anti-monopolists came to nothing. The various interest groups involved never managed to co-ordinate anything remotely resembling a sustained campaign of action, and their petitions had little effect upon those in government.[17] However, their efforts did serve to focus attention upon the question of the Company's contribution to the domestic economy, and considerable thought was devoted to how the Company could improve the performance of its commercial operations within the existing organizational framework and terms of reference. The anti-monopolists thus did not themselves monopolize the debate about the Company's trading activities. A number of writers, some of whom of course were closely connected with the Company,[18] were to be found well to the fore in the defence of the status quo.

Among these writers was Thomas Mortimer who launched a vigorous attack on those who advocated opening a 'free' trade with India. Advancing on a broad front, he argued that the claims of the anti-monopolists belonged to an economic world of the past. More specifically, he argued that the Company itself had put the Indian trade on a new footing since the 1750s and now sent to the subcontinent 'a considerable quantity [of goods], consisting of a variety of articles'. In Mortimer's view, this development represented part of the revolution that had occurred in British overseas trade since the 1750s.[19] In its Asian context this revolution was closely related to, and, indeed, dependent upon, the transformation that had taken place in the Company's political

---

[15] NLW, Clive MSS 52, p. 152: report sent to Clive by his close friend and aide Luke Scrafton.   [16] *Gazetteer*, 22 Mar. 1768.

[17] See, for example, Lord North's response to a petition presented to the House of Commons by the inhabitants of Ilminster, Somerset on 16 Dec. 1768, BL, Eg. MSS 216, p. 16.

[18] For a vigorous defence of the Indian trade as organized and conducted in the early 1770s see A. Dalrymple, *A General View of the East India Company* (1772).

[19] Mortimer, *Elements of Commerce, Politics and Finance*, pp. 130–1.

and economic role in Bengal. The old commercial patterns, principles, and methods, which have been fully examined and analyzed by K.N. Chaudhuri,[20] were reshaped and revised in order to serve the new purpose of transferring the territorial revenue surplus to Britain. A great stimulus was given to the Indian trade as attempts were made to improve the quantity and quality of goods in order to put the *Diwani* revenues 'in train'.

The hopes of the anti-monopolists can be seen to have suffered a significant setback when new and very different conditions and patterns of British trade with India were established after 1765. If the Company's monopoly was now broken, not only would the Indian trade be restructured, but the Company's position as revenue collector would be undermined. Even if the trade was only partially opened to independent British traders such action would deny the Company access in some degree to the goods and markets that were necessary to lubricate the entire revenue collection and transfer system. In effect, the acquisition of the *Diwani* confirmed, for the time being at least, the Company's position as a monopolistic commercial organization. The Indian trade was not the concern only of the Company, for the territorial revenues were now perceived in many quarters as being a national and not a sectional asset.[21] To interfere with the state–Company relationship by adjusting the conduct and organization of the India trade would upset the financial arrangements by which, after 1767, the nation derived a direct, fixed, financial contribution of £400,000 a year from the Bengal revenues. Thus, despite Beckford's threats, there was never any real prospect of any concessions being made to the free trade lobby: far too much was at stake. Few in government would not have endorsed the sentiments of the pamphleteer who wrote in 1770 that 'A renewal of their [the Company's] charter will be the surest means of securing their acquisitions to this country, and promoting its trade to [India].'[22] It is hardly surprising that the free trade question was placed on the very margins of political debate after 1766: developments in Bengal had in fact overtaken the anti-monopolists. At no time was the Company's privileged position more secure than in the mid-1760s. It remained that way until the 1790s.[23]

[20] Chaudhuri, *Trading World of Asia*.
[21] See, for example, *An Address to the Proprietors of India Stock, Showing from the Political State of Indostan the Necessity of Sending Commissioners to Regulate Their Affairs Abroad* (1769), p. 30; Speech of Richard Fitzpatrick during the debate on the Address: 26 Nov. 1772, BL, Eg. MSS 242, p. 14.
[22] *An Essay on the East Indian Trade and its Importance to This Kingdom: With a Comparative View of the Dutch, French, and English Companies* (1770), p. 65.
[23] P.J. Marshall, *Problems of Empire: Britain and India 1757–1813* (1968), pp. 90–1.

By the late 1760s India had been well and truly woven into the economic fabric of the British empire. Of course the Indian connexion had always been valued in its commercial context, but the financial benefits derived from territorial acquisition on the subcontinent were now held to play an increasingly important part in the workings of the domestic economy. At a time when the level of national debt appeared to be spiralling ever-upwards, the prospect of partial relief in the form of overseas revenue collections was welcomed in most quarters. Thomas Pownall noted this in 1773 when he observed that

People now at last begin to view those Indian affairs, not simply as financial appendages connected to the Empire; but from the participation of their revenues being wrought into the very composition and frame of our finances...people in general from these views begin to see such an union of interest, such a coexistence between the two, that they tremble with horror even at the imagination of the downfall of this Indian part of our system; knowing that it must necessarily involve with its fall, the ruin of the whole edifice of the British Empire.[24]

There was some justification for this view, especially in light of the fixed sum the Company was supposed to pay into the Treasury each year. Even so, the net value of the contribution made to the domestic economy by finance, corporate or private, derived from Bengal should not be exaggerated. The Company could not sustain for long the level of payment to the state agreed in 1767, and recent detailed research has exposed the myth of vast personal fortunes flooding into the country from Bengal following the revolution of 1757. The notion, for example, that the industrial revolution was initially funded by the ill-gotten gains of a handful of nabobs is fanciful.[25]

Nevertheless, contemporary financial experts such as George Grenville were firm in their belief that wealth derived from India did much, or could do much, to relieve the burden imposed upon government by the national debt. Indeed, in 1769 he went as far as to claim that India represented 'perhaps the last stake of our finances'.[26] Similarly, the anonymous author of a well-received pamphlet on Indian affairs wrote in 1773 that the loss of India would lead to 'national bankruptcy; or, which is the same thing, a stop to the payment of interest on the national debt'.[27] Such concerns were well-founded and quite legitimate, for East

---

[24] Pownall, *The Right, Interest, and Duty of Government*, p. 4.
[25] P.J. Cain and A.G. Hopkins, 'The political economy of British expansion overseas, 1750–1914', *Economic History Review*, 2nd ser., XXXIII (1980), 464 (n. 8), 471.
[26] See, for example, his speech of 27 Feb. 1769, BL, Eg. MSS, 242, pp. 172–9. Quotation from p. 176.
[27] Author of *The Present State of the British Interest in India: With a Plan for Establishing a Regular System of Government in that Country* (1773), quoted in *Monthly Review*, 48

India Company finance played a key, if not leading, role in the London money market, and events in India often served to condition general price trends. As Thomas Mortimer remarked, 'The return of great wealth, derived from Asiatic commerce and territorial jurisdiction [is one of] the chief events which may make the funds rise above five per cent from the concourse of purchasers, who will find no other channels for employing their money to equal advantage.'[28]

With the Company's stock worth about £11 million at market prices in 1769, a setback in India could place a considerable amount of investment capital at risk. Grenville remarked upon this in February 1769 when he observed in the House of Commons that in the event of the commencement of war in India the 'whole eleven millions of money should be blown up into the air at once'. Consequently, he doubted whether the City in general could survive such a heavy loss.[29] His theory was soon put to the test because, only three months later, India stock prices crashed following the arrival in London of news of military reverses suffered by the Company in the Carnatic at the hands of Haidar Ali. Many speculators sustained heavy losses, and other prices fell, but, fortunately for the City, a general financial crisis was averted.[30] Even so, an incident such as this served only to draw attention to the indirect financial consequences of imperial activity, and this led Grenville and like-minded observers to argue that the state should assume greater responsibility for the Company's general security.[31] Others who were perhaps less well informed were to receive a rude awakening in 1772 when the Company came very close to financial collapse and ruin.

To many of those in Parliament news of British success in Bengal was a welcome but rather surprising and unforeseen development. The few MPs with expert knowledge of the Company's operations thus found themselves addressing an audience who understood very little about the realities of the situation in the east: there was a need for very basic information to be made available. Accordingly, when Lord Clive made his maiden speech in the Commons he took it upon himself to describe at length to the House 'the vast importance of this Company to the nation'.[32] The effect of this speech upon Clive's audience may be judged from Edmund Burke's reaction to it. After Clive had presented a detailed exposition of the economic benefits derived from the Company's

(1773), 99. For a similar view see J.H. Grose, *A Voyage to the East Indies*, quoted in *Gentleman's Magazine*, 36 (1766), 308.

[28] Mortimer, *Elements of Commerce, Politics, and Finance*, p. 409. For the movement of average annual stock prices see P.E. Mirowski, 'The rise (and retreat) of a market: English joint-stock shares in the eighteenth century', *Journal of Economic History*, XLI (1981), 569–70.   [29] BL, Eg. MSS 218, pp. 175–6.

[30] See below, pp. 76–7.   [31] BL, Eg. MSS 218, p. 177.   [32] *Ibid.* p. 149.

trading operations and revenue collection, Burke rose to thank him for his great service to the House. In doing so, Burke indicated that Clive had opened for the first time many Members' eyes to the economic potential of India. 'He has', said Burke, 'laid open such a world of commerce; he has laid open so valuable an empire, both from our present possessions and future operations; he has laid open such additional manufactures and revenues, as I believe never was laid before any committee in so short words.' 'The Orient sun', he concluded, 'never laid more glorious expectations before us.'[33]

Burke, of course, was later to develop a keen interest in, and knowledge of, the Indian empire,[34] but in these early days he was particularly impressed by the material advantages that he thought could be derived from the Company's activities in Asia. In 1772 he quantified these advantages for the benefit of the House of Commons, and in passing he contrasted the situation in the east with other parts of the empire. The Company, he declared, have 'extended the commerce, they h[ave] given you an army of thirty thousand men, they h[ave] given you fifteen millions of subjects, they h[ave] given you a fleet of ninety sail. They h[ave] given you four hundred thousand pounds wh[ich] is more than the surplus you draw [from] all the other parts [of the empire] put together.'[35] Others were not convinced, and argued that the cost of maintaining, supporting, and protecting the Company far outweighed these advantages[36] but, superficially at least, the Indian empire was beginning to represent an attractive economic proposition to many British politicians. They had only to consider the deepening political crisis in North America in order better to appreciate the benefits accruing from British activity in India. While successive ministries became embroiled in conflict with the American colonists over revenue collection and the payment of officials' salaries,[37] there were, or seemed to be, no such problems within an Indian context. From 1767 the state was supposed to receive a substantial annual sum from the Company without being drawn into areas of imperial activity such as revenue collection or territorial administration. To ministers this must have

---

[33] *Ibid.* p. 162.
[34] For the development of Burke's views see P.J. Marshall, *The Impeachment of Warren Hastings* (Oxford, 1965), pp. 1–2; and P. Langford (ed.), *The Writings and Speeches of Edmund Burke*, II: *Party, Parliament and the American Crisis 1766–1774* (Oxford, 1981), 23–4.   [35] Speech of 30 March, BL, Eg. MSS 239, pp. 265–6.
[36] See, for example, Isaac Barré's speech in the House of Commons on 27 Feb. 1769 in which he calculated that it had cost the state £4½ million in aid to enable the Company to achieve its present position in India, *ibid.* 218, p. 124.
[37] See, for example, P.D.G. Thomas, *The Townshend Duties Crisis: The Second Phase of the American Revolution 1767–1773* (Oxford, 1987), pp. 242–6, 253–4.

seemed to represent the ideal form of imperial relationship: wealth without responsibility, and empire without expenditure.

In view of Bengal's changing economic status within the imperial order, and given that from time to time during the late 1760s Britain's North American possessions appeared to be on the point of being lost,[38] it became imperative to some that India be more securely attached to the empire. Imperial integration was taking place within a financial context in the sense that resources from India were being transferred for use within the metropolitan economy, but there was now a need further to develop integration in both an administrative and a strategic sense as well. It was necessary to consider India as something more than simply an economic asset out on a very distant geographical limb. As one pamphleteer reminded his readers in 1769, 'the Company's dominions in the East are part of the British Empire, and that unless the state views the transactions of that country as that of the great body of the nation, there is wanting that harmony and universal bond of interest which secures the prosperity of national affairs'.[39]

Close observers of imperial politics such as Clive, Thomas Pownall, and Sir George Colebrooke identified a pressing need to consider British overseas interests as a single entity and not as a series of independent administrative and commercial units. Of course Britain, and London in particular, already acted as an entrepôt, but if the far-flung possessions and colonies could be brought together in a better-organized and well-ordered system of trade one important benefit would be a general tightening of the imperial knot. In this way losses in one sphere of operations could be offset by commercial gains and profits in other areas.

Colebrooke, Chairman of the East India Company, made this point in the Commons in 1769. Warning that diverse, economically independent colonies bred inevitable weakness, he called for strength through trade: 'Open a connexion between the East Indies and America... You cannot be sovereigns in one part and merchants in another. All India should be combined into one system.'[40] A similar, albeit isolated, appeal was made by Pownall who called for government assistance and intervention in order to place trade between India and the British Atlantic empire on firm, well-regulated, and permanent foundations.[41] But such pleas fell on deaf ears and, when an attempt was made in 1773 to open the North American market to Company tea, it was not intended as the

[38] Letter from Clive to Claud Russell, 10 Feb. 1769: NLW, Clive MSS 61 (no foliation). The letter continues in vol. 62.
[39] *Address to the Proprietors of India Stock*, p. 30.
[40] Speech of 27 February, BL, Eg. MSS 218, pp. 134–5.
[41] Pownall, *Administration of the Colonies* (4th ed., 1768), pp. 306–7.

development of a larger system of trade. Instead it was little more than a short-term expedient measure designed to reduce the massive tea stockpile in the Company's London warehouses.[42]

Clive complained in bitter terms in 1769 that few politicians had the breadth of vision that was necessary to develop an overview of British imperial interests. In fact he went as far as to declare that Lord Chatham and George Grenville were 'the only men capable in my opinion of embracing such ideas which ... are extensive ones'.[43] During the last few years of his life Clive became increasingly frustrated by the fact that most contemporaries continued, quite correctly in many ways, to view the North Atlantic empire and the newly won Indian empire as representing very different and discrete forms of imperial activity. This state of affairs was reflected at the most simple of levels in the structure of the government's decision-making machinery in London and, although Pownall made repeated calls for the establishment of a colonial office,[44] there was little or no attempt to consolidate and rationalize the many offices, agencies, and departments to which the problems of empire were referred. Indeed, in some ways the situation became worse rather than better following the creation of a new American Department under Lord Hillsborough in January 1768. Previously North American and Indian affairs had both been handled in the first instance by Lord Shelburne's Southern Department, but the two areas of policy-making were now separated, with only the latter remaining under the Southern Secretary's supervision. As if to add further to this division of administrative labour, domestic East India Company problems continued to be dealt with by the Treasury. Throughout the period, therefore, no minister was ever able to keep himself fully informed about Britain's fluctuating worldwide imperial fortunes.

The basic problem confronting those who had a vision, however blurred or partially formed, of a global British empire incorporating the recently acquired Indian possessions was that of overcoming sectional interests and prevailing prejudices. No matter how great the benefits derived from the Indian empire were thought to be during the late 1760s, it remained an undisputed fact to most contemporaries that British imperial strength was founded primarily upon the North Atlantic connexion. Furthermore, the association with the North American colonies had been strengthened over the course of two hundred years or so by a number of cultural, intellectual, and political

---

[42] See below, pp. 151–3. This issue is discussed in its North American context by Thomas, *Townshend Duties Crisis*, pp. 246–57.

[43] Clive to Claud Russell, 10 Feb. 1769, NLW, Clive MSS 62 (no foliation).

[44] Pownall, *Administration of the Colonies* (4th ed., 1768), pp. 10, 14–15, and 121.

ties that were not to be found in the relationship with India.[45] Such ties were not easily cast aside.

That North America was perceived to be in a pre-eminent position in the imperial order is revealed by the comparisons some observers made of the relative importance of India and the American colonies to Britain. The publication in 1770, for example, of the anonymous pamphlet *The Importance of the British Dominions in India Compared with that in America* prompted a vigorous and detailed response from Thomas Mortimer. Mortimer, as already noted, was well aware of the full potential value of the East India Company's possessions, but he nevertheless refuted the contention that Bengal is 'capable of yielding to Britain in return for her small share of attention, not only more rich, but also more durable benefits than all her other foreign possessions'.[46] Instead he argued in forceful terms that not only did North America yield greater benefits to Britain than India but, ironically in view of what was to happen a few years later, that they were more stable and durable than those to be found in Asia. 'Upon the whole', he concluded, 'our American colonies are established upon the truest principles of commerce and they are the primary source of the maritime strength, riches and prosperity of Great Britain; and that our East India factories are the second efficient cause of her immense opulence.'[47]

The Chancellor of the Exchequer, Lord North, made a similar point in December 1768 when he declared to the House of Commons that there were 'two great national questions, the state of the East India Company and the affairs of America'. He then added the important qualification that they were 'great in a different degree; for important as the East may be, in point of revenue it cannot be put in competition with America'.[48] This was a widely held belief and it served to condition much contemporary political thought on imperial issues. The attention of most observers in the 1760s was still firmly fixed on the west and on the problems of empire in British North America.

Even though India was destined to be cast in the political and imperial shadow of North America until the loss of the thirteen colonies in 1782, there was nevertheless a remarkable upsurge in interest in the subcontinent during the immediate post-*Diwani* period. However,

[45] F.D. Van Aalst, 'The British view of India, 1750–1785', unpublished Ph.D thesis, University of Pennsylvania, 1970, pp. 4–5.
[46] Mortimer, *Elements of Commerce, Politics and Finance*, p. 162.
[47] *Ibid.*, p. 170.
[48] Speech of 7 Dec. 1768 on William Beckford's motion for papers relating to unrest in America; R.C. Simmons and P.D.G. Thomas (eds.), *Proceedings and Debates of the British Parliaments Respecting North America 1754–1783* (6 vols., New York, 1982 to date), III, 36.

much of this interest was extremely narrow in focus, and it was concentrated not on Indian society as such, but rather upon the East India Company and its various points of contact with the indigenous population, economy, and culture. As the *Annual Register* noted in 1767, 'Everything relative to them [the Company] was now laid before the public; the exact state of their immense property became known to all persons; their most private secrets were unveiled; their charters, their rights, their possessions, their conduct at home and abroad, their dispatches and their utility to the nation were now matters of eager and public discussion.'[49]

The reading public had access to a wide range of travel and topographical books and articles about Asia, but knowledge of Indian languages, customs, art, and literature remained limited, and to a large extent restricted to the few who benefited from the scholarly or practical application of such information.[50] On the other hand, as perceptions of India's economic potential altered, so details of revenue collection, customs duties, and commercial activities were provided through pamphlets and articles written by those with an inside knowledge of the Company's affairs. This resulted in a better understanding of the nature of the British presence in India, a point made by MP Isaac Barré in 1769 when he reminded the House of Commons that before 1767 'not only Parliament, but the nation at large, were perfectly ignorant of the state of our affairs in India, knew nothing of the expenses that the Company were put to in the different establishments, knew nothing of the revenues rising from the territories in their possession'.[51]

Disputes between Company servants in India prompted the production of many partisan books and articles designed to influence public opinion, and these works provided much incidental information related to the general context of the Company's activities. Books written by disaffected servants such as William Bolts, Alexander Dow, Henry Vansittart, and Harry Verelst were well received by a reading public that was already outraged by reports of the vast personal fortunes accumulated by some leading British figures in Bengal. Indeed, such was the influence of these works that they played an important part in the events leading up to the establishment of the parliamentary Select Committee on Company affairs in 1772.[52] But, in the main, however, this interest in India was prompted by general concern about the Company's affairs, and there were, for example, few expressions of concern about the effects of British activities upon the indigenous

---

[49] *Annual Register*, 1767, p. 43.
[50] P.J. Marshall and G. Williams, *The Great Map of Mankind: British Perceptions of the World in the Age of Enlightenment* (1982), pp. 74–8.
[51] Speech of 27 Feb. 1769, BL, Eg. MSS 218, p. 114.   [52] See below pp. 95–6.

population. From time to time passing reference was made to the downtrodden nature of Indian society, but the issue remained a secondary one and no sustained case was ever made against the Company's administration on humanitarian grounds.

These perceptions of British activity in India, indeed of British imperial activity in general, conditioned the nature of the political response to problems related to the East India Company between 1766 and 1773. At first most politicians were preoccupied with extracting a direct financial return from the Company, and they refused to be drawn into areas of debate or decision-making related to reform or regulation of British administrative, commercial or political activity on the subcontinent. It was only during the early years of Lord North's administration that the realization slowly dawned in ministerial circles that for the nation to derive sustained economic benefit from India, the very foundations of the relationship between state, Company, and territorial possessions would have to be almost entirely rebuilt.

3   The policy-makers: Parliament and the East India Company

South Asian issues had not figured prominently in Westminster politics during the first half of the eighteenth century, and therefore most parliamentary politicians were ill-equipped to tackle the problems related to British activity in India that emerged in the 1760s. Members of both Houses had great difficulty in placing such unfamiliar issues in their proper context, and they chose instead to define the Indian problem as something that should be dealt with by the East India Company as an internal matter. Indeed, few parliamentarians, especially before 1772 or 1773, would have accepted that they had any part to play in the formulation of British policy as it applied to India. To an extent this is understandable. Of all the Members elected to the Parliament of 1768 only nineteen, seven of whom were directors of the Company, had actually been to the subcontinent.[1] The remainder lacked even the most elementary knowledge of the subject. This state of affairs prevailed throughout the period under study and beyond and, while there is much evidence that those in key executive positions sought to educate themselves on Indian issues, most ordinary parliamentarians remained ill-informed about events in Bengal.

Ignorance, however, could not be excused on the grounds that information on Indian affairs was either scarce or unavailable. A wealth of printed material was available to those seeking insights on British activity in South Asia and, in 1767, the first of several parliamentary inquiries examined various aspects of the Company's affairs at home and abroad. But, as Clive complained to Richard Becher, a member of the Bengal Council, in March 1768, 'it is certain that both the Directors and Parliament are superlatively ignorant of our affairs abroad, notwithstanding the great lights received in the late enquiries, yet still they remain in the dark and comprehend nothing about it'.[2] This was not simply an expression of Clive's own personal frustration with the

---

[1] Sir L. Namier and J. Brooke (eds.), *History of Parliament. The House of Commons 1754–1790* (3 vols., 1964), I, 151.   [2] NLW, Clive MSS 61 (no foliation).

shortcomings of those who supervised and directed the Company's activities. In January 1773 the Marquess of Rockingham complained to Edmund Burke in similar terms about the conduct of Indian affairs. 'The general rate of understanding in the House of Commons is not very acute', he observed.[3] Indeed, ten years later a House of Commons Select Committee conceded that an understanding of Indian affairs and issues was beyond the grasp of most ordinary Members, who 'are fatigued into such a despair of obtaining a competent knowledge of the transactions in India, that they are easily persuaded to remand them back to that obscurity, mystery, and intrigue out of which they have been forced upon public notice by the calamities arising from their extreme mismanagement'.[4] In short, Indian issues were neither popular nor well understood.

But, while few in Parliament were well informed about India or the problems of empire in the east, many MPs did have close political or financial links with the East India Company. Some 23 per cent of all the members of the 1768 Parliament owned Company stock at one time or another between 1764 and 1774, and there were, on average, 118 sitting Members holding stock at any given time between 1768 and 1774.[5] This strong financial connexion between parliamentarians and the East India Company also manifested itself in the upper House where thirty-four peers owned stock between 1764 and 1774. Of course, for many of these individuals India stock represented an attractive financial investment which offered a rate of return of between 6 and $12\frac{1}{2}$ per cent a year. For others, however, the political application of Company voting rights (bestowed upon each owner of £500 stock) was of primary importance. In particular the great struggle between Lord Clive and Laurence Sulivan for control of the Company during the 1760s resulted in a marked change in stockholding patterns, and parliamentarians were to be found well to the fore among those seeking to build up and sustain political groups and factions at India House.[6]

Events in Bengal must have seemed remote in the extreme to many politicians, but the fortunes of the East India Company in general were of great interest to those with a financial stake or political interest in the

---

[3] *The Correspondence of Edmund Burke*, II: ed. L.S. Sutherland (Cambridge, 1960), 402.
[4] *Ninth Report of the Select Committee of the House of Commons on East India Company Affairs* (1783), pp. 377–8.
[5] H.V. Bowen, '"Dipped in the traffic": East India stockholders in the House of Commons, 1768–1774', *Parliamentary History*, V (1986), 40–2.
[6] H.V. Bowen, 'Investment and empire in the later eighteenth century: East India stockholding, 1756–1791', *Economic History Review*, 2nd ser., XLII (1989), 196–204. The definitive account of the Clive–Sulivan power struggle is to be found in Sutherland, *East India Company*, chs. 4 and 5.

Company. This was reflected in the conduct of East India Company business in the House of Commons, where the participation of stockholders in the legislative process was well out of proportion to their actual numbers in the House. In the two main areas of decision-making, the debates and the committees of inquiry established to consider the state of the Company, India stockholders were well to the fore. Of the thirty-one members of the Select Committee established on 16 April 1772, fifteen were stockholders, as were six of the thirteen MPs who served on the Secret Committee appointed in November of the same year. Of the 129 MPs who spoke on Indian issues in the Commons between 1768 and 1774 75 (or 58.2 %) owned India stock, and of 1,614 speeches made on the subject during the same period 792 (49 %) were made by stockholders.[7] The speakers ranged from George Johnstone and George Dempster who made 117 and 85 speeches respectively, to John Robinson, Sir Eyre Coote, and Sir James Cockburn who made their sole intervention during the Parliament of 1768 on the subject of Indian affairs (see Table 1). Many who spoke on Indian affairs were simply making available much-needed expert advice which had been acquired during periods of Company or military service on the subcontinent, and thus individuals such as Lord Clive, General John Carnac, Robert Gregory, and Thomas Rumhold made all or the majority of their parliamentary speeches on matters related to India and the East India Company. Indeed, Indian issues attracted the regular attention of a small well-defined group of MPs, most of whom were stockholders, and it was essentially these individuals who determined the content and quality of debate, as well as the general nature of the parliamentary response to the problems of the East India Company.

The presence of a large group of Members in the House with close financial and political ties with the East India Company has prompted historians, over many years, to attempt to define an East Indian lobby or 'interest' in Parliament. However, the complexities and cross-currents of Company politics have rendered such an attempt fruitless, and it is impossible to identify anything which remotely resembles an homogeneous East Indian interest group during this or any other period. Members divided in the House according to their primary, long-established, political allegiances. They did not eschew such affiliations lightly and, in general, they did not allow loyalties to the Company or any Company interest group to override their parliamentary connex-

---

[7] The figures related to speeches on Indian and Company affairs have been calculated from an examination of all the known reports for debates, as listed in P.D.G. Thomas, 'Sources for debates of the House of Commons, 1768–1774', *Bulletin of the Institute of Historical Research*, Special Supplement no. 4 (1959).

Table 1. *Leading speakers on Indian and Company issues in the House of Commons and the General Court (recorded number of speeches)*

House of Commons (1768–74)		General Court (1769–73)	
Lord North	164	William Crichton	38
*George Dempster	117	†Sir George Colebrooke	34
*George Johnstone	85	†George Johnstone	34
*William Dowdeswell	66	†George Dempster	32
Jeremiah Dyson	51	Keane Fitzgerald	30
John Burgoyne	47	†Laurence Sulivan	25
*Alexander Wedderburn	41	†Henry Crabb Boulton	17
Sir William Meredith	39	James Adair	17
*Hans Stanley	39	Thomas Rous	16
Edmund Burke	38	Duke of Richmond	15
*Laurence Sulivan	36	General Richard Smith	14
*Sir Richard Sutton	35	Sir James Hodges	12
Thomas Townshend jnr	34	Stephen Le Maitre	10
*Lord Clive	33	†Lauchlin Macleane	8
William Pulteney	32	Joseph Salvador	8
Charles Jenkinson	32	'Mr Elliot'	8
*Charles W. Cornwall	30	†Peregrine Cust	7
*Sir Gilbert Elliot	30	Aaron Franks	6
Edward Thurlow	28	†William Burke	6
*Richard Fuller	27	†Henry Vansittart	6

* = Company stockholder   † = Member of Parliament.

ions.[8] There is no evidence, for example, of stockholding MPs voting, speaking, or acting as a *bloc*, and there were only a few of whom it could be said, as Edmund Burke said of Laurence Sulivan in 1769, 'His consequence in the India House is much more material to him than his rank in Parliament.'[9]

The influx of politicians, factions, and interest groups into the East India Company between 1750 and 1773 had significant repercussions upon the political complexion of the Company's executive body, the Court of Directors. Those individuals or groups seeking influence over Company policy or its relations with the state sought to gain a foothold in the Directorate through the election of themselves or their nominees

---

[8] See, for example, the case of George Dempster (the MP for Perth Burghs), as described by Edmund Burke to Lord Rockingham, 6 Nov. 1769, *Burke Corr.*, II, 106–7. Attempts to define an East Indian 'interest' in the House of Commons have been made by J.M. Holzman, *The Nabobs in England 1760–1815: A Study of the Returned Anglo-Indian* (New York, 1926), pp. 103–22; and C.H. Philips, *The East India Company 1784–1834* (Manchester, 1940), pp. 307–47.   [9] *Burke Corr.*, II, 106–7.

to that body. Similarly, those already serving as directors endeavoured to reinforce their position by cultivating a following in the General Court, the forum where the stockholders met to discuss and determine the broad outlines of Company policy. Between 1760 and 1773 this developed into a debilitating two-way process: factionalism in the one Court fuelled factionalism in the other.

The background, abilities, and experience of those sitting in the Court of Directors altered quite significantly during the 1760s and 1770s. The Court was no longer the preserve of the London mercantile community, and its base was broadened to include a greater number of representatives from the world of high finance, and metropolitan and national politics.[10] In addition, the traditional long terms of service within the Directorate were reduced as the Company became a battleground for several powerful factions: in 1754 twelve of the twenty-four directors had served in the Court for more than ten years in total, while by 1765 only three of the incumbents had done so.[11] Finally, because most directors owed their election to the support of patrons or factions it would seem that loyalty to the corporate interest of the Company was gradually eroded in the years after 1750.[12] Indeed, the prevailing political climate within the Company was such that very few directors retained any significant level of independent action or thought. One notable exception to this, however, was John Manship, who in 1772 played a leading part in exposing mismanagement and corruption within the Court.

An annual ballot among Company stockholders led to the appointment of twenty-four of their number as directors, provided that they owned £2,000 of stock and were 'natural born subjects of England'. Even so, this did lead to the establishment of a fairly cosmopolitan Court of Directors.[13] Their term of office was for one year in the first instance, but throughout the 1760s argument raged over whether this term should be extended so as to avoid the annual disruption to the Company's affairs caused by the replacement of a significant number of directors each April. In 1769, for example, eleven individuals who had not been directors the previous year were elected to the Court, and there were twelve such directors the following year. Both Clive and Laurence Sulivan recognized the disruptive effect that this had on the development of long-term Company policy and strategy.[14] However, there were those

[10] J.G. Parker, 'The directors of the East India Company, 1754–1790', unpublished Ph.D. thesis, University of Edinburgh, 1976, esp. chs. 2 and 3.
[11] *Ibid.*, p. 333.   [12] *Ibid.*, p. 382.
[13] The restrictive nationality clause had ceased to be applied long before the middle of the century, and a number of directors of Irish and Scottish descent rose to prominence during the period under review.   [14] See below pp. 45–6.

who contended that a one-year appointment was preferable to a longer term of office. They found an advocate in Edmund Burke who argued in the House of Commons in 1769 that 'this Company has grown up under such directors: it is become a great and glorious Company'.[15] In making a thinly veiled reference to the ongoing debate over the need for annual or triennial parliaments, he observed that 'men, continually watched over by their constituents, are worked into a vigour'.

Individuals were not permitted to serve as directors for more than four consecutive years. This was intended to avoid the perpetuation of oligarchy among the directors, but influential individuals such as Sir George Colebrooke were able to make a successful return to the Directorate after the statutory year's absence. Colebrooke served as a director from 1767 to 1770 and then again in 1772, being Chairman in the last three of these years and Deputy-Chairman in 1768. The appointment of a Chairman was made by the directors at their first full meeting after the annual election, and the Chairman was then permitted to nominate a deputy to act in his absence at meetings of the General Court as well as the Court of Directors. Each director was paid an attendance allowance of £150 per annum for his services to the Company, while the additional responsibilities undertaken by the Chairman and his deputy were reflected in an annual payment of £350.

Under the terms of the Company's charter of 1698 the directors were obliged to meet in full Court on a weekly basis. This they did in the committee rooms at India House, but they also met before every General Court meeting and whenever else the Chairman thought it necessary. However, the bulk of the Company's executive business was dealt with by ten specialized sub-committees of directors. Each director was required to serve on between two and five of the committees, with the Chairman and his deputy serving on all of them. Over the years the committees had been graded in order of seniority and this categorization was adhered to during the 1760s and 1770s, even though it was somewhat outdated and did not reflect the Company's new priorities.

The Committees in descending order of seniority were those of Correspondence, Law Suits, Treasury, Warehouse, Accounts, Buying, House, Shipping, Private Trade, and Prevention of Private Trade. In addition, in times of emergency or crisis a small Secret Committee was established to liaise with the administration of the day.[16] The appointment of directors to these committees was usually on the grounds of seniority, and thus, as Company Secretary Peter Michell

[15] Speech of 27 Feb. 1769, as reported in BL, Eg. MSS 218, pp. 163–4.
[16] C.H. Philips, 'The Secret Committee of the East India Company', *Bulletin of the School of Oriental and African Studies*, X (1940–2).

reported to Parliament in 1773, the committees were 'generally composed in each year of the same members'.[17] For example, John Manship, who was a director in 1765, 1767, and between 1769 and 1772, was always a member of the Correspondence, Treasury, and Warehouse Committees, while Robert Jones (director 1766–9 and MP for Huntingdon) was always a member of the Committees of Correspondence, Shipping, and Treasury. This at least ensured some degree of continuity in areas of specialized decision-making.

In spite of the existence of ten directors' committees within the Company's administrative structure, it was generally understood that for practical purposes three committees were of central importance and influence in the decision-making process. They fulfilled vital executive functions and provided the full Court of Directors with the specialist advice that was necessary for the shaping of Company policy both at home and abroad. The Committee of Correspondence received the dispatches from overseas, examined them, and drafted the replies to the Company's servants. Needless to say, much of the Company's overseas policy was formulated in this committee. The Committee of Treasury conducted and sanctioned many of the Company's financial transactions. It negotiated with the Bank of England for loans, purchased bullion, and was instrumental in recommending the level of dividend that the directors proposed at the March and September quarterly meetings of stockholders. Finally, the Committee of Accounts assessed and maintained control over the Company's general financial position. In order to do this the Committee fulfilled the vital function of attempting to regulate the numbers of bills of exchange drawn on the Company by individuals in India for eventual redemption in London. Regular projections of the Company's financial position were made, and up-to-date accounts were presented to the directors when required.

Orders prepared for dispatch to India required the signature of at least thirteen directors, and thus business originating in the ten sub-committees was presented at the weekly full Court meeting for discussion and approval. The minutes of the Court of Directors give an indication of the wide range of the business that came before the Court, but it appears that no rigid rules of procedure were observed.[18] Precedence, however, was always given to business conducted with Parliament or the administration of the day. At each meeting correspondence, dispatches from overseas, and the recommendations of the sub-committees were read out, listed in the minutes, and debated. On the rare occasions that the Court was divided on an issue or failed to

[17] *RCHC*, IV, 384.
[18] The Court minutes for the period 1766–73 are to be found in IOR, B/82–9.

determine an appropriate course of action, the matter was resolved by means of a ballot of all the directors present.[19] The Chairman did not have a casting vote but, in the event of a tied ballot, provision existed for the question to be decided by the drawing of lots. When decisions had been made, the appropriate resolution was recorded in the minutes and orders were drafted before being signed by the requisite number of directors.

The sub-division of the Company's administrative organization and its supporting secretariat corresponded to that of the directors' ten committees. Thus, for example, the warehousekeepers were responsible to the Committee of Warehouses, and the Accountant and his staff were answerable to the Committees of Treasury and Accounts. Long-standing employees such as Peter Michell (Company Secretary from 1769), Charles Coggan (Clerk to the Committee of Shipping), and John Hoole (Auditor from 1769) had risen through the ranks at India House,[20] and their experience and skills played no small part in helping the Company, and the directors in particular, to come to terms with the many and varied problems of the period. Even so, only a few individuals possessed full knowledge of all aspects of the Company's activities. The most notable exceptions to this were the Chairman and his deputy who, as members of all ten committees, were in a position to participate in all areas of decision-making. They were able to influence what business was brought before the full Court of Directors, and they were armed with the important advantage of possessing prior knowledge of decisions brought forward from the sub-committees. This advantage was reinforced by the convention that the minutes of two of the most important committees, those of Treasury and Secrecy, were not available for scrutiny by directors who did not serve on them.[21] The Chairman and his deputy were thus in a position of unrivalled authority and influence.

To the Chairman's wide-ranging power was added one other important function which served to extend his role to incorporate the very grounds upon which Company-state relations were conducted. During negotiations between the Company and the government of the day proposals were carried to the ministry by the Chairman and his deputy. From time to time other directors, or even ordinary proprietors, were appointed to accompany the Chairman in order to assist with negotiations, whether they were with the First Lord of the Treasury or

---

[19] See, for example, Sutherland, *East India Company*, p. 204.
[20] Michell had previously been deputy to the Secretary Robert Jones, while John Hoole had served a long apprenticeship as Deputy Auditor. Annual lists of the Company's permanent employees are to be found in the *Court and City Register* and *Royal Kalendar*.   [21] *RCHC*, IV, 384.

with the full Treasury Board.[22] Even so, these discussions tended to focus very much on the Chairman, and he came to represent the official voice of the Company.[23] This, of course, placed him in a position of the greatest influence, and, although he was answerable to the proprietors and directors for his actions, he had often during the course of negotiations to rely upon his own commercial and political judgement to determine what best served the interests of the Company. Needless to say, a compliant and favourably disposed Company Chairman could be of immense benefit to the ministry during the course of negotiations, and this became all too evident to successive administrations between 1766 and 1773.

The fact that almost a quarter of MPs purchased India stock reflected the important part that the East India Company's General Court played as a well-established and influential political forum in its own right. As the Company's position in India had changed since the 1750s, so the conduct and organization of Company politics in Britain had undergone a profound and lasting transformation. Even though executive control and the day-to-day administration of the Company in London was vested in the Court of Directors, all major policy decisions were determined in the Court of Proprietors, otherwise known as the General Court.

The General Court was the ultimate sovereign body within the Company, and it was the forum in which the stockholders debated, discussed, and decided upon policy and the regulation and administration of the Company's overseas and domestic affairs. The Court served to define the general nature of the relationship between the Company and the state, and the proprietors proposed and sanctioned financial agreements with the government of the day. Moreover, because successive ministries proved reluctant to take a positive lead in Indian affairs, the origin of much of the East India Company legislation enacted during this period was to be found in proposals submitted to the government by the Company.

A well-defined method of procedure was established by which East Indian political business was often dealt with before it even entered the parliamentary arena. In 1766, 1768, 1772, and 1773 the ministry or Treasury Board gave advance warning to the directors that Company

---

[22] In January 1768, for example, it was decided that Henry Crabb Boulton and George Dudley should join the Chairman, Thomas Rous, in negotiations with the ministry; IOR, B/83, p. 530.

[23] In 1773, however, the Chairman Sir George Colebrooke ran into difficulties over the definition of his role as Company spokesman. He mistakenly assumed that several conversations with Lord North were part of the ongoing negotiations with the administration, but the minister was adamant that the meetings had been of a private and personal nature.

affairs would be the subject of parliamentary scrutiny during the forthcoming session. The Company was invited to draw up proposals related to regulatory measures or financial matters. Directors' committees then drafted proposals which were submitted to the General Court where they were ratified or amended. Having been finalized, the proposals were formally presented to the ministry who, if they deemed the terms broadly acceptable, recommended their submission to Parliament. On most occasions little fundamental reconstruction or reshaping of the proposals was necessary in the House of Commons. Details were sometimes added or deleted, but the general outline or framework of legislation was always first determined during the course of lengthy negotiations between the Company and the ministry. Agreements between the two parties were more or less rubber-stamped by the House of Commons, especially when the ministry had a large majority in the chamber, as was the case after 1770. This situation meant that the General Court played as important a part as the House of Commons in the legislative process as it applied to Indian affairs.

Contemporaries were well aware of the significance of events at the General Court. Lord Beauchamp commented to Horace Walpole in 1767 that 'all mankind are thinking of what passes there', and two years later the Earl of Chatham's failure to come to terms with East Indian issues prompted him to complain to the King that recent General Courts had adopted the role of 'little parliaments'.[24] Far-reaching decisions were taken in the Court, and the repercussions were felt not only in London but also half way around the world in Asia where the lives of millions of Indians were affected, albeit indirectly, by the actions and votes of the Company's stockholders. But whether the stockholders understood the full extent of their responsibilities is open to question. For most of them the General Court represented a forum in which domestic political and financial decisions were made and, as Adam Smith observed of joint-stock company investors in general, 'the greater part of those seldom pretend to understand anything of the business of the Company; and when the spirit of faction happens not to prevail among them, give themselves no trouble about it, but receive contentedly some half-yearly or yearly dividend, as the directors think proper to make to them'.[25]

Few would have accepted that one of the Court's primary functions was to shape the general manner in which British rule was applied to the indigenous population in areas under the Company's influence. This

---

[24] *The Yale Edition of Horace Walpole's Correspondence*, ed. W.S. Lewis (48 vols., Oxford, 1939–84), XXXIX, 18; *The Autobiographical and Political Correspondence of Augustus Henry, 3rd Duke of Grafton*, ed. Sir William Anson (1898), p. 237.
[25] *Wealth of Nations*, p. 741.

imperial dimension to stockholding did not receive much attention from contemporary observers although Horace Walpole, who displayed more concern than most for the natives of Bengal, did refer to it in passing in 1769 when he wrote of the General Court, 'People trudge to the other end of town to vote who shall govern empires at the other end of [the] world.'[26] By attending, speaking at, or voting in, the General Court such individuals, drawn in the main from the well-to-do sections of metropolitan society,[27] were contributing to the development of Company policy and, in the long term, to the making of the British empire in India.

The relevance of the East India Company to national politics in the post-Plassey period was reflected in an increase in the number of individuals who purchased stock and participated in the proceedings of the General Court. There are several statistical indicators of this trend. Not only did the total number of stockholdings rise from 2,160 in 1748 to 2,826 in 1773, but the proportion of proprietors owning the minimum voting qualification of £500 stock rose from 31 per cent to 48 per cent of the total during the same period.[28] That more proprietors were utilising their stock purchases in order to participate in Company politics is beyond doubt: there was a four-fold increase in the number of voters at the annual election between 1758 and 1773. The average number of voters during the 1750s was 288; by the 1760s it had risen to 838; and, for the period 1770–3, the average reached 1,063.[29]

Whereas contested elections had been rare before 1758, they became standard practice during the 1760s when the Clive–Sulivan power struggle took place. Vote-creation techniques, particularly the 'splitting' of stock into units of £500 for distribution to friends and supporters, became refined and this played a major part in increasing the number of voters participating in the annual election of directors. Nevertheless, there are other signs that more importance was now attached to the proceedings of the General Court. Because Courts could be convened at the behest of either the directors or the proprietors, the frequency of stockholder meetings serves as a useful indicator of the level of debate within the Company.

---

[26] *Walpole Corr.*, XXIII, 133.

[27] Bowen, 'Investment and Empire', pp. 194–5.

[28] The figures for 1748 are taken from P.G.M. Dickson, *The Financial Revolution in England: A Study in the Development of Public Credit 1688–1756* (1967), p. 287. The figures for 1773 are based on *A List of the Names of all the Proprietors of East India Stock; Distinguishing the Principal Stock Each Proprietor Now Holds and the Time When Such Proprietors Became Possessed Thereof* (9 March 1773).

[29] Figures derived from Company election results as recorded in the General Court minute books (1702–73), IOR, B/255–8.

When the political crisis confronting the Company was at its peak in 1773 the General Court met on five occasions between 20 and 30 April, and on six occasions between 14 and 27 May. Over a longer timescale, the unique nature and extent of the problems of the 1760s and 1770s can be placed into proper perspective by comparing the average number of Court meetings per year during this period with the average number for the earlier decades of the century. During the 1740s there were an average of 5.4 meetings per year, and the 1750s were little different with 5.8 meetings per year. However, by the 1760s the average number of meetings had risen to 13.3 per year, and during the period 1770–3 the figure rose to 22. The figures for the 1740s and 1750s rose barely above the statutory minimum requirements of the Company's charter and they reflect periods of uncontested annual elections, economic stability and, for the most part, limited conflict in India. They stand in marked contrast to the figures for the 1760s and 1770s when not only did the Court meet more often, but it also often sat for up to twelve hours a day.

A similar point can be made about the frequency of ballots at the General Court. Because they only took place when demanded by nine or more proprietors, their frequency reflects the level of debate and disagreement within the Company. This, in turn, is indicative of the increase in the Court's political importance. In the fifty years before 1766 there were only seven ballots at the Court, while in the seven years after 1766 there were ballots on no fewer than forty-five occasions. An average of 277 proprietors (around 8 to 10 per cent of the total) voted at these ballots, the highest figure being 893 at the ballot of 8 April 1767. All the signs, therefore, point to the fact that after the 1750s Company politics became far more partisan in nature, and that this in turn prompted a marked increase in the numbers who actually participated in the Company's decision-making process.[30]

Members of Parliament were well to the fore among those seeking representation at the General Court, and they played a variety of roles there. Some, like Clive, Sulivan, or Sir George Colebrooke, led their own large factions and sought to carve out a position of dominance for themselves in both the General Court and Court of Directors. Some acted as distributors or receivers of 'split' votes, while others held a vote but, like the Paymaster-General Richard Rigby, seldom if ever used it, and did not apply their political talents to the Court on a regular basis.[31]

Alongside these parliamentarians were to be found aspiring politicians who, for one reason or another, had been denied access to Parliament or

---

[30] Figures for Court meetings and ballots derived from *ibid.*
[31] Rigby made this point in the Commons on 8 June 1773; BL, Eg. MSS 250, p. 7.

the Court of Common Council. For them the General Court offered a convenient platform from which they could make themselves and their views known. Publicity was guaranteed because the proceedings of the Court were fully reported in the London press after 1769, and all that was necessary was the initial outlay for £500 nominal stock and the nerve to stand and debate alongside men like the Duke of Richmond, Henry Crabb Boulton, and William Burke. Indeed, in general terms, a fairly broad cross-section of metropolitan society was represented in the General Court. Parliamentarians rubbed shoulders with established City politicians such as James Adair; with ex-Company military personnel such as General Richard Smith and Colonel John Caillaud; with representatives of the business community such as Joseph Salvador and Aaron Franks; and with the large number of ordinary investors, male and female, who often balloted and voted, but seldom spoke in debate.[32] This provided a rich and sometimes volatile mixture of personalities in the General Court, and the generally high standard of debate bears testimony to this.

Nevertheless, it would be wrong to describe the Court, as John Robinson, the Secretary to the Treasury, did in 1778, as 'the most democratic body that ever existed'.[33] Although there were no restrictions on who could purchase stock and contribute to Company politics, the actual number of participants at routine Court meetings was small. The annual election of directors sometimes attracted over a thousand voters, but the ordinary meetings at which Company policy was debated and determined were seldom attended by more than a couple of hundred stockholders and, on occasions, only a handful were present.[34] Furthermore, the number who actually contributed to the proceedings and debates was even more limited, and only seventy individuals have been identified as speaking at the Court between 1766 and 1773. An influential coterie of twenty or so leading speakers monopolized the proceedings, and among these were some of the politicians who led the way on Indian issues in the House of Commons: George Dempster, George Johnstone, Laurence Sulivan, and Sir George Colebrooke. Indeed, nine of the most frequent speakers at the Court between 1766 and 1773 were parliamentarians (see Table 1). It was these experienced politicians who gave a lead to the ordinary shareholders, and they

---

[32] Women voted but did not speak at the Court. For an analysis of their political activity at India House see H.V. Bowen, 'British politics and the East India Company, 1766–1773', unpublished Ph.D. thesis, University of Wales, 1986, pp. 38–41.

[33] 'Consideration of East India Affairs' (1778); BL, Add. MSS 38398, ff. 108–17, printed in Marshall, *Problems of Empire*, p. 118.

[34] Bowen, 'British politics and the East India Company', pp. 47–55.

defined the manner in which Company politics were conducted: they played a crucial part in the development of corporate policy and strategy.

There was quite a considerable overlap between the participants in debate in Parliament and the General Court, yet there is little evidence of any ministerial spokesmen presenting the administration's case or viewpoint to the stockholders in their own assembly. Lord Weymouth attempted this in 1769 but his actions, which were not endorsed by his colleagues, were perceived by the stockholders as a direct threat to the Company's independence and were not repeated.[35] On the other hand, speakers such as Johnstone and Dempster who identified themselves with the opposition in Parliament, were often successful in putting across their ideas to a proprietary which, throughout this period, felt threatened by the incursions of the ministry into East Indian affairs.

Indian issues and Company politics offered the followers of Lord Rockingham, who were ineffective in Parliament during the early 1770s, a subject and an arena which they could use to harass and embarrass the ministry. Rockingham himself reported news of negotiations between the Company and the administration to Edmund Burke in February 1773, and he advanced the view that 'there must soon arrive various opportunities – either in Parliament or the E.I. Court for some steps to be taken to thwart the measures intended'.[36] Accordingly, James Adair briefly found himself in the role of co-ordinator of a Rockinghamite group within the General Court.[37] Some keen observers of the situation recognized what was going on, and it was noted in March 1773 by John Caillaud that Dempster, Richmond, and Johnstone had acted in close union to 'hamper' the directors in their attempts to secure an agreement with the ministry on the issue of reform of the Company's affairs.[38]

The reasons for such actions were not to be found in Company politics alone, and it was believed that they served a much wider purpose. Caillaud observed to Warren Hastings that 'the real views of this party, under the plausible pretence of being the sacred guardians of the Company's charted rights is to get the matter for forming a strong opposition in Parliament against administration'.[39] That was a fair comment for, by raising the standard of opposition in the General Court, the Rockinghams were hoping to make life as difficult as possible for the ministry. In doing so, however, they also created numerous problems for the directors, many of whom by 1773 were favourably disposed towards the administration and were dependent on them for support at the annual election. As Sir George Colebrooke (Chairman of

---

[35] For details of this episode see below, pp. 80–1.   [36] *Burke Corr.*, II, 423.
[37] WWM, R1–1425.   [38] BL, Add. MSS 29133, f. 445.   [39] *Ibid.*

the directors in 1772–3) later recalled, Richmond, Dempster, and their associates used all of the available opportunities presented by General Court debates to contest the directors' proposals 'inch by inch'.[40]

The evolution of Company policy was thus often a painfully slow process: the problems of empire became caught up in the cut and thrust of domestic politics. On several occasions the directors concluded terms and agreements with the ministry following lengthy negotiations, only to find that they were confronted with a hostile and obstructionist General Court when the time came for ratification. Members of factions, such as Dempster and Johnstone, or outspoken independent proprietors such as William Crichton, could always count on support in the Court, and they were able vigorously to contest issues. By doing so they were often able to set the agenda for debate and discussion: they amended or deleted the directors' proposals; they argued their case; and they advanced their own alternative schemes of arrangement. And, more often than not, they won their point, for, as well as commanding considerable debating skills, they also possessed detailed knowledge of the Company's affairs. In 1772, for example, when the directors presented to the proprietors a plan recommending that supervisors be sent to the Company's territories in India, George Johnstone 'showed even such a knowledge of the legal parts of it that they underwent an immediate alteration from behind the bar in consequence'.[41] Individuals such as these played a key part in the formulation of all Indian legislation enacted during this period. They first applied themselves to the task in the General Court, and then those with seats in the Commons took a prominent part in the subsequent Indian debates in Parliament. In effect the ministry had to negotiate two difficult legislative hurdles.

Because the General Court was granted, albeit temporarily, a prominent position in national political life, much depended upon how it coped with the new demands placed upon it. It had functioned relatively efficiently during lengthy periods of peace and stability earlier in the century, but it now had to be able as an institution to handle the influx of a large number of new stockholders, many of whom were experienced political campaigners. The Court's rules and regulations had to be sufficiently watertight to ensure that abuses and malpractice were kept to a minimum. Unfortunately for the Company, and for those seeking a swift response to Indian problems, the framework provided for the conduct of business within the General Court proved to be wholly inadequate to deal with the realities of political life in the 1760s and

---

[40] Sir G. Colebrooke, *Retrospection: Or Reminiscences Addressed to My Son Henry Thomas Colebrooke Esq.* (2 vols., 1898–9), II, 26.
[41] *London Evening Post*, 19 Nov. 1772.

1770s. At the heart of the problem lay the question of the nature of the relationship between the General Court and the Court of Directors.

The directors and the stockholders had coexisted harmoniously during the first half of the century and this was reflected in the conduct of Company politics. Elections were usually a formality; there were few Court meetings, and even fewer divisions or ballots. Contentious issues were few and far between and, in general, the directors were able to keep a firm grip on the Company's affairs in Britain. However, the relationship between proprietors and directors was recast in 1758 when the latter lost much of their effective control over the General Court. First, on 15 March, they lost an adjournment motion, and they were then further embarrassed when their decision regarding the appointment of a Governor for the Bengal Presidency was overturned. This uneasy though not unprecedented situation was then exacerbated when the annual election of directors was contested for the first time since 1735 and the outgoing Court of Directors suffered a heavy defeat.[42] This defeat was itself important, but still more so was the re-establishment of a contested annual election fought between a 'house' list of candidates (approved by the directors) and an alternative list sponsored by a group of proprietors. The implications for continuity and stability within the Company and its overseas operations were obvious, as some contemporaries observed.[43]

The General Court had identified itself, as the Company's charter had originally intended it should, as the ultimate sovereign body within the Company. However, because routine administration of the Company's affairs still remained with the Court of Directors, this led to an often uneasy relationship between the directors and their constituents. As one observer noted in 1769, 'The choice of directors was, and still is, in the body of proprietors; the appointments abroad and plan of conduct in the Court of Directors.'[44] In other words, the directors were not free to act as they wished because, ultimately, they were dependent on the support of a majority of the stockholders. The threat of removal from office, either through the electoral process or by impeachment for mismanagement, remained an effective curb on irresponsible behaviour by the directors, either collectively or as individuals.

Consequently, the annual election of directors became an event of the greatest importance in the political calendar because it provided the

---

[42] Sutherland, *East India Company*, pp. 66–73.
[43] J.Z. Holwell, *Important Facts Regarding the East India Company's Affairs in Bengal From the Year 1752 to 1760* (1764), p. 159.
[44] Anonymous author of *A Letter to a Late Popular Director (L—S—Esq.) Relative to Indian Affairs and the Present Contests* (1769), p. 3.

opportunity for the stockholders to express their faith in, or disapproval of, the manner in which the Company's business was being conducted. Even so, the flawed nature of this electoral system became apparent to all of those with a close interest in the Company's affairs. Clive sketched out the nature of the problem when he wrote to Claud Russell in February 1769:

> The East Indies also I think cannot remain long to us if our constitution be not altered. A direction for a year only and that time entirely taken up in securing directors for the year to come cannot long maintain that authority which is requisite for the managing and governing such extensive, populous, rich and powerful kingdoms as the East India Company are possessed of.[45]

Laurence Sulivan, who, ironically, had helped to initiate the 'revolt' of the proprietors in 1758 and had then waged constant electoral warfare against Clive during the 1760s, was even more forthright in his analysis of where the root of the constitutional problem lay. 'General courts', he wrote in 1767, 'as they have been, and may be, are the springs of all our mischiefs.'[46] As a remedy he proposed restricting the influence of the stockholders so that 'no general courts shall have powers to control the directors, but upon such matters...that puts their estate in danger or criminality that lays the directors open to discussion.' It was an ominous warning for the General Court that these two leading figures within the Company had both identified a major weakness in the constitution and in their demands for reform advocated a curb on the Court's influence.

The nature of the relationship between the General Court and the Court of Directors was not the only flaw in the Company's structure. The organizational framework provided by the charter and by-laws proved to be far from adequate in establishing firm guidelines for the regulation of the proceedings of the General Court. There was little detail relating to the conduct of business in the Court. Indeed, of the thirty-one original Company by-laws only six related directly to the regulation of the General Court or the conduct of elections. Before the 1760s the limitations of these by-laws had been masked by the lack of debate or dissension within the Company. By contrast, during the political upheavals of the 1760s and 1770s weaknesses within the Court's operational framework were continuously and ruthlessly exploited as procedural anomalies were seized upon and taken up as weapons in fiercely fought debates and elections.

The Company lacked the necessary means or will to correct this

---

[45] NLW, Clive MSS 61 (no foliation). The letter continues in volume 62.

[46] 'Laurence Sulivan's paper to Lord Shelburne on the condition of the East India Company and an outline of a plan of reform' (1767), Clements Library, Lansdowne MSS 90, f. 84.

situation, despite the existence since 1709 of a standing committee of proprietors whose task it was to examine and supplement the by-laws when necessary. Indeed, between 1749 and 1768 no additions or amendments were made to any of the by-laws.

As a result of this failure to put its own house in order, the Company sought and received parliamentary legislation which was designed to tighten up practice and procedure at India House. Between 1767 and 1770 three Acts (7 Geo. III, c. 48, 7 Geo. III, c. 49, and 10 Geo. III, c. 47) established detailed guidelines for the conduct of business in the General Court and Company elections. But these Acts were no more than expedient measures designed to correct blatant and specific abuses such as the 'splitting' of stock. Many other anomalies came to light and were seized upon and exploited by experienced politicians during the vigorous debates that characterized Court proceedings between 1766 and 1773.[47]

The problems confronting the General Court and, indeed, the Company in general between 1766 and 1773 were often to be found closer to home than issues relating to the regulation of activities in Bengal. Hampered by the lack of satisfactory procedures, the Company had first to put its internal affairs in order before proceeding to issues of a wider and more important nature. For a number of reasons, undivided attention could not be given to the problems of empire.

[47] See, for example, the debates reported in *The Gazetteer*, 15 Nov. 1766, and *London Evening Post*, 25 Aug. 1772, 23 and 27 Feb. 1773.

4 Crown and Company (I): the *Diwani* and the inquiry of 1767

Contemporaries often spoke or wrote about the East Indian problem or question, but in 1766 this meant many different things to different people. Indeed, an initial failure to identify and define the scope of the problem in precise terms led to a confusion of purpose which lasted until 1772. Until then, the Company and the ministry tackled very different sets of Indian priorities. They often failed to agree as to what exactly was on the political agenda; they often worked at cross purposes; and they were often forced into positions of confrontation and conflicting interest. There is little evidence to suggest that the ministry and the Company ever worked for long in close harmony towards a common goal or aim during this period. Instead, a prolonged war of attrition developed between the two parties as they both sought to protect their own position and interests.

Following the Company's acquisition of the *Diwani*, the directors sought immediate reform of their administrative, judicial, and commercial affairs in Bengal.[1] They held this to be imperative if recent gains were to be consolidated. In particular, they needed to establish new trading and revenue collection systems in order to maximise corporate investment and secure the return of as large a revenue surplus as possible to Britain. These were essentially practical problems, but the solutions often required support and reinforcement in the form of parliamentary legislation. Ministers, however, neither wished nor sought to be drawn into new areas of imperial legislative activity or responsibility. The problems of empire were held to be, initially at least, the problems of the East India Company and not of the British government. Most ministers were thus content to define the East Indian problem within very narrow terms of reference as a constitutional and legal problem. They sought no more than to assert the British Crown's

---

[1] See chapters 6 and 7. A few parts of this chapter were first published in H.V. Bowen, 'A question of sovereignty? The Bengal land revenue issue, 1765–67', *Journal of Imperial and Commonwealth History*, XVI (1988), 155–76. I am indebted to the editor for permission to reprint them.

'right' to a share of the revenues now being collected by the Company in Bengal, Bihar, and Orissa.

This unsatisfactory state of affairs arose in large part from the manner in which the first parliamentary inquiry into the East India Company's affairs was conceived and prosecuted in 1766 and 1767. The minister responsible, Lord Chatham, chose quite deliberately to secure for the hard-pressed Exchequer a share of the Company's new riches. In doing so, Chatham and his cabinet colleagues found themselves drawn into an extremely complex legal problem centred upon the Company's right to procure and retain territories and revenues. The inquiry of 1766–7 became preoccupied with this issue to the exclusion of all other aspects of the Indian problem. The Crown and the Company put forward competing legal claims to the territorial revenues of Bengal, Bihar, and Orissa, and by doing so they were forced into ever more entrenched positions. They became, in effect, rivals for the same financial prize. Consequently, attempts by the Company to enlist the help of the ministry with problems such as recruitment for their armies foundered in an atmosphere of hostility and suspicion between the two parties. Eventually a financial agreement was struck between the state and the Company, but it was no more than a short-term solution which caused more problems than it solved. Despite Clive's impassioned plea in 1769 for a partnership of equals between the ministry and the Company, there was never any real prospect of such an arrangement being entered into willingly by either side. The financial stakes were far too high.

Chatham's objective in 1766 was a simple one, and it reflected the nature of his interest in Indian and Company issues. He hoped that during the course of a parliamentary inquiry into the Company's affairs the ministry would be able to secure a declaration that the legal right to the recently acquired territorial revenues and possessions in Bengal lay not with the Company but with the British Crown. His aim was to establish this most fundamental principle and then permit the Company to maintain its privileged position in India in return for annual payments (a share of the revenues) to the Treasury. By accepting such an arrangement the state would procure a satisfactory financial return from the Company without being drawn into the complexities and burdens of imperial administration and territorial responsibility on the subcontinent. The Company would remain as the sole legal representative and vehicle of British activity in India.

Such was the theory, but in practice Chatham's administration was unable to secure the necessary and prerequisite definition of the legal and constitutional relationship between the state, the Company, and the territorial possessions in India: a declaration of the British Crown's rights to the Bengal revenues was not forthcoming. In seeking to explain Chatham's failure, historians have focused in the main upon political factors. The ministry was handicapped by its weak position in the House of Commons, and any unity of purpose within the cabinet was undermined by erratic behaviour from senior ministers Charles Townshend, the Chancellor of the Exchequer, and Henry Seymour Conway. Chatham himself, having declared his intentions to his colleagues, never fully explained how the ministry's objectives were to be secured.

This wholly unsatisfactory state of affairs was then made much worse when Chatham, suffering from the effects of illness, withdrew from public business and left the ministry in the hands of a reluctant and somewhat unsuitable caretaker, the Duke of Grafton. Finally, the ministerial designs upon the Company were identified by the opposition as belonging to the long-running debate about the sanctity of chartered rights. In particular, the ministerial attempt to assert what was believed to be the doctrine of unrestrained parliamentary sovereignty over the property of a chartered body struck a chord with the Bedfords, Grenvilles, and Rockinghams. By placing the problem in this familiar context not only were they able to interest back-bench MPs in East Indian issues, but they were also able to find common ground against the administration. They formed a 'union of the opposition' which forced Chatham's beleagured colleagues even further onto the defensive.[2]

These political factors, all of great significance in their own right, only partly explain why Chatham's East India policy eventually ended in compromise, confusion, and recrimination. The legal problems confronting the ministry also require due emphasis. Of particular importance is the question of how, within the context of the inquiry, Chatham intended to define the legal status of the Company's possessions. Above all, did he have a legitimate claim to endorse his fundamental assertion, as expressed to Grafton in February 1767, that 'the question of right... cannot (under any colourable pretence) be in the Company'?[3] This was the central issue raised by the inquiry of 1767 because, in the final analysis, there were a number of crucial ambiguities surrounding the Company's legal right to procure and retain territory, and they served to deflect the ministry from its course of action.

In 1766 well-informed observers believed that large financial benefits

---

[2] See, for example, J. Brooke, *The Chatham Administration 1766–1768* (1956), pp. 77–9, 90–2, 99–102; P. Lawson, 'Parliament and the first East India inquiry, 1767', *Parliamentary History*, I (1982), 101–10; Sir L. Namier and J. Brooke, *Charles Townshend* (1964), pp. 158–72; Sutherland, *East India Company*, pp. 152–3, 160–2.

[3] *Grafton Autobiography*, p. 112.

would accrue to the Company as a consequence of their new position as *Diwan* in Bengal. The estimates of these were later realized to have been overinflated, and there is little doubt that Clive played a full part in the creation of an atmosphere of unjustified optimism amongst the Company's stockholders and the nation at large.[4] For, although the directors of the Company were extremely cautious and realistic in their assessment of the Company's new economic position in Bengal, the public was subjected to all manner of speculation on the question of how vast the size of the revenues was likely to be.[5] But, far more importantly, influential politicians and ministers received private reports and estimates of the financial return that Clive had secured for the Company. Both the Marquess of Rockingham and Lord Chatham were informed that the Company would receive a net balance of over £2 million from the territorial revenues by the end of 1766.[6] For ministers with one eye on an enormous national debt this was a particularly interesting development and, as noted earlier, some public figures were swift to link the nation's financial redemption with the Company's success in India. One such was William Beckford, who advanced a simple formula for the solution of the prevailing national economic crisis: '"Look to the rising sun", cried perpetually the Alderman, "Your Treasury coffers are to be filled from the east, not the west."'[7]

Beckford was a close political associate of William Pitt (later Lord Chatham) who had himself taken a close interest in the Company's affairs since the late 1750s when he had served as Secretary of State for the South. Pitt had met Clive and had been in receipt of letters from him, and this relationship had undoubtedly helped to shape and define his views on the nature, purpose, and direction of British activity in India. Indeed, following a meeting with Pitt and Newcastle in 1761, Clive recorded that 'Mr Pitt seems thoroughly convinced of the infinite consequence of the trade of the East India Company to the nation; he made no scruple to me of giving it the preference to our concerns in America.'[8] However, more importantly in view of what was to happen in 1767, Pitt had learned from Clive in January 1759 that recent political and military developments in Bengal had brought with them a whole

---

[4] See below, p. 104.
[5] See, for example, *Lloyd's Evening Post*, 20 Mar. 1767.
[6] PRO, 30/8 (Chatham papers), 99, part 3, f. 178; WWM, R-66: Clive to Rockingham, 6 Sept. 1766.
[7] Colebrooke, *Retrospection*, II, 108. Beckford had substantial economic interests in the West Indies.
[8] Memorandum of a meeting between the three printed in Sir J. Malcolm, *The Life of Robert, Lord Clive; Collected from the Family Papers Communicated by the Earl of Powis to Major-General Sir John Malcolm* (3 vols., 1836), II, 203–4.

host of problems which the Company was ill-equipped to deal with. 'So large a sovereignty', Clive had written, 'may possibly be an object too extensive for a mercantile company; and it is to be feared they are not of themselves able, without the nation's assistance, to maintain so wide a dominion.'[9]

This candid statement found an echo from Pitt seven years later. John Walsh, MP for Worcester and a close friend of Clive, spoke to Pitt as he left the House of Commons shortly after news of the acquisition of the *Diwani* had become public knowledge. Upon hearing Walsh's account of the Company's recent achievements, Pitt remarked that Clive had 'acquired great honour, but that they [the new possessions] were too vast: it was some time he had been dissatisfied with our proceedings there'.[10] Walsh's opinion was that 'due attention may be paid to him [Pitt]', and he warned that 'one word from him would go in making or unmaking the Company'. In view of this, it could not have come as a great surprise to the Court of Directors when, within six weeks of the establishment of a ministry headed by Pitt (now Lord Chatham), they were informed that the Company's affairs would be brought under the consideration of Parliament during the forthcoming session.[11]

It soon became known to the public that the ministry intended to undertake an examination of the Company's affairs, but nobody knew what form the inquiry would take. Such confusion was understandable and, from the time that the issue was first raised, even the members of the cabinet remained uncertain as to Chatham's intentions. He was reluctant to declare his proposed plan of action to even his closest cabinet colleagues. As Grafton later remarked, 'Lord Chatham never did open to us, or the Cabinet in general what was his real and fixed plan.'[12] However, while the Prime Minister might have remained distant from his colleagues, he was nevertheless actively pursuing his objective of securing for the state a share of the Company's new revenues. The problem he was confronting was that of determining upon what legal grounds his case should be based.

Among Chatham's papers are to be found several briefing documents presented to him in 1766 and 1767 on the subject of the Company's right to the territorial revenues derived from the *Diwani*.[13] Some of them, including one from Laurence Sulivan,[14] recommended decisive action

[9] *The Correspondence of William Pitt, Earl of Chatham*, ed. W.S. Taylor and J.H. Pringle (4 vols., 1838–40), I, 389–90.   [10] NLW, Clive MSS 52, p. 87.

[11] IOR, B/82, pp. 151–2. For the preliminaries to the formation of the Chatham administration see Brooke, *Chatham Administration*, pp. 1–4.

[12] *Grafton Autobiography*, p. 98.   [13] PRO, 30/8, part 3, ff. 245–8, 263.

[14] *Ibid.*, f. 263.

against the Company's privileges, and, from a study of these papers, evolved Chatham's notion of subjecting the Company to a parliamentary inquiry and therein deciding upon the right to the revenues. This course of action was approved by some of his most loyal supporters, such as Thomas Walpole MP for Ashburton, who told Chatham in September 1766 that the recent gains in Bengal should be consolidated, and that if the Company proved to be incapable of performing this task then the state should intervene and assume the responsibility itself.[15] However, other supporters of the ministry, such as the procedural expert Jeremiah Dyson, warned that the administration should proceed with extreme caution because a legal decision relating to the revenues was not part of the 'ordinary business of the House of Commons'.[16] Chatham nevertheless remained fixed in his determination to proceed with an inquiry and a subsequent declaration of right, but his plan soon became beset with unforeseen problems and difficulties.

The question of the British Crown's sovereignty over the Company's possessions in India as 'English settlements' was never in doubt. The 'sovereign right, power and dominion' over the Company's 'forts, places, and plantations' had been reserved to the Crown in perpetuity by the Company's charter of 1698, a document which simply confirmed provisions incorporated in the charters of 1683 and 1686.[17] Even so, the whole issue of British sovereign rights in India had been clarified in 1757 in an opinion delivered by the Attorney- and Solicitor-Generals, Charles Yorke and Charles Pratt. In that year, following a number of disputes between Company servants and some of the regular army officers who had recently arrived in India to assist in the struggle against the French,[18] the directors had petitioned the King for a grant to enable the Company to retain all booty and plunder captured during the course of hostilities. They also requested the right to hold any territories within the limits of their trade that were gained by any legitimate means from any enemy, and to be empowered to dispose of the possessions as they so pleased, 'subject nevertheless to your Majesty's disposition and

---

[15] *Chatham Corr.*, III, 61.
[16] Undated paper submitted to Lord Shelburne, Clements Library, Lansdowne MSS, 90, f. 467.
[17] A.B. Keith, *A Constitutional History of India, 1600–1935* (1936), pp. 9–20. See also S.V. Desika Char (ed.), *Readings in the Constitutional History of India, 1757–1947* (Oxford, 1983), p. xxxii. The charter of 1698 was granted to the 'new' East India Company. When the new Company merged with the old in 1709 the charter of the former became the charter of the United Company.
[18] There had been a number of disputes between the Company's servants in India and regular army officers over the division of the spoils of war. See, for example, details of the serious altercation between the Madras Council and Colonel Aldercron in August 1756; Malcolm, *Life of Robert, Lord Clive*, I, 134–40.

pleasure, as to lands as may be acquired by conquest from the subjects of any European power'.[19] Pratt and Yorke were asked for their opinion, and they reported their recommendations on 24 December 1757.

The first part of the petition met with little objection, and the right to the plunder was granted to the Company subject to three restrictions: the plunder had to be captured within the limits of the Company's trade; it had to be taken in a defensive action; and the act of capture had to be made by the Company's troops acting alone, and not in conjunction with any regular army units. The second part of the Company's request, that relating to the 'holding or retaining fortresses and districts already acquired, or to be acquired by treaty, grant, or conquest', proved rather more difficult for the law officers to deliberate upon. As they noted, 'many objections occur to it, more material than to be weighed'. They conceded, therefore, that their judgement could not be regarded as a definitive statement, because it was not possible by precedent nor practicable through policy considerations to make a general grant to a trading company with respect to any future conquests taken from either an Indian or a European power. However, Pratt and Yorke did differentiate between territories and possessions taken from Indians by conquest, and those procured by the Company through treaty or negotiation. In the former instance the Crown obtained sovereignty and actual possession of the land, but in the latter case it only acquired sovereignty over the Company's acquisitions as 'English settlements'. Possession of the land itself was granted to the Company.[20]

Nine years later, this opinion gave hope to those defending the Company's rights,[21] as well as to those supporting the Crown's claims to the territorial revenues. Just as one pamphleteer could write 'that they [the Company] have obtained sovereignty is easily asserted, and is easily denied',[22] so too could equally valid rival claims be made on the question of the right to the territorial revenues. The Chathamite MP

---

[19] Copies of the Company's petition and the subsequent Pratt-Yorke opinion are to be found in S. Lambert (ed.), *House of Commons Sessional Papers of the Eighteenth Century* (147 vols., Wilmington, Delaware, 1975), XXVI, item 1. The following quotations relating to the opinion have been taken from this source.

[20] This distinction was later used in relation to questions of land ownership in North America. The Pratt-Yorke opinion of 1757 was used as the basis of the arguments of those contesting the Crown's claim to land granted to settlers by American Indians. See J.M. Sosin, *Whitehall and the Wilderness: The Middle West in British Colonial Policy 1760–1775* (Lincoln, Neb., 1965), pp. 229–35, 259–67.

[21] In October 1766 it was reported to George Grenville by Thomas Whately that Sir George Colebrooke had mounted an 'extraordinary defence' of the Company's right to the revenues that was based on the Pratt-Yorke opinion; BL, Add. MSS 42084, ff. 188–9.

[22] *A Letter to the Proprietors of East India Stock, Containing a Relation of the Negotiations with Government from 1767 to the Present Time, Respecting the Company's Acquisitions in India* (1769), p. 3.

Colonel Isaac Barré commented upon this in the House of Commons in December 1766. In delivering the benefits of his military experience to the House, he declared that 'the artillery of the law he saw was brought down on both sides; but, like artillery had not done much hurt'.[23] Barré read Pratt's and Yorke's opinion in the context of the recent acquisitions and judged it favourable to the Company, even though the law officers had declared 'for what might follow, policy must take time to consider'. This, he concluded, implied that they did not understand the conquests as 'granted away by the charter'. Barré also noted that Charles Yorke, recently relieved of the burdens of office having resigned as Attorney-General in August, now defended the Company 'as entitled from the charter to their present acquisitions'. As if to complicate matters, Charles Pratt, now Lord Camden, stood on the other side of the argument and served as Lord Chancellor in Chatham's cabinet. Edmund Burke later recalled, 'the lawyers equivocated when the question was agitated',[24] and such equivocation did not strengthen Chatham's case.

On one hand it could be argued that the territorial revenues had been acquired by the Company through a direct grant from the Mughal Emperor. The grounds of this argument, it was later recalled, were that the Company 'held their possessions in India, not as an absolute property, but as a farm granted to them by the Great Mogul, and according to the constitution of the [Mughal] Empire subject to an annual rent'.[25] If this was so, was it not the case that the revenues were held by the Company within a legal context over which the British Crown and Parliament had no jurisdiction? Because the Company had freely acknowledged the Emperor as *de jure* sovereign in Bengal, it was difficult for some observers to perceive upon what grounds the ministry could base the Crown's claim to a share of the revenues.

On the other hand, supporters of the ministry argued that the grant from the Emperor had stemmed from a protracted war of conquest fought by the Company with a substantial amount of state assistance. The territorial revenues belonged to the spoils of war. Peregrine Cust, a staunch friend of the Company, admitted this in the House of Commons when he declared that 'the government was entitled to expect a return from the Company, as their settlements had been preserved by the navy, and depended upon the protection of the public'.[26] Isaac Barré reinforced this view in 1769 when he calculated that it had cost the nation four and a half million pounds 'to enable this Company to acquire

[23] Speech of 9 Dec. 1766, as reported in Horace Walpole, *Memoirs of the Reign of King George III*, ed. G.F. Russell Barker (4 vols., 1894), II, 288–9.
[24] Speech to the House of Commons, 23 Mar. 1773 reported in W. Cobbett, *Parliamentary History of England from...1066 to...1803* (36 vols., 1806–20), XVII, col. 821.
[25] Macpherson, *History of the European Commerce*, p. 193.
[26] Walpole, *Memoirs*, II, 288.

an extensive dominion greater than that of most crowned heads in Europe'.[27] Chatham himself made a similar point four years later, although he never publicly defined his stance in such precise terms in 1766 or 1767. In May 1773 he wrote that he had always believed in a 'mixed right' to the territorial revenues, 'the state equitably entitled to the larger share, as largest contributor by fleet, men, etc.'.[28] This represented an extension of the argument that had been advanced by Peregrine Cust, but it was an interpretation for which there was very little factual foundation.

Although the state had supported the Company in an auxiliary capacity, as Cust admitted, it had played no direct part in the important and decisive campaigns of 1764 and 1765. In fact there were no land-based Crown troops serving in Bengal during most of the war against Shuja-ud-daula and Mir Kasim. The regular army units that had fought against the French during the Seven Years War had been disbanded, recalled to Britain, or assimilated into the Company's own army.[29] The Company had taken all the military risks (the campaign had been by no means a foregone conclusion), and had carried the enormous financial burden of the war.[30] One supporter of the Company's rights had this point in mind when he asked in 1767 about the entitlement to the new riches of Bengal. Did the revenues belong to 'they who alone gained the battle against Sujah Dowlah which decided everything in the Company's favour; or they whose troops were not only not present, but were not in the country at the time of the action ... they, in short, to whom the Mogul granted the Duanship, or they to whom he did not grant it'?[31]

The question that lay at the very heart of the Bengal revenue issue was a simple one, and a contemporary framed it most succinctly in 1767. Should the Company's territorial acquisitions and revenues be considered as a 'mercantile purchase or acquest by mutual bargain and reciprocal treaty, or the fruit of arms and of terms imposed by conquerors through the terror of military force, and coercion over a naked and defenceless possessor and inhabitants[?]'[32] The answer was to be found as much in factual interpretation of recent events in Bengal as in evaluation of legal definitions and judgements. The debate focused on whether or not the Company had actually fought a war of territorial

---

[27] Speech in the House of Commons, 27 Feb. 1769, BL, Eg. MSS 218, p. 124.
[28] *Chatham Corr.*, IV, 264.
[29] A. Broome, *A History of the Rise and Progress of the Bengal Army* (1851), p. 392.
[30] The Company's military expenditure in Bengal rose from £346,413 in 1762/3 to £886,090 in 1765/6, RCHC, IV, 60–1.
[31] *Letter to the Proprietors of India Stock*, p. 15.
[32] Anonymous author of the pamphlet *A Letter to George Grenville* quoted in *Monthly Review*, 36 (1767), 148.

conquest in 1764 and 1765.[33] Certainly the Company had become the
dominant military force in the region, but its ambitions had not
extended to the assumption of sovereign status. In this strict sense it
could be argued that the Company had not made any tangible territorial
acquisitions. Of course the reality, as outlined in chapter 1, was quite
different, but the Company had gone to elaborate lengths to acknowledge
Shah Alam's sovereignty. Furthermore, the *Diwani* had not simply been
extorted from the Emperor under the terms of an imposed or dictated
peace settlement. Shah Alam had in fact been trying to offload the office
of *Diwan* onto the Company for almost six years, for his own prospects
of receiving a regular income in the form of a tribute from the provinces
of Bengal, Bihar, and Orissa were better served by the British than by
the Nawab. On the other hand, if it was accepted that the Company had
fought a war of conquest then the pertinent question was whether they
could, with or without the support of the regular army, conquer on
behalf of anyone other than the Crown.

Chatham's position was quite clear: the Company had fought a war of
conquest, the *Diwani* belonged to the spoils of that war, and the Crown
had an undeniable right to a share of those spoils. As the Court
officeholder and MP Hans Stanley later remarked, 'Mr Pitt looked upon
India as a British conquest.'[34] Thus, in 1769, when Isaac Barré recalled
the proceedings of the inquiry two years earlier, he explained that what
the Chathamites had intended to do was 'to decide the right that this
country had to those territories, they being undoubtedly in the minds of
the most dispassionate, the effects of conquest, derived from the
operations of war and of course to be given to this country'.[35] Chatham,
who as Secretary of State for the South in 1757 had framed the
ministerial response to the Company based upon the Pratt-Yorke
opinion, did not lose sight of the fact that the Company could only
derive a right to property and territory gained by conquest through a
grant from the Crown. It was this belief that formed the cornerstone of
his whole attitude towards the Company and its territorial revenues in
1766.

The parliamentary session of 1766–7 began on 11 November and,
although a week later William Beckford moved for a Committee of
inquiry into the Company's affairs,[36] it was not until the following

[33] For a contemporary review of the arguments see *Annual Register* (1767), pp. 42–3*.
[34] Speech to the House of Commons, 9 Mar. 1773, BL, Eg. MSS 244, p. 278.
[35] Speech of 27 Feb. 1769, *ibid.*, 218, p. 115.
[36] The aggressive, even wild, manner in which Beckford introduced the business
prompted much comment from observers, and caused much dismay in Company
circles. See, for example, Walpole, *Memoirs*, II, 279–80; Verelst, *A View of the Rise*, pp.
80–1; John Scott to Shelburne, 29 Nov. 1766, cited in Brooke, *Chatham Administration*,
p. 74, n. 1.

March that the Committee finally began its proceedings. A number of circumstances contributed to this five-month delay. In particular, divisions within the cabinet hampered progress, because from the outset both Charles Townshend and Henry Seymour Conway favoured a negotiated settlement with the Company. Yet this should not be interpreted as an indication that they questioned the validity of the Crown's claims to the revenues.[37] The divisions within the cabinet instead stemmed from differences of opinion over the tactical approach to the question, and both Townshend and Conway sought to avert a head-on collision between the Company and the ministry.

Townshend, who was considering ideas on American taxation at this time, was well aware of the practical difficulties surrounding any declaration of right in favour of the Crown, and he devoted considerable thought to the subject. Once such a declaration had been made the state would have to assume ultimate responsibility for the Company's territorial possessions. Thus, if at any time the Company was to prove incapable of exercising adequate supervision over those territories, the state would have no alternative but to intervene and establish itself as revenue collector and defender of British interests in Bengal. This was eventually to become a viable option by the middle of the nineteenth century, but no eighteenth-century government possessed either the necessary resources or strength of purpose to effect such a transfer of responsibility. However, Chatham refused to consider or even acknowledge the potential long-term dangers inherent in his proposed plan of action, and it was thus left to Townshend to point out the 'impracticability of substituting the Public in the place of the Company in the collecting, investing, conducting, and remitting the revenue'.[38] A declaration of right in favour of the Crown could at some future date place an intolerable burden upon the nation for, despite the optimistic estimates about the size of the *Diwani* revenues, there was as yet no way of determining whether the benefits derived from India would ever offset the enormous cost of maintaining the British position there.

Although it has been held, and cannot be denied, that Townshend's speculative activities in India stock played no small part in conditioning his whole approach to the Indian problem,[39] there is no doubt that he made a far more realistic appraisal of the issues involved than many of his colleagues. He stressed the need for a financial deal, a settlement of

---

[37] See, for example, Conway's pronouncement on the subject in 1772, BL, Eg. MSS 240, p. 311. For a detailed account of the period between Nov. 1766 and Apr. 1767 see Bowen, 'British politics and the East India Company', ch. 4.

[38] Sentiments expressed in letters written to Grafton and Chatham in early 1767 cited in Namier and Brooke, *Charles Townshend*, p. 161.   [39] *Ibid.*, pp. 159–60, 167.

'reciprocal advantage', to be struck between the state and the Company. If the right was not declared the Company could remain in place, at no cost to government, as the vehicle of revenue collection in Bengal, and the state could then receive a significant financial return from its activities. Thus, as the Duke of Grafton later recalled, both Townshend and Conway 'were for waving [*sic*] the decision on right and for bringing on a negotiation with the Company, without entering on this essential point, which Lord Chatham together with the rest of the Cabinet wanted to see decided in the first place'.[40]

In spite of a majority of the cabinet falling into line behind Chatham, the initiative eventually passed to those favouring a negotiated financial settlement. The Company, encouraged by the apparent weakening of the ministry's resolve, submitted, amended, and resubmitted proposals that were intended to form the basis of a satisfactory settlement between the two parties. This process took an inordinate length of time and the opening of the inquiry was repeatedly postponed while the outcome of negotiations was awaited.

Throughout much of this period, which lasted from December 1766 to March 1767, Chatham was absent from London recovering from illness, and he was far from satisfied with the manner in which the business was conducted by his colleagues. As if further to undermine the ministry's position, numerical weakness in the House of Commons ensured that the opposition was able to harass and threaten to defeat the embattled administration in the division lobby. Indeed, on 27 February the ministry suffered an embarrassing setback when it lost a division on the land tax by 206 votes to 188. The effects of this defeat must not be overstated, because the land tax was an emotive tissue which cut across normal political loyalties, but, even so, it did illustrate just how vulnerable the ministry could be if the opposition took care to prepare its ground and co-ordinate its efforts.[41] Indian affairs offered them ample opportunities to do just that.

Notwithstanding all the difficulties confronting the ministry, the central issue of the right to the revenues was kept firmly in sight by Chatham's associates. Thus, in spite of the lead given by moderate elements within the cabinet, and even when the directors of the Company and the Treasury were in the middle of protracted negotiations in February 1767, Beckford was prepared to make a motion in the Commons declaring that 'all districts, provinces and revenues, acquired by the East India Company since the year 1748 do not, of right, belong

---

[40] *Grafton Autobiography*, p. 109.
[41] Brooke, *Chatham Administration*, pp. 105–10.

to the said Company.'[42] He was prevented from doing so when tactical considerations prompted delay,[43] but Chatham himself remained adamant that whatever bargain was struck between the Company and the ministry, the right to the revenues would first have to be determined.[44]

At the beginning of March, as if to give a belated lead to his frustrated colleagues, Chatham prepared detailed instructions on how the business was to be conducted when the inquiry eventually began.[45] These instructions underlined once again his firm commitment to a declaration of right, and they demonstrated upon what grounds such a declaration was to be made. The Committee was to begin by stating facts based upon two fundamental premisses: namely, that the Company, according to the terms of all its charters, had been instituted as no more than a trading company; and, secondly, that all the revenues and territories obtained in India had stemmed from 'actual and extensive operations of war'. A satisfactory declaration of right would follow in due course. Then, having made this last statement on Company affairs, Chatham withdrew from public life and left consideration of the 'transcendent object' to his subordinate and divided cabinet colleagues.

Even as Chatham formulated his instructions he acknowledged that the ministry's weak political position undermined his hopes for success. The recent defeat on the land tax issue represented a shattering blow to confidence, and meant that any attempt to force the question of right to a decision in the Commons might pose a serious threat to the future of the ministry. Delay was counselled and Chatham's instructions were designed to gain time for the ministry while the political temperature was lowered. On the one hand, some political observers felt that Chatham was being forced to the negotiating table. Edmund Burke adopted this view of the situation and predicted that he 'will find some way of quitting his ground of a claim of right on the Company and will at length negotiate a treaty'.[46] Others, however, including some within the Company, still firmly believed that the question of right would eventually have to be settled by the Committee of inquiry.[47]

---

[42] *Chatham Corr.*, III, 201–2.
[43] *Ibid.*, III, 212. Two weeks earlier Chatham had conceded that with a negotiation pending there was little prospect of any question for deciding the right being 'duly supported', *ibid.*, III, 181.   [44] *Grafton Autobiography*, p. 98.
[45] 'East India plan for motion as recommended by Lord Chatham', Clements Library, Lansdowne MSS, 90, f. 441. From internal evidence this paper can be dated as 6 Mar. 1767.
[46] *The Correspondence of Edmund Burke*, I: ed. T.W. Copeland (Cambridge, 1958), 300. The Duke of Newcastle came to the same conclusion, BL, Add. MSS 32980, f. 304.
[47] John Walsh to Clive, 26 Mar. 1767, IOL, MSS Eur. G. 37, box 44 (no fol.).

Nobody understood the realities of the situation better than the Chairman of the Company, George Dudley. In a perceptive analysis of the situation, he sketched the outlines of the ministry's position. 'They seem to me', he wrote to Clive in March, 'to determine in their own minds that the right is in the Crown and therefore if the Company has a desire to preserve a share in it they must acknowledge that right.' Accordingly, any proposals for a negotiated settlement that were formulated by the Company had, above all else, to serve the purpose of preventing a 'tryal of right'.[48] The directors recognized the considerable threat to the Company's position and thus sought to remove the danger by offering the ministry a satisfactory settlement which did not hinge upon a solution of the problem of territorial rights.

The realities of the political situation were such that several members of the cabinet, apart from Conway and Townshend, became more receptive to such an idea. With a resurgent opposition in Parliament concentrating on the popular issue of the threat to chartered rights, any attempt to force a solution to the revenue question in the House of Commons was fraught with very serious difficulties; a negotiated settlement offered the ministry an alternative but acceptable way out of a tight political corner. A significant financial return from the Company could still be secured and that, after all, was the overriding concern. This whole state of affairs was summed up by Lord Shelburne, who reported to Chatham in mid-March that 'the situation of the House of Commons, too bad to be described, appears to make what passes in the City [i.e. the negotiations] very material'.[49]

Even so, while circumstances dictated that the cabinet consider a negotiated settlement, Chatham's staunchest supporters bided their time and awaited the opening of the inquiry. When the Committee eventually began its work they then made a sustained and concerted attempt to obtain the necessary declaration of right, and that attempt was almost successful. As Chatham had originally intended, a full and detailed examination of the right to the Company's revenues and territorial acquisitions in Bengal was undertaken.

The Committee began its proceedings on 20 March.[50] The first witness to come before the House was Henry Vansittart, the former Governor of Bengal, who was examined for four hours on 27 March on the subject of the Company's activities since 1756. In particular, he was

---

[48] *Ibid.*   [49] PRO, 30/8, 56, ff. 76–8.
[50] Unlike its successors in 1772 and 1773 the Committee did not produce any reports. The most complete record of its proceedings is to be found in BL, Add. MSS 18469, 'Evidence taken before the Committee, 27 March–13 April 1767'. This copy was sent by Robert Gregory to Sir Hugh Inglis on 19 April 1802.

questioned on the nature of the Company's possessions, the manner of their acquisition, and their estimated value.[51] These lines of questioning were then repeated with most of the remaining witnesses: the inquiry became preoccupied with the revenues and the Company's territorial expansion in Bengal.[52] 'All they do', complained Edmund Burke of the ministry, 'is run a blind muck at the Company's right to their acquisitions, without knowing the practicability or regarding the justice of the measure.'[53] However, it was by 'running a blind muck' at the central issue of right that the Chathamites gradually wore down the resistance of the parliamentary opposition and the dissenters within the cabinet.

Horace Walpole soon thought that the ministry was nearing its objective: 'every single evidence has brought forth in stronger and stronger colours the right of the crown to the conquests made by the Company. This was thought to be a great problematic and ticklish question. There is now the highest probability the government will carry that point.'[54] This was a view shared by the Duke of Newcastle, who reported to Rockingham on 14 April that Conway was now 'concerned of the *Right*'.[55] He also noted a major change of attitude among the directors in the face of this pressure: 'I am afraid my Lord Chatham will carry his point in the East India affairs. The directors will give up their point of right and, they say, when their bargain is fixed the right signifies nothing to them. They will make a new proposal to the ministry, and such, as I hear, will be accepted.' Chatham was close to his objective.

Although it was widely held that the ministry's stance on territorial rights had been strengthened during the course of the inquiry, a number of difficulties remained unresolved. To the old question of whether or not the Company's acquisitions represented a conquest or a grant was now added a new problem: where and exactly how should the declaration of right be made? Was an expression of parliamentary opinion sufficient to secure such a declaration, or should the issue be tried in a court of law? Supporters of the Company argued that not only was the ministry attempting to infringe the Company's basic chartered privileges, but

---

[51] BL, Add. MSS 32980, f. 394; *ibid.*, 18469, ff. 2–11. Questions from the ministerial side were put by Beckford, Dyson, Sir Gilbert Elliot, Lord Clare, the Attorney-General William de Grey, Lord Barrington and Isaac Barré. Questions from the opposition were put by Grenville, Charles Yorke, and Lord Catherlough. Neither Townshend nor Conway were present.
[52] See, for example, the questioning of John Zephaniah Holwell and Warren Hastings on 30, 31 March, and of George Dudley on 9 April, BL, Add. MSS 18469, ff. 12–30, 56–62.   [53] *Burke Corr.*, I, 303.   [54] *Walpole Corr.*, XXII, 504.
[55] WWM, R1-774.

that Parliament was not the correct venue in which to decide upon the right to the territorial revenues.[56]

This new legal problem was brought into the open during a debate on 14 April when the ministry successfully staved off, by 213 votes to 157, an opposition attempt to put an end to the inquiry.[57] Prominent among the speakers were those well versed in legal affairs: even William Blackstone, the great jurist, made one of his rare parliamentary speeches on this occasion.[58] Jeremiah Dyson had already warned ministers that the issue of right should not be resolved in the Commons, and many others appear to have had similar reservations. Two years later George Grenville recalled that 'the House in general seemed to express an earnest wish that the decision [of right] might not be made here in Parliament'.[59] Instead, Grenville had advocated ('I mentioned it') that a 'proportionate sum should be taken [from the Company] by way of a tax'. This solved a number of problems and took away the 'odious office of being legislators and judges both'. As if to reinforce the advisability of securing such a compromise, a number of objections were also raised on 14 April against trying the issue of right in court.[60] The House resigned itself to await developments in the negotiations between the Company and the Treasury.

On 28 April and 2 May representatives of the Company met with ministers to discuss a negotiated settlement. They presented a set of proposals that had been much amended and revised since they had been first drafted in February. Indeed, it had taken until 8 April for the proprietors to resolve the issue, for only then had they voted by 546 to 347 to accept the directors' proposals, and not those of Laurence Sulivan, as the basis of a settlement with the ministry.[61] Although many of the details still needed to be finalized, and were to be the subject of protracted bargaining over many weeks, one fundamental feature was established and accepted by both sides. The directors presented their proposals on the condition that 'such an agreement must depend on the Company's enjoyment of the *Diwani* of Bengal, Bihar, and Orissa'.[62] This was now deemed acceptable by the ministry and Townshend indicated as much to the Chairman and Deputy-Chairman on 2 May.[63]

[56] *Annual Register*, 1767, p. 43*.   [57] *CJ*, XXXI, 306.

[58] For a full account of the debate see P.D.G. Thomas (ed.), 'The parliamentary diaries of Nathaniel Ryder 1764–7', *Camden Miscellany*, XXIII, Royal Historical Society, Camden Fourth Series, VII (1969), 338–40.

[59] BL, Eg. MSS 218, pp. 173–4.

[60] See, for example, the speech of the Attorney-General William de Grey; Walpole, *Memoirs*, III, 2.   [61] IOR, B/83, p. 3.

[62] *Ibid.*, B/82, pp. 480–2; B/83, pp. 9, 11–12, 28–9.

[63] *Ibid.*, B/83, p. 30. see also BL, Add. MSS 32981, f. 254.

Chatham's intention of declaring the right had been laid to rest because, notwithstanding appearances in the Committee of inquiry, several ministers still held very strong reservations about their ability to secure such a declaration in Parliament.[64] Thus, when the Company offered them suitable terms, and an annual payment of £400,000 was fixed upon in lieu of a decision of right, they were only too glad to accept such a settlement.

It is not clear how or why this particular figure of £400,000 a year was arrived at, but both William Pulteney and Laurence Sulivan proposed several times in the General Court that such a sum would represent an appropriate annual payment from the Company to government. Sulivan's motives are unclear. He had close links with Chatham's colleague Lord Shelburne and may have been a ministerial Trojan Horse inside India House or, on the other hand, he may have been courting popularity among the proprietors as part of his long-running campaign to secure election to the Court of Directors. Most contemporary observers favoured the latter interpretation, and saw Sulivan's actions as little more than a crude attempt to coax the ministry into relaxing their recently imposed restrictions on the level of Company dividend payments.[65] This was most definitely not a tactic favoured by the directors, and Colebrooke was later of the opinion that Sulivan's interference cost the Company £100,000 a year, because at one stage in the negotiations the ministry had been quite prepared to accept an annual payment of £300,000.[66] Whatever the reasons, and here the Company's political history is at its most impenetrable,[67] it is worth pointing out that £400,000 a year just about compensated government for the revenue lost because of the reduction of the land tax rate from 4s. to 3s. in February. Perhaps, quite simply, ministers saw this form of East India settlement as the best short-term method of balancing the Treasury's books.

In fact, the Company had acted just in time, for when the Committee of inquiry reconvened after the Easter recess on 1 May it became known that William Beckford had prepared eight motions to put before the House.[68] However, Beckford was thwarted when it was announced that an agreement between the Company and the ministry was close at hand. As the Company's revised proposals had 'received such approbation'

---

[64] Walpole, *Memoirs*, III, 8, 11.

[65] Thomas Bradshaw to Grafton, 15 May 1767, *Grafton Autobiography*, p. 180. The 'Dividend Bill' had been introduced in the Commons on 11 May. It was eventually enacted as 7 Geo. III, c. 49.   [66] Colebrooke, *Retrospection*, I, 116.

[67] The final framing of the settlement is discussed in detail in Bowen, 'British politics and the East India Company', pp. 403–8.   [68] *Burke Corr.*, I, 310.

and were 'generally thought advantageous to public and Company',[69] Chatham's ally was denied the opportunity to put his motions to the Commons. The following year he complained about this to the House in bitter terms: 'You ought not to have taken the £400,000. I was not supported by government who ought to declare the right.'[70] On the other hand, most other politicians, members of the government and opposition alike, were satisfied with the compromise solution that had been found to the problem: a two-year agreement between the ministry and the Company found expression in statute (7 Geo. III, c. 57). The Company retained all of its territorial possessions and, as agreed, it undertook to pay £400,000 a year into the Treasury.

The architect of the inquiry, Lord Chatham, made no recorded public comment on his ministers' failure to declare the Crown's right to the Bengal revenues. Nevertheless, there is evidence which suggests that he was far from satisfied with the course that recent events had taken. When precisely he made his dissatisfaction known is not clear, but at some point in 1767 he criticized in no uncertain terms the bargain struck with the Company by Townshend. 'The proposal', he declared, '... deserves the highest disapprobation of Parliament ... It bargains away in effect the great right and interest of the nation (which if duly and wisely asserted would have brought effectual relief) for the convenience of the present minute.'[71] In a sense Chatham was correct, for most observers assumed that the ministry's failure to secure a declaration of right meant that the Company had won its point and had confirmed its position as sole legal British territorial proprietor in Bengal. Events were later to prove that this was not in fact the case, but in the confused political circumstances of 1767 it is difficult to see what other course of action Chatham's ministers could have followed.

The East India legislation of 1767 settled very little; it served only as a forerunner to further parliamentary intervention in the Company's affairs, and it postponed permanent solutions until a later date. The inquiry had served to highlight the intractable legal difficulties surrounding the Company's position as a territorial proprietor in India, yet the means were not at hand to secure a solution to the problem. In spite of all its various political weaknesses, the Chatham ministry had come as close as it possibly could to its primary objective, a declaration of right. The ground was well prepared in the inquiry, and many

---

[69] James West to the Duke of Newcastle (undated), BL, Add. MSS 32981, f. 307. See also Walpole, *Memoirs*, III, 11–12; Thomas, 'Ryder Diaries', p. 341.
[70] BL, Eg. MSS 216, p. 19.
[71] From a paper endorsed 'East Indies. Lord Chatham's own in Pretyman MSS, Orwell Park' quoted in B. Williams, *The Life of William Pitt, Earl of Chatham* (2 vols., 1913) II, 235. I have been unable to locate the original document.

observers had believed that the issue would be resolved in favour of the Crown. However, what could not be determined was exactly how, where, and by whom the matter should be decided. In the final analysis these factors, together with the failure to secure a clear-cut definition of the Company's acquisitions as being the product of either conquest or a Mughal grant, led to the failure of Chatham's strategy. Too many legal arguments and procedural difficulties remained unresolved, and a redefinition of the Company's status was deferred until a later date. The Company's right to collect the territorial revenues of Bengal, Bihar, and Orissa thus continued on the basis of an ill-defined and disputed legal position, and Chatham bequeathed to his immediate successors a political, constitutional, and imperial problem of the greatest magnitude.

5 Crown and Company (II): foreign relations, 1766–1769

The events leading up to Clive's assumption of the *Diwani* in 1765 opened up new political, military, and economic horizons for those in control of the East India Company's affairs in India. Those same events also highlighted some of the weaknesses within the informal and ill-defined relationship between the Company and the British government.

The Company had cast itself in the new role of territorial proprietor in Bengal, yet it had done so with little or no reference to its nominal political masters in Whitehall and Westminster. The assumption of the *Diwani* had been presented by Clive to all parties as a *fait accompli*, and there had been no consultation on the matter with the directors of the Company, let alone with the ministry. While few objected to this at the time, the possibility was raised that in future Company servants might procure, or attempt to procure, territory that was unwanted, difficult to defend, and a burden to the nation as well as the Company. Accordingly, two important and related questions came to the fore during the late 1760s. How far, and in what form, should the Company extend its power and influence? And, secondly, what permanent voice should the ministry be given in future deliberations related to the Company's strategic planning and operations?

Such were the burdens of new responsibilities that some felt that it was no longer possible to allow the Company alone to chart the course of political and military events on the subcontinent. The recently awakened interest in India as a national economic asset demanded a much closer day-to-day supervision of the Company's affairs by ministers, and thus during the late 1760s a steady erosion of the Company's freedom of political and diplomatic action occurred. Nothing better symbolized this than the appointment of Sir John Lindsay in 1769 as Crown Plenipotentiary in the Indian Ocean and surrounding area. He was to act as the ministerial 'voice' in the region, a development which represented an important first step towards the establishment of a permanent non-Company British representative in India.

The unrivalled strength of British arms in north-eastern India by

1765, and the collapse of the Wazir of Awadh's capacity for resistance, enabled individuals within the Company to entertain thoughts of a further extension of their influence and territory. Schemes were considered whereby the Mughal Emperor, supported by the Company, would undertake the conquest of Awadh and the province would thereafter be supported and defended by British arms. In return for this help the Emperor would grant the Company the right to collect the revenues of Benares, the *zamindari* of Bulwant Singh.[1] Although this rather fanciful scheme was eventually rejected, the very fact that it was considered at all is indicative of the underlying tensions between those within the Company who were prepared to countenance an extended interventionist policy, and those who strove for the consolidation of the Company's position within the frontiers of Bengal.

Yet, while it would be quite wrong to argue that anything like a 'forward' school of thought existed among Company decision-makers,[2] consideration of ventures such as the annexation of Awadh did undoubtedly take place from time to time during the late 1760s. Moreover, such debate was not confined to those in India, and there were some in London within the highest Company circles who were carried away on the general wave of enthusiasm created by Clive's success in Bengal. These individuals could see no remaining restraints upon the geographical scope of the Company's activities and, as Laurence Sulivan warned in 1767, some directors might be tempted 'to extend their conquests, perhaps to China (an easy acquisition)'.[3] In a broader context, a pamphleteer discussing the Company's affairs in 1772 reminded his readers that it was held to be a general maxim of all imperial activity that 'Extension of dominion is an irresistible desire.'[4]

In the short term such fears proved to be unfounded. Thoughts of future conquest found no place in the corporate Company mind, despite what may have been discussed in private by individual directors. The Secretary of the Company, Robert James, stated a general principle when he told the parliamentary Committee of inquiry in 1767 that 'We don't want conquest and power; it is commercial interest only we look for.'[5] The peaceful cultivation of extended commercial links was sanctioned by the authorities in London; military conquest was not. Thus commercial projects were founded upon a desire to open up trade links with Tibet and Western China; and a factory establishment was

---

[1] Verelst, *A View of the Rise*, p. 53.   [2] Marshall, *Problems of Empire*, p. 63.
[3] Anonymous paper written in the unmistakable hand of Laurence Sulivan: PRO, 30/8, vol. 99, pt. 3, f. 263.
[4] Dalrymple, *A General View of the East India Company*, p. vi.
[5] BL, Add. MSS 18469, f. 77, quoted in Marshall, *Problems of Empire*, p. 17.

sought on the island of Balambangan off north-east Borneo.[6] At the same time, the annexation of Awadh was eventually rejected in favour of the creation of a strong buffer state, well disposed towards the Company, against the Marathas and Afghans.[7] History provided several examples of the fateful consequences of unrestrained territorial aggrandizement, and the Chairman of the Company, Sir George Colebrooke, reminded the House of Commons of this in 1769: 'By extension of territory the Roman Empire was dissolved. Let us try to give a permanency to these acquisitions, and by doing so secure the prosperity of Great Britain.'[8]

'Permanency' and a curb on territorial expansion became synonymous, for it was only by concentrating exclusively upon trade and commerce that the Company and, indirectly, the nation could benefit from the acquisition of the *Diwani*. A 'wild project' such as a march on Delhi in support of the Mughal Emperor could only serve to threaten the Company's long-term economic prosperity by burdening the Company with additional expenditure and weakening the defences of established settlements.[9] Thus the bounds of the Company's activities were set at the borders of the province of Bihar. 'The [River] Carmanassa is our boundary', Clive told Claud Russell of the Bengal Council in 1767, 'and nothing but the most obvious necessity should carry us beyond it.'[10] Such sentiments were representative of the official line which found frequent expression in the dispatches sent from London, and Indian rulers were reassured that the Company had 'no further object than to maintain the tranquility of the Bengal province'.[11] 'It is not our wish to acquire further possessions', the directors reminded the Council at Fort William in June 1769, 'but to advert [sic] to the good management of those we have.'[12] Indeed, throughout the late 1760s the directors appear to have been quite content to focus their thoughts on Bengal alone, and the Presidencies of Madras and Bombay were only seldom deemed worthy of sustained consideration and debate. It was only when the Company's campaigns in the Carnatic region of Southern India against Haidar Ali of Mysore began to fail in 1768–9 that the directors were shaken out of an almost obsessive preoccupation with events in Bengal. Clive expressed a commonly held, and hardly

---

[6] *FWIHC*, V, 81, 142. The development of British contact with Tibet is examined in A. Lamb, *British India and Tibet, 1766–1810* (2nd revised ed., 1986), ch. 1.

[7] *FWIHC*, IV, 144–5, 183.

[8] Speech of 27 Feb. 1769; BL, Eg. MSS 218, f. 134.

[9] *FWIHC*, V, 10. See also Verelst, *A View of the Rise*, pp. 53–4.

[10] NLW, Clive MSS 61 (no fol.).   [11] *FWIHC*, V, 10–11.

[12] *Ibid.*, V, 208. The question of the maintenance of law and order in Bengal has recently been examined by G.J. Bryant, 'Pacification in the early British raj, 1755–85', *Journal of Imperial and Commonwealth History*, XIII (1985), 4–19.

surprising, belief when he wrote in 1767 of 'Bengal being an object of much greater importance than any of the other Company possessions'; while, two years later, Sir George Colebrooke went one step further and declared to the House of Commons in emphatic terms that 'there is no province but Bengal worth preserving'.[13]

Such arguments were incorporated in directives issued by the Company's London-based executive, but they had little effect upon the general situation in India. In particular, the Company's servants at Fort St George did not take kindly to what they perceived as a deliberate attempt by the directors to reduce their Presidency to second-class status. The directors had in fact always had the greatest difficulty in securing acceptance by their overseas servants of even the broadest policy guidelines. Orders were sometimes ignored, while on other occasions they were rendered useless by the passage of time between their issue in London and their arrival in India. The former problem was referred to by the Chairman of the Company, Thomas Rous, when he told the parliamentary Committee of inquiry in 1767 that 'We [the directors] have never had our orders complied with – not a quarter, nor a fifth, or a sixth for these ten years past.'[14] But, even allowing for the fact that this unsatisfactory and rather debilitating state of affairs was as much a geographical matter as anything else, there were elements of an important and inherent contradiction to be found in the orders issued from London as they related to the central question of the consolidation and/or expansion of the Company's activities. It was difficult if not impossible to extend trade and commerce into new markets or territory without military assistance and support. When, to use an example already cited, the scheme to open trade links with eastern Indonesia was set in motion the first step taken was the dispatch of a cruiser to 'take possession' of the island of Balambangan.[15]

All the Company's experiences to date pointed to the fact that in the last resort their trade was an armed trade in which, when necessary, force or the threat of force played a full part in the exploitation of commercial opportunities.[16] Indeed Laurence Sulivan remarked in the House of Commons in February 1773 that the Company could only ever

[13] NLW, Clive MSS 59, p. 4; Colebrooke (speech of 27 Feb. 1769), BL, Eg. MSS 218, f. 135. The distressed state of the Bombay Presidency during the third quarter of the eighteenth century has been examined by P. Nightingale, *Trade and Empire in Western India, 1784–1806* (Cambridge, 1970), ch. 2.

[14] BL, Add. MSS 18469, f. 68. Rous had been elected Chairman of the Company the previous day.

[15] *FWIHC*, V, 142. For a full account of the 'Borneo Enterprise' and its ultimate failure see V.T. Harlow, *The Founding of the Second British Empire, 1763–1795* (2 vols., 1952 and 1964), I, 70–97.

[16] For a full discussion of this issue see Chaudhuri, *Trading World of Asia*, pp. 109–20.

make the native population pay their debts 'by compulsion'. There were, he held, no other means by which the Company could possibly conduct its trading and revenue-collection operations.[17] From this state of affairs it was only a short step to the assumption of primary administrative responsibilities.[18] The directors were thus confronted at all times with the almost impossible task of achieving a fine balance between territorial consolidation in Bengal, and commercial expansion elsewhere. Further military conquest was prohibited, but the careful exercise of military power in support of trade was not. These two central tenets of the directors' broad policy guidelines were almost irreconcilable and, in practice, many Company servants proved to be incapable of making a distinction between the two. They were able to perceive grounds upon which they might justify armed activity well beyond the Company's prescribed spheres of influence.

The orders and appeals for restraint from the directors had particularly little effect upon those Company servants who were engaged in their own private-trading activities. Private inter-Asian trade by Company servants had been permitted since the seventeenth century, and a steady increase in its volume had occurred since then, with more rapid growth occurring after the Battle of Plassey.[19] The search for new private-trade openings had often set these servants against the interests of the Company they nominally represented, as well as against the interests of the native population. Indeed, a whole series of private-trade-related disputes had contributed in large part to the outbreak of war between the Company and the Nawab Mir Kasim in 1763.[20] Time and again the servants in India had to be reminded about the geographical limitations of, and treaty restrictions upon, British trading activity.[21] It was to no avail, and throughout the 1760s, for example, Company servants participated in the production and distribution of salt in areas well beyond the Company's jurisdiction.[22] Such commercial enterprise represented an informal extension of British activity that had not been sanctioned by any metropolitan authority within the Company.

[17] Speech of 2 June 1773; BL, Eg. MSS 249, p. 168.
[18] P.J. Marshall, *East Indian Fortunes: The British in Bengal in the Eighteenth Century* (Oxford, 1976), pp. 112–15.
[19] *Ibid., passim.* See also I.B. Watson, *Foundations for Empire: English Private Trade in India, 1659–1760* (New Delhi, 1980) and J.D. Nichol, 'The British in India 1740–1763: a study of imperial expansion into Bengal', unpublished Ph.D. thesis, University of Cambridge, 1976.
[20] Marshall, *East Indian Fortunes*, pp. 124–8; Dodwell, *Dupleix and Clive*, pp. 214–25.
[21] See, for example, *FWIHC*, V, 9, 11–12.
[22] B. Barui, *The Salt Industry of Bengal, 1757–1800: A Study in the Interaction of British Monopoly Control and Indigenous Culture* (Calcutta, 1985), pp. 85–6; Marshall, *East Indian Fortunes*, p. 16.

It was a development that could not be controlled, and it brought with it a whole host of problems for the directors.[23] Indeed, in 1767 Clive identified private-trade disputes as the 'foundation of all the bloodsheds, massacres, and confusion which have happened of late years in Bengal', and few contemporaries would have disagreed with this diagnosis of the Company's ills.[24] Similar arguments later played an important part in sustaining the case of those in Parliament who questioned the manner in which Company servants conducted themselves and their business in India.

Throughout the period the directors were confronted with a wide and complex range of problems related to the future scope of the Company's activities. In order for the newly acquired territories to realize economic benefits for the nation as well as the Company's stockholders, British possessions now had to be consolidated, cultivated, and protected. This meant that civil and military resources had to be channelled in the first instance into those areas where the Company was now de facto sovereign. At the same time, and wherever possible, the Company's legitimate trading activities had to be expanded without securing the addition of further political and administrative burdens. Finally, the unauthorized and often dangerous private-trading schemes and projects of individual Company servants had to be strictly controlled, if not eliminated altogether.

Any attempts to consolidate the Company's territorial possessions and cultivate extended commercial operations were heavily dependent upon the maintenance of peaceful relations with Indian powers and rival European trading companies. By 1765 the military threat posed by the French and Dutch to the Company had almost disappeared but, nevertheless, fears of a French resurgence were ever-present in the thoughts of the directors. 'The French', they told the Bengal Council in November 1768, 'will undoubtedly leave no arts unpractised to open a way for regaining their former influence in India.'[25] News of Choiseul's designs kept the directors on their mettle, even though his schemes were often fanciful and unrealistic. In 1770, for example, a complex plan to destabilize the Company in London through the purchase and distribution of vast amounts of India stock ended in farcical circumstances when one of the central figures in the plot was uncovered and gaoled for the non-payment of debts.[26]

In a commercial context Company policy was directed towards denying other European companies any opportunity to re-establish their

[23] Nichol quite appropriately defines such a process and its ramifications as 'sub imperialism': 'The British in India', pp. 4–5, 304.   [24] FWIHC, V, 282.
[25] Ibid., V, 143.
[26] Calendar of Home Office Papers of the Reign of George III 1770–2 (1881), pp. 244–6.

former position of economic strength on the subcontinent, and any new trade outlet that the Company could secure was held to be a setback to their rivals. However, the directors did not seek direct confrontation with the French and Dutch in their attempts to keep them 'within proper limits'. Instead they relied upon the application of pressure from native ministers and officials who were urged by the Company to remind other Europeans of the extent of their treaty obligations and commercial privileges.[27] The directors also strove (with little apparent success) to prevent 'the cargoes of the French and Dutch ships being more valuable than ours',[28] and this served in part to underpin the sustained campaign for the exportation of better quality goods to London. Such maxims about the general conduct of trading policy found repeated expression in the directives sent from London in the 1760s but, at the same time, it was also stressed that unnecessary commercial disputes were to be avoided at all costs. To illustrate the point, in 1767 the directors consented to the supply of salt to Jean Law, Governor of the French Company's settlement at Pondicherry, 'as a good harmony with the French will be the means of preventing any disagreeable altercations in point of trade'.[29]

In broad strategic terms the threat posed by the French was perceived to be a very real one indeed.[30] As events in 1769 were to prove, any reports, false or otherwise, of French collusion with native princes could have a disastrous effect upon India stock prices.[31] Such reports, or news of an increased French presence at Isle de France (Mauritius), were therefore never taken lightly.[32] In November 1768 the directors exhorted their servants in India to exercise the 'utmost vigilance to disconcert their [the French] intrigues with the country powers and to render ineffectual their design for involving us with them'.[33] At all times a careful balance between alertness, firmness, and conciliation had to be maintained by the Company when dealing with other European trading organizations.

It was not only the Company that had an interest in keeping other European powers in check on the subcontinent. India had been an important sphere of operations during the Seven Years War, and Crown forces had made a significant, if not decisive, contribution to the elimination of European challenges to the Company. Moreover, the ministry perceived French activity in India as only a part of a global strategy designed to exploit British weaknesses. The Southern De-

[27] *FWIHC*, V, 142.   [28] *Ibid.*, V, 43.   [29] *Ibid.*, V, 19.
[30] For a detailed study of the real and perceived nature of the French threat to India during this period see N. Tracy, 'Parry of a threat to India, 1768–1774', *Mariner's Mirror*, 59 (1973), 35–48.   [31] See below p. 76.
[32] Tracy, 'Parry of a threat to India', pp. 35–9.   [33] *FWIHC*, V, 143.

partment kept a close eye on military developments in India, and the Secretary of State was often swift to intervene if he thought that the Company had overstepped the mark and undertaken actions which might provoke other European powers. This was very much the case in 1768-9 when the King, via Lord Weymouth, expressed his disquiet at the manner in which the seizure of Balambangan had been executed without the prior approval of the ministry. It was feared that the Company's actions might 'interfere with the subsisting treaties with other states, or give umbrage to those powers which he [the King] is upon terms of amity'.[34] The Company was reminded in no uncertain terms that it had to respect existing national diplomatic and strategic considerations. Its freedom of action was in theory limited by what was, or was not, acceptable to the ministry.

In particular the ministry sometimes deemed it necessary to remind the Company of the various treaty obligations of other European powers as they applied to India. Such was the case when, contrary to the terms of the Peace of Paris, the Company allowed the French to undertake a limited reinforcement and rearmament of their settlements in 1765–6.[35] A number of European troops and sepoys were stationed by the French company at Chandernagore; a defensive wall or barricade was built; and the deployment of twenty cannon was permitted 'for the purpose of securing themselves and their effects from the inroads and attacks of the enemies to the country powers, and of imposing a proper respect on the people of the country'. The British Company did, however, reserve the right to withdraw such privileges if they were abused in any way.

The Southern Secretary, Lord Shelburne, was informed of these developments in November 1767, and two months later he wrote to the directors to inform them of 'His Majesty's surprise' at 'so extraordinary a transaction with a foreign power'. The directors were censured not only for granting 'so hazardous a concession', but also because they had not sought ministerial advice on the matter. The minister then reminded the directors that the 'severe' terms of the Paris peace treaty as they related to India had been requested by the Company itself so that French influence and strength could be reduced. 'To soften the strong prohibitory letter and spirit of a treaty' was considered to be dangerous to 'both the Company and to the public'. Even so, Shelburne decided that to withdraw the French privileges after they had been in force for two and a half years would be an unnecessarily provocative gesture by

---

[34] *Calendar of Home Office Papers of the Reign of George III 1766–9* (1879), p. 386.
[35] Under the terms of the Treaty of Paris, Britain and France had restored to one another all the territories they had possessed at the beginning of 1749. The French also undertook not to maintain troops or construct fortifications in Bengal. See article 11 (the only one relating to India) of the treaty, printed in *CJ*, XXIX, 578.

the British government. He decided that the status quo should be maintained, but he informed the directors that the ministry expected that the Company should in future 'keep a most watchful eye on the conduct of the French in Bengal so that upon the slightest appearance of any insidious machination in consequence of the permission granted to them you and your servants in Bengal shall be ready to assert your rights of withstanding it'.[36]

A resolute response along the lines advocated by Lord Shelburne was deemed necessary the following year, 1769, when not only were the French reported to be digging a ditch around Chandernagore, but they were also thought to be sending reinforcements to Mauritius. The French claimed that the ditch was being built for simple drainage purposes, but the British Company interpreted its construction as part of an attempt to strengthen the city's defensive fortifications. The ensuing crisis in Anglo-French relations soon passed, following a flurry of diplomatic activity in London and Paris, and the filling in of the ditch, but for a time in 1770 it appeared that the French actions might lead to war. The North ministry, already embroiled in a serious dispute with France and Spain over claims to the Falklands Islands, had resolved to defend British interests in India against further French encroachment.[37] Once again the French were perceived to have been engaged in simultaneously threatening British interests and possessions in several quarters of the globe, and their actions in Asia were held to have been particularly dangerous. India was beginning to play an important part in British strategic considerations and this, coupled with the realization that Bengal had become an important national economic asset, helps to explain the trend towards a much closer ministerial supervision of the Company's overseas activities during the 1760s.

Prior to 1763 the British government had not developed any regular contact with Indian rulers or sovereigns. India remained well outside the sphere of normal British diplomatic activity, and the conduct of such relations had, through practical necessity as much as anything else, devolved upon the Company and its servants. In the final analysis policy decisions related to negotiations, agreements, and treaties with Indians rested with the Court of Directors. The formulation of policy was thus to be found within the Company's own political and decision-making machinery, and it was not subject to any formal ministerial supervision or control.

Nevertheless, within a diplomatic context it is possible to detect an

---

[36] *FWIHC*, V, 122–4. This was enclosed with the directors' letter of 16 Mar. 1768 to the Bengal Council.

[37] Tracy, 'Parry of a threat to India', pp. 37–8. The Company's correspondence relating to the Chandernagore ditch incident is to be found in *FWIHC*, XIV, 213–20.

underlying change beginning to occur in the state–Company relationship after 1763. When the Treaty of Paris was signed the ministry recognized for the first time the sovereign status of two Indian rulers: the Nawab of Arcot, Muhammed Ali Khan, and the Subah of the Deccan, Salabat Jang.[38] This raised a number of questions. Could the British monarch allow relations with these sovereign figures to be conducted by the officials of a private trading company rather than by Crown representatives? If not, then how could diplomatic channels be opened and maintained in an area where the Crown had no official representatives? If such channels were to be opened, would the ministry then be obliged to develop its own policy initiatives in India? For much of the 1760s issues such as these were obscured because revenue matters were of more immediate importance. But, in 1769, the whole question of the conduct and regulation of British external issues in India came to prominence when the new Southern Secretary Lord Weymouth took up the matter. In his response to a confused state of diplomatic affairs it is possible to discern signs that for the first time, in areas other than those related to military operations, a government minister was attempting to develop his own policy on British activity in India.

The various underlying tensions in the Crown–Company relationship were brought to the surface in 1769 when news of the Company's failures against Haidar Ali became known in Britain. Haidar had met with considerable early success and, having captured the fort of Malbagal from the British on 4 October 1768, he soon found himself in a position to threaten Fort St George and the town of Madras. These events were first reported in London at the end of May 1769 and an atmosphere of crisis soon prevailed in both India House and the money markets. Other factors contributed to the creation of such an atmosphere because the dispatches from India carried yet more bad news: a general scarcity of specie was reported in the Madras Presidency and, more immediately alarming, the directors were told that in the north the Wazir of Awadh, Shuja-ud-daula, had been recruiting and drilling large numbers of troops.[39] And all the time, in the background, stood the French, who were actively seeking to improve their position in India at the Company's expense. All this soon became public knowledge and, when coupled with misrepresentation and scaremongering in the press,[40] it prompted a spectacular fall in the price of Company stock, an

---

[38] *CJ*, XXIX, 578.

[39] Report of the dispatches read to the General Court on 1 June; *London Chronicle*, 3 June 1769.

[40] See, for example, the speculative comments made in *ibid.*, 27, 30 May, and 1 June. Unbeknown to those in London, Haidar Ali had reached Madras on 27 Mar. 1769, and had agreed a peace treaty with representatives of the Company on 4 April.

occurrence which some contemporaries likened to the bursting of the South Sea Bubble in 1720.[41] At a stroke, so it seemed, the Company's long run of political and military success had been halted and reversed.

The directors' response to this difficult situation was threefold. First, in an attempt to calm stockmarket fears, they presented a confident face to the stockholders. Making light of the news from India and expressing surprise at its effect within the City, they placed the blame for the panic firmly at the feet of stockjobbers and 'designing and interested men'.[42] Secondly, naval reinforcements were requested from the ministry on the grounds that the French had 'hostile ideas...against us'.[43] Finally, the directors undertook an immediate review of all aspects of the Company's affairs, and the Committee of Correspondence met throughout the first week of June to consider a response to the recent dispatches.

The Committee were in no doubt as to the cause of the recent setbacks in India. The full Court of Directors were told on 8 June that there had been a 'manifest disobedience' of their orders and the 'appearance in many instances of misconduct, not to say criminality in many of the Company's servants'.[44] They were particularly critical of the decision to open hostilities against Haidar Ali. Accordingly, in the Committee's view, the sending of a 'superintending power' to India had become an 'indispensable measure' because it would lead to a better supervision of the Company's servants. This in turn would enable Company strategy in all three Presidencies to be better co-ordinated, and it would ensure that general policy could be implemented in accordance with the directors' wishes. The idea appears to have originated with Clive, although Sir George Colebrooke later claimed the credit for it.[45] Whatever the case, the directors approved the scheme and the ministry was asked to make a frigate available to transport the supervisors to India.[46]

It was decided that the Supervisory Commission should comprise three commissioners and, after some initial jockeying for position, it was agreed that representatives of the major political factions in the Company should be included. Representing the Sulivan interest was Henry Vansittart, the former Governor of Bengal, who was anxious to restore his personal finances following substantial losses in the recent stock crash. Clive was represented by his close friend and aide Luke Scrafton.

[41] *Middlesex Journal*, 3 June 1769. The financial implications have been examined by Sutherland, *East India Company*, pp. 191–3, 209–212.
[42] *London Chronicle*, 30 May 1769.   [43] PRO, CO, 77/21, ff. 159–61.
[44] IOR, Court Minutes, B/85, p. 64.
[45] BL, Add. MSS 42087, f. 32; Colebrooke, *Retrospection*, I, 140. Clive had been invited by the Committee of Correspondence (of which Colebrooke was the Chairman) to suggest ways in which the Company should tackle its problems.
[46] IOR, Court Minutes, B/85, p. 64.

The third place went to the Company military officer Francis Forde, whose role was intended to be somewhat akin to that of an arbiter between the other two commissioners. With a number of other factions putting forward candidates for the Commission, the selection contest was often acrimonious,[47] but nevertheless the appointment of Forde, Scrafton, and Vansittart was approved by the directors on 14 June. A month later on 12 July, after significant opposition in the General Court,[48] the appointments were endorsed by the stockholders. The role of the commissioners, as defined by the Company Secretary Peter Michell to Robert Wood, Under-Secretary at the Southern Department, was to be threefold.[49] First, they were to conduct all negotiations with native princes; second, they were to direct and regulate the activities of all the Company's civil and military servants; and, finally, they were to control all matters relating to trade and revenue collection. In short, they were to provide a panacea for all the Company's ills.

At this point, the issues surrounding the appointment of a Supervisory Commission and the Company's requests to the ministry for naval support became intertwined. The Company had been resisting Haidar Ali without any military assistance from the Crown, but they now found that Lord Weymouth, spurred into action by the rumours of a French threat, was attempting to assert an unprecedented degree of influence over the development of the Company's affairs in India. This first became apparent on 11 July when the Company was informed that the ministry intended to send a naval officer to India with 'full powers' from both King and Company to command the latter's marine forces.[50] But the proposed role for this 'sea officer of experience' was not restricted to naval matters. He was to have the power to 'treat and settle matters in the Persian Gulf and also with the Marathas and Haidar Ali or with any other maritime powers', so far as such power did not interfere with the prerogative of the supervisors or the Councils of the Company's Presidencies.

There is evidence to suggest that Weymouth's measures had their origins in representations made to the ministry by the Nawab of Arcot via his agent in London, John Macpherson.[51] The Nawab asked that the Company servants' right to negotiate with native princes be limited, and that discussions related to matters of war and peace should be conducted by officers of the British Crown.[52] Sir George Colebrooke identified this

---

[47] Sutherland, *East India Company*, pp. 195–6.

[48] *London Chronicle*, 20 June 1769.   [49] IOR, HMS, 100, pp. 273–6.

[50] PRO, CO, 77/21, f. 80.

[51] John Macpherson (1745–1821), Governor-General 1785–6, Bt. 1786.

[52] J.D. Gurney, 'The debts of the Nawab of Arcot, 1763–1776', unpublished D. Phil. thesis, University of Oxford, 1968, pp. 87–90.

connexion between the Nawab and the proposals advanced by Weymouth, and he later recalled that the Duke of Grafton was persuaded by the 'nonentity' Macpherson to listen to the complaints of the Nawab. Then, according to Colebrooke, 'to the utter astonishment of the Company', the directors received a letter from Weymouth stating that it had become necessary to grant 'extraordinary and plenipotentiary powers' to the naval commander-elect, Sir John Lindsay.[53] Somewhat surprisingly, the directors decided at once that 'such an officer be sent out as soon as possible'.[54]

Bearing in mind that the directors had requested naval assistance to deal with a French and not a native threat, and that for years the Company had jealously guarded its right to make war and peace with Indian princes, it is remarkable that Weymouth's proposals met with so little opposition. On the strength of one meeting and a demand from the minister, the directors had permitted a significant erosion of the Company's independence of action on the subcontinent. However, the directors soon realized the full implications of their actions, and they effected a swift *volte face* on 21 July when they decided that the powers granted to the naval officer were of 'too extensive a nature'.[55] Five days later Robert Wood was told by the directors' Secret Committee that the Company would not sanction the appointment of an officer in a 'ministerial capacity', but that they were quite content for one to be sent out 'with as extensive powers as you ever gave to any admiral in India'.[56] When Weymouth heard of this he told the directors in rather indignant terms that he was disappointed that 'any offers of the assistance of government, with a view to strengthen and add weight to the Company's negotiations in India and proposed with so much caution not to interfere with the powers of her servants abroad, should be rejected'.[57]

Relations between the Company and the Southern Department deteriorated rapidly during the second half of July. Already, on 17 July, Weymouth had accused the directors of deliberately concealing information from him about the situation in India, a charge which was rejected in no uncertain terms.[58] Then once more, on 27 July, the directors outlined their objections to the naval officer's role as 'sole plenipotentiary' for dealing with the native princes.[59] The stage was set for an acrimonious dispute, and at stake was the very basis upon which future Indo-British diplomatic relations were to be conducted.

Matters came to a head in early August when Weymouth, armed with

[53] Colebrooke, *Retrospection*, I, 140–1.   [54] PRO, CO, 77/21, f. 80.
[55] IOR, Court Minutes, B/85, p. 121.   [56] PRO, CO, 77/21, ff. 78–9.
[57] *Ibid.*   [58] IOR, HMS, 100, pp. 311, 315, and 317.
[59] PRO, CO, 77/21, f. 68.

an opinion from Sir Fletcher Norton,[60] declared that the commission given by the Company to their supervisors was illegal on the grounds that 'it suspends the established judicatures and the ordinary governments...and establishes nothing in their places'.[61] He insisted that it be amended before he would permit the supervisors to set foot aboard any Crown frigate supplied for their passage to India. At the same time, the Company was asked to produce a commission for Lindsay which would conform with the instructions he had been given by the ministry. The Company complied with both these requests on 4 August, but defiantly declared once again that they would not accept any government assistance in determining relations with native Indian powers.[62]

Weymouth, losing patience fast, then seized the initiative and, in doing so, gave events an extraordinary twist. On 10 August he requested that the directors 'take the sense' of the Company's stockholders on the question of involving the naval Commander-in-Chief in negotiations with the native powers. He astutely linked this issue with a request that the General Court had made on 27 July for a naval force 'consisting of ships of the line as well as frigates' to be sent by the ministry to help the Company in India. The context in which this force was to be used was not specified by the proprietors,[63] but Weymouth pointed out that at the Peace of Paris the King had recognized 'the legal title of certain princes in India to their respective dominions'.[64] He then declared that he could not dispatch a naval force to India which might be employed 'contrary to those engagements'. His main concern was that Crown forces might be brought, through their support of the Company's interest, into unwanted conflict with those Indian sovereigns acknowledged by the King in 1763. The minister decreed that the King's ships would only be used in actions in which the 'officers of the Crown [be given] that share in the deliberations and resolutions upon peace and war, which is necessary where His Majesty's forces are employed'.

The implications of this were clear. The diplomatic obligations of Crown and Company were considered to be quite separate, and Weymouth was not prepared to allow the King's forces to be dragged into conflicts against sovereign powers on the coat tails of Company servants. He demanded a say in the development of policy and strategy in situations where Crown interests and resources were at stake. The subtleties of this argument were lost on most observers and, instead,

---

[60] Norton, Lord Chief Justice in Eyre above the Trent, was soon to become Speaker of the House of Commons.   [61] IOR, HMS, 100, p. 383.
[62] Ibid., 100, pp. 387–8.
[63] IOR, B/85, p. 121; resolution of General Court, 27 July.
[64] IOR, HMS, 100, p. 443.

criticism was directed against the minister's tactical approach to the problem. By appealing directly to the General Court he was considered by many to be involving the ministry in the internal affairs of the Company to an unwarranted, unprecedented, and dangerous degree.[65]

The dispute continued throughout August and into September although, not surprisingly, most political attention was focused on the frenzied extra-parliamentary activities organized on behalf of John Wilkes who, in April, had been unseated by the Commons as the Member for Middlesex. The Company's commission for the supervisors was eventually amended, and it was debated at length in the General Court before being approved on 14 September.[66] At the same time, because of great opposition from the Company's stockholders, Weymouth was forced to modify his position on the intended role of the Plenipotentiary in the Gulf. His rather heavy-handed tactics had provoked a hostile response from the friends of the Company, many of whom were already uneasy about the level of ministerial interference in India House affairs.[67] Indeed, leading opposition politician George Grenville was told by Thomas Whately on 19 August that he would hardly believe the 'contempt and resentment' that had arisen from Weymouth's threatening letters.[68]

The minister had miscalculated the level of support he thought he would find within the Company and, on 13 September, the proprietors refused, by 177 votes to 95, to sanction ministerial interference in negotiations between the Company and the Indian powers in any area other than the Persian Gulf. Weymouth could not in the first instance develop any ministerial policy initiatives in India without the Company's co-operation, and, in view of this, he conceded that he now desired only that the Commander-in-Chief should 'assist those [servants] of the Company in joint negotiation, and not that he should be sole plenipotentiary'.[69] In using a more conciliatory tone than at any other stage of the proceedings, Weymouth argued that great advantages would accrue to both the Crown and the Company from the 'mere appearance' of the Company and royal servants working side by side in diplomatic negotiations. He declared that the ministry did not wish to interfere in

[65] It appears that Weymouth did not have the full support of his cabinet colleagues. It was rumoured that Lord Camden 'openly disapproved' of his tactics and was prepared to speak out in Parliament against them; letter from Mrs Anderson to the Earl of Loudoun, 22 Aug. 1769, Mount Stuart, Loudoun MSS, 1769, bundle 1 (no foliation).
[66] IOR, Court Minutes, B/85, pp. 214, 226–8.
[67] See, for example, the pamphlet *Vox Populi Vox Rei: Lord Weymouth's Appeal to a General Court of Indian Proprietors Considered* (1769). Weymouth on the other hand found a rather unlikely ally in the *Middlesex Journal*. See, for example, the issue of 15 Aug.   [68] BL, Add. MSS 57817B, f. 105.
[69] IOR, Court Minutes, B/85, pp. 169–72.

the Company's affairs, and that it desired only a 'share in the deliberations and resolutions...merely with regard to the two objects of peace and war when His Majesty's forces are to be employed'. On the face of it, he now offered little more than a re-statement of the traditional role of the royal Commander-in-Chief in India.

In public Weymouth accepted the decision of the General Court, and Sir John Lindsay was given instructions for his mission in accordance with commissions prepared for him by both the Crown and the Company.[70] In private, however, Lindsay was presented with a set of secret instructions which defined the Commander's role along the lines originally desired by Weymouth.[71] Lindsay was told that it was 'highly improper' that the King should 'trust the execution of engagements which he has contracted with other crowned heads to the Company servants'. In particular, and as a direct consequence of the representations of John Macpherson, Lindsay was instructed to make the 'strictest inquiry' into the Company's relations with the Nawab of Arcot.[72] Lindsay was warned not to enter into any conflicts with the Company's servants when performing this task, and he was told that an appearance of unity was to be maintained at all costs. While Weymouth's instructions suggested that a clash of ministerial and Company interests was almost inevitable, Lindsay was ordered to postpone such an event for as long as possible.[73] In short, Weymouth was developing his own ministerial initiatives with regard to British affairs in India and, to all intents and purposes, he had succeeded in breaking the Company's diplomatic and political monopoly. In spite of all his claims about unity of purpose, Weymouth's actions set a pattern for the development of future separate, and sometimes conflicting, Company and ministerial interests on the subcontinent. This situation, an uneasy partnership at the best of times, was not finally resolved until the Company's affairs were wound up in the aftermath of the Indian mutiny of 1857.

In the immediate future it remained to be seen whether or not the representatives of the directors and the ministry would help better to regulate relations with the country powers, bring the servants under control, and establish the Company's commercial and revenue operations upon sound administrative foundations. While the routine government of the Company's settlements was to continue on long-

---

[70] IOR, HMS, 101, p. 59.
[71] It is not clear how long these instructions remained secret, but a copy is to be found among the Company's records, *ibid.*, 101, pp. 101–31.
[72] *Ibid.*, 101, p. 111. The instructions made specific references to complaints made by the Nawab to the King. The Company was also concerned with the state of the Nawab's debts and the directors mentioned them in their instructions to their supervisors; Gurney, 'The debts of the Nawab of Arcot', p. 85.
[73] IOR, HMS, 101, p. 128.

established lines, the three commissioners 'were to have a superintending and controlling power over the whole in like manner as if the
Court of Directors were...present upon the spot'.[74] Even so, although
it was hoped that the activities of the three Presidencies could now be
based upon 'one uniform plan of action', the directors made it quite
clear to the supervisors where they expected their attention to be focused
during their time in India. 'The preservation and security of Bengal',
they were told, 'is...the most important object and consideration of the
Company.'[75] Thus when the supervisors sailed for India upon the
Aurora at the end of September 1769 they carried with them the
directors' hopes that Company policy for Bengal, as determined in
London, would now be implemented with far greater consistency,
moderation, and good sense than had been the case during the previous
decade or so.

[74] *FWIHC*, V, 216.   [75] IOR, HMS, 100, p. 404.

6   Attempts at reform (I): civil, military and judicial affairs, 1767–1772

The appointment of three supervisors in 1769 represented only one of several attempts made by the directors to reform the Company's civil, military, and judicial systems in India. It had been recognized long before the mid-1760s that important aspects of the Company's operational framework were unsatisfactory, but these shortcomings could not be tolerated at all after the acceptance of territorial responsibilities in 1765. A significant modification, or even a complete overhaul of the Company's overseas administrative machinery, was thought to be necessary and, in 1766, the directors set in motion a comprehensive review of all aspects of the Company's activities in India. They sought in an institutional context to consolidate the newly won position in Bengal but, in keeping with the importance of their new responsibilities, they also endeavoured to encourage new standards of behaviour and service among their servants: individual attitudes as well as corporate practices and procedures required attention and change. As John Pybus remarked to Robert Palk in April 1767, the Company now required above all else 'very able heads and honest hearts for supporting with honour and advantage the whole vast superstructure which has been so suddenly and successfully raised'.[1] Herein lay a particularly thorny problem, for Company employees were being asked to become imperial administrators and guardians of an important national asset. This caused an almost inevitable conflict of interest as they continued to go about their everyday affairs as representatives of a commercial organization, and as private traders and businessmen.

Yet despite the directors' good intentions, they at first received very little assistance or encouragement from the King's ministers. The East India Company legislation of 1767 was restricted in scope to the transfer of a share of the Company's territorial revenues to the state, and to the correction of a number of specific weaknesses evident within the management structure of the Company in Britain.[2] The ministry did not

---

[1] *Historical Manuscripts Commission, Report on the Palk MSS* (1922), p. 50.
[2] See below, p. 88.

attempt to come to terms with the many problems related to the Company's activities in Bengal that had been brought to light during Clive's governorship of the Presidency, and which had later resurfaced during the parliamentary inquiry. The line of state intervention was very firmly drawn by an administration that was already confronting a whole host of colonial difficulties in North America. A similar attitude was adopted by the Grafton ministry in 1769 when the agreement between the state and the Company was extended for a further five years. It was only in 1772, when the Company finally proved itself to be incapable of reforming its own affairs, that the North ministry intervened in order to lay down very basic guidelines for the conduct of the Company's overseas activities. By then it was perceived by those in government that Bengal was in very real danger of being lost.

Clive's governorship of Bengal between 1765 and 1767 had been notable not only for the important territorial and political advances made by the Company, but also for the astounding revelations that had been made about corruption among many of the senior servants who had formerly been stationed in the Presidency. Indeed, the primary purpose of Clive's reappointment as Governor had been to restore order to the administrative chaos prevailing at Fort William. Servants had abused trading privileges and had repeatedly ignored directors' orders prohibiting private trade. Moreover, when Clive arrived in Calcutta he discovered that, following the death of Mir Jafar in February 1765, sums of money worth £112,000 had been paid to the Council by the three contenders for the position of chief minister to the new Nawab, Najm-ud-daula.[3] It was hardly surprising, wrote the new Governor to Joseph Fowke in September 1765, that the 'name of the English stink in the nostrils of a gentoo or a mussalman'.[4] Accordingly, Clive had begun the 'cleansing of the Augean stables', and a steady stream of Company servants, including members of the Council, was sent back to Britain. Some of these individuals, such as Ralph Leycester and John Johnstone, became implacable enemies of Clive, and they sought to clear their names in the Company's General Court.[5] This added an important extra dimension to the factional politics of India House during the late 1760s and, in turn, the conflict helped to focus public attention on Clive's own receipt of presents, as well as a *jagir* payment of £26,000 a year which

[3] Marshall, *East Indian Fortunes*, pp. 130–9, 168–75, 237.
[4] NLW, Clive MSS 236, p. 21.
[5] They achieved this at the Court of 6 May 1767 when the charges against them were dropped: IOR, B/83, p. 41. Others who had been dismissed included Charles Playdell, Ascanius Senior, Samuel Middleton, George Grey, and John Spencer. John Johnstone was brother of the prominent Company politician, George Johnstone.

had been granted to him by Mir Jafar following the overthrow of Siraj-ud-daula in 1757.[6]

When Clive and his Select Committee reviewed the activities of their predecessors in September 1765 they were unequivocal in their condemnation of John Spencer's administration. They reported to the directors that 'Every spring of this government was smeared with corruption, that principles of rapacity and oppression universally prevailed, and that every spark of sentiment and public spirit was lost [or] extinguished in the inordinate lust of unmerited wealth.'[7] The directors, once more placing complete faith in Clive's judgement, accepted this appraisal of the situation, and they replied in May 1766 that they too were deeply concerned about 'the most complicated scene of corruption in which we have the unhappiness to see most of our principal servants involved'.[8] Yet again they found themselves addressing the problem of presents or gifts extorted from Indians, and yet again they found that they were obliged to regulate, if not eliminate, the private trade and commercial activities of Company servants. They moved at once to eradicate one particular type of abuse when they prohibited their servants from landholding or involving themselves in revenue farming or collection.[9]

This hard line was then reinforced by a decision to begin legal action against several Company servants who had disobeyed their instructions. It was ordered that any property remaining in Bengal which belonged to John Johnstone or John Spencer should be seized, and the opinion of the Attorney- and Solicitor-Generals was sent to Calcutta with respect to 'the measures to be taken with our servants [still] in Bengal for the disobedience to the resolution of the General Court and of our orders in consequence of it'. Armed with this opinion, the Council were to bring offenders to trial at Fort William.[10] This was intended to be a salutary reminder to all Company servants that they were not operating beyond the scope or jurisdiction of English law. Moreover, the directors acknowledged that they had an obligation to offer some protection to the native population against unreasonable or offensive behaviour by Company servants. As they observed, it was both in the Company's interest and part of their duty 'to protect and cherish the inhabitants and to give them no occasion to look on every Englishman as their national enemy'.[11] The Select Committee were told that 'if our servants presume

---

[6] A *jagir* was a grant assigning land revenues to an individual. The political controversy surrounding Clive's *jagir* is examined in B. Lenman and P. Lawson, 'Robert Clive, the "black jagir", and British politics', *Historical Journal*, XXVI (1983), 801–29.

[7] *FWIHC*, XIV, 164.   [8] *Ibid.*, IV, 187.   [9] *Ibid.*, IV, 186.

[10] *Ibid.*, IV, 190–1.   [11] *Ibid.*, IV, 189.

thus to call into question our most direct and positive orders, enforced by the general voice of the whole body of proprietors, it is time for us to exert the authority vested in us and to do justice to the injured natives, to our own honour, and to the national character'.[12]

No-one could predict with any certainty whether such warnings would be heeded because in the past similar statements had been ignored and ridiculed. The directors fully recognized this, and they also acknowledged that a better type of Company servant would not be created until the moral and ethical atmosphere in which he worked and lived was improved.[13] The purging of the Bengal administration between 1765 and 1767 offered the Company a golden opportunity to create such an atmosphere through the establishment of a new and very different code of conduct and service for those (many of whom were transferred from Madras) appointed to fill the numerous vacancies at Fort William. As the directors remarked in March 1767, 'We apprehend there must be a total change of manners in the settlement before we can expect a rising set of valuable servants.'[14] Accordingly, a whole series of recommendations were made on how the Company's Bengal servants should conduct themselves: private trade was prohibited; duties were defined; activities were restricted; and dress, drink, and accommodation were regulated.[15] Quite simply, it was hoped that such attention to detail would lead to 'luxury and extravagance' being replaced by 'simplicity and economy', particularly among the Company's younger servants.[16]

At first the Company attempted to solve problems related to its activities in Bengal without recourse to any outside help. Solutions evolved within the Company's decision-making machinery in the tried and trusted manner. However, when it became known in the autumn of 1766 that the Chatham ministry was preparing to begin a full-scale parliamentary inquiry into the Company's affairs, the proprietors decided to ask for assistance with their problems in Bengal.[17] Indeed, several observers were now of the opinion that the Company might not be able to retain its recently extended possessions without a significant amount of aid and encouragement from the state.[18] A far-sighted minister such as Charles Townshend, who thought along these lines, was able to identify a number of important legislative areas in which the

[12] Ibid., IV, 186.   [13] Ibid., IV, 190.   [14] Ibid., V, 7.
[15] Ibid., V, 22–3. See also pp. 56, 58.
[16] Ibid., V, 7. For a description of British life in Bengal at this time see Spear, The Nabobs, ch. 2.
[17] The issue was discussed at the General Courts of 14 Nov., 17 and 31 Dec., and on the last date it was resolved that the Company should 'treat' with the ministry on this and other matters; IOR, B/82, pp. 270–3, 318–19, 337.
[18] See, for example, the letter of 'Candidus' in London Evening Post, 5 Jan. 1767.

government might be able to help the Company as it endeavoured to strengthen its grip on Bengal.[19]

When the Company and the ministry began to negotiate a settlement of the *Diwani* issue in early 1767 the directors sought assistance with several specific problems. Formal proposals were submitted by the Company in January and April and, on both occasions, the ministry was asked, among other things, to help with improving the recruitment of Europeans for the Bengal army, and with 'strengthening the hands of the Company if necessary for the better and more effectual government of their civil and military servants or others abroad, and for preventing their accepting or receiving presents'.[20] In both cases there were strong grounds for the Company seeking statutory reinforcement of proposed reforms, yet the ministry steadfastly refused to take up the matters.

Negotiations between directors and ministers centred on the financial aspects of the state–Company relationship. Eventually some aid was offered in the form of customs concessions designed to help the Company's tea trade; proceedings at the General Court were regulated; and voting qualifications in joint-stock companies were amended in an attempt to eliminate stock 'splitting'.[21] However, the ministry drew the line at interfering in the Company's overseas affairs.[22] In a sense this was quite understandable. The parliamentary session of 1766–7 had been an extremely difficult one for the ministry, and they had encountered numerous obstacles in their attempt to secure a share of the Company's territorial revenues: at times it had even seemed likely that the Chatham administration would not survive at all. Because of this, ministers (apart from Townshend) had refused to create yet another Indian rod for their backs by involving themselves in what they perceived as being essentially secondary administrative issues related to the Company's internal affairs. When the Company emerged from the first parliamentary inquiry it was left in no doubt that it would be expected singlehandedly to deal with any problems arising from its activities in Bengal.

The directors noted the ministry's attitude and, after the parliamentary business of 1767 had been completed, they began a formal review of the Company's situation in India. For this purpose they enlisted the services of distinguished Company servants such as John Caillaud and Stringer Lawrence. Clive, who had returned from Bengal in July 1767, was also invited to assist in this task even though he made little attempt to hide his contempt for the directors, many of whom were

---

[19] Letter of December 1766 cited in Namier and Brooke, *Charles Townshend*, p. 161.
[20] The proposals submitted in January are to be found in *Chatham Corr.*, III, 164–5, and those submitted in April are in IOR, B/82, pp. 480–2.
[21] 7 Geo. III, c. 48, 49, and 56.   [22] IOR, B/83, pp. 118–19.

his long-standing political opponents.[23] In August 1767 he was asked by the Chairman, Thomas Rous, for a 'complete plan' relating to 'important concerns political, civil, and military' but, because of ill-health, he was unable to comply with the request. Nevertheless, he did produce a detailed paper on military affairs within a few weeks[24] and, three months later, he met the Committee of Correspondence at Bath in order to enlarge upon his ideas.

Clive's formal discussion paper contained two central themes which were to condition a great deal of the Company's thought on reform over the next few years. First, he advocated that military resources be concentrated in Bengal for the simple and obvious reason that the Company's extended territorial role there demanded considerably more manpower than the other Presidencies. For this purpose he recommended a distribution of the Company's European troops in an approximate ratio of 7:5:3 between Bengal, Madras, and Bombay.[25] Second, and as a direct consequence of this proposed restructuring of the armed forces, he urged that the Company's recruitment system for its European troops be reformed at once, a measure that he had been advocating since 1764.[26] The situation in India required two thousand additional European troops to be sent out immediately, twelve hundred of them to Bengal, because many units were well below strength; but, in the longer term, Clive recommended that the Company should seek to maintain a permanent establishment of two battalions of troops in Britain. These men would be used for recruitment and training purposes, and could themselves be dispatched to India during times of emergency.

This was a bold and expensive plan, but Clive had long been a critic of the poor quality of the recruits who entered the Company's service after being enlisted by contractors appointed by the directors. Such men were often unfit for active service, and the methods used by the contractors occasionally left much to be desired as they sought swiftly to make up companies of 300 men. Recruitment needed to be strictly monitored and regulated, and Clive was convinced that his plan could not be implemented without the active involvement of the government. He needed their assistance to ensure the passage of suitable legislation

[23] NLW, 59, p. 21.   [24] *Ibid.*, 59, pp. 1–12.
[25] This recommendation was put into effect by the directors the following year: *FWIHC*, V, 89 ff.
[26] *RCHC*, IV, 577. Parts of the following discussion of the Company's recruiting problems were first published in H.V. Bowen, 'The East India Company and military recruitment in Britain, 1763–1771', *Bulletin of the Institute of Historical Research*, LIX (1986), 78–90. I am indebted to the editor for permission to reprint them.

through Parliament, but the securing of such assistance proved to be a major stumbling block for the Company.

Clive's plan was accepted in principle by the directors but, while it did result in a concentration of manpower resources in Bengal, it did not lead immediately to a reform of the Company's recruiting system. It was not until the summer of 1769, when news of Haidar Ali's successes in South India reached Britain, that the pace of reform quickened. In October Clive noted with the 'greatest satisfaction' that his ideas for recruitment of 1764 and 1767 were now in the final process of being adopted by the Company and drafted into a proposed measure for submission to the ministry.[27] Clive, Stringer Lawrence, and Eyre Coote helped the directors produce a detailed proposal; and, again, a central feature was that one or two units should be permanently established in Britain. The directors could then 'make draughts as occasion might require'.[28] The intended effect of the measure, the directors were told, was that 'your soldiers would then arrive at their place of destination fit for duty and you would no longer depend on the precarious supply of undisciplined and often unfit levies'.[29]

Having adopted this plan, the directors consulted the Southern Department, indicated their intentions, and sought royal approval for their actions.[30] On 31 October 1769 Lord Weymouth wrote to the directors and reported that he had spoken to the King about 'such regulations as it might be proper to lay before Parliament for the better government and security' of the Company's possessions in India. The King had ordered that the ministry should pay 'the most particular attention' to the Company's proposals and, consequently, Weymouth urged that the directors lose no time 'in suggesting whatever you may think conducive to the valuable acquisitions in India, that your ideas on a matter of such importance may be properly digested and considered before the meeting of Parliament'.[31] Having received royal approval and an assurance about the ministry's cooperation, the directors lost no time in completing the drafting of their recruiting proposals. On 24 November detailed copies of two proposed plans were forwarded to Weymouth.[32]

The first of the two plans simply proposed that the Company be granted the right to recruit 'by beat of drum' in all parts of the King's dominions.[33] Once sworn in and attested, the troops would then become

---

[27] NLW, Clive MSS, 59, p. 71.   [28] Ibid., 59, p. 76.
[29] This idea was also incorporated in a plan Clive submitted to Lord North in 1770; IOL, Sutton Court Collection, Strachie Papers, Eur. MSS. F. 128, box 4 (no fol.).
[30] IOR, HMS, 101, p. 311.   [31] Ibid., 101, p. 312.
[32] Copies of the plans are to be found at ibid., 101, pp. 341–6.
[33] For a description of recruitment by beat of drum see J.A. Houlding, Fit for Service: The Training of the British Army, 1715–1795 (Oxford, 1982), p. 117.

subject to the terms and conditions of the Mutiny Act. The second plan was far more extensive and was based upon the proposals drafted by Clive. Under this scheme the directors would be permitted to maintain a permanent body of troops in Britain for the purpose of enlisting and training recruits. This corps was not to exceed 1,800 men and it would be officered by men holding royal commissions.

The first plan formed the basis of a bill presented to Parliament in April 1770, and the War Office assisted with the final drafting of the measure.[34] The foundations for this cooperation had been laid in March when Weymouth had written to the Secretary at War, Lord Barrington, asking that he assist the Company 'in carrying such a [recruiting] measure through the House of Commons'.[35] However, this had only been a qualified offer of assistance to the Company, for Weymouth had warned Barrington that he should not cooperate at all if he considered that the Company's proposals might in any way 'materially affect the recruiting for the King's services'. In addition, he had indicated to the War Office that there were 'strong objections' to both of the Company's plans.

Barrington must have perceived little real threat to regular army recruitment but, despite his cooperation, the repeated adjournment of the reading of the Committee report on the Bill meant that the proposal was lost towards the end of the session through a lack of available parliamentary time in which to complete the business.[36] This setback does not appear to have unduly concerned the Company, for their favoured proposal was the second plan and they reserved their efforts in order to secure its passage the following year.

Unfortunately for the Company, the adoption of the more extensive recruiting plan served to lose them the support and cooperation of the military establishment. Both Barrington and the Adjutant-General Edward Harvey set themselves resolutely against the Bill in a manner which contrasted with their behaviour the previous year. Horace Walpole recognized that while Lord North and the ministry took no part in the proceedings, 'the officers had taken great objections to it [the Bill], as preventive of their recruiting'. In particular, Walpole noted the prominent role played by Harvey who instilled 'those prejudices' of the military into the King. He was in no doubt that the opposition of the military lobby was the main reason for the failure of the Bill, although

---

[34] The Bill was drafted by Company Chairman Colebrooke, Deputy-Chairman Peregrine Cust, Secretary at War Lord Barrington, and Adjutant-General Edward Harvey: *CJ*, XXXII, 875.   [35] PRO, WO1/680, p. 57.
[36] *CJ*, XXXII, 964, 969, 971.

at the same time he did acknowledge that 'many good men approved it'.[37]

The opposition of the regular army to the second Bill arose not from a desire to prevent the Company from recruiting at all, but rather from the specific methods proposed. Their cooperation with the directors the previous year had illustrated that they were quite prepared to assist the Company, but only if recruiting for the royal regiments was not adversely affected. In the East India Military Recruiting Bill presented to the House of Commons by Sir George Colebrooke on 18 February 1771 they perceived a significant threat.[38] They felt that the number of men who would join the regular army would be substantially reduced if a more attractive form of military employment existed. Such an alternative, they argued, would be provided by the creation of a permanent regiment of East India Company troops based in Britain.

This fundamental objection to the Bill was seized upon by military personnel in the House of Commons and used repeatedly during debates on the measure in February, March, and April 1771.[39] Moreover, opponents of the Bill also played upon traditional fears about the exercise of unrestrained military power within the realm. In the House on 4 March Barrington drew attention to the dangers associated with having substantial numbers of troops operating outside direct royal supervision, while on the same day Lord Rockingham's associate George Dempster spoke of the general fear about the possible creation of a standing army of catholics and foreigners.[40] The end for the Bill finally came on 23 April after, in Horace Walpole's words, 'many long debates'.[41] When the question was put that the Bill be read for the third time the House divided, with 45 Members on each side. The speaker, Sir Fletcher Norton, then intervened and, claiming that any alternative was better than the present method of recruiting, he cast his vote in favour of the third reading.[42] By the time the motion to pass the Bill was put there were slightly more members present in the House, but the outcome was just as close: the motion was passed in the negative by 51 votes to 50.

In the final analysis the Company had been unable to overcome the opposition of the military lobby to the measure in the House, but perhaps more important in the long term was the fact that the ministry

[37] Walpole *Memoirs*, IV, 212. For a similar assessment see Colebrooke, *Retrospection*, I, 195.
[38] See, for example, the detailed (undated) critique of the Bill written by Barrington; Suffolk Record Office, Barrington MSS, HA174:1026/6c/1.
[39] The military personnel who spoke in debate against the Bill included Barrington, Harvey, Barré, Lord George Germain, and General John Burgoyne.
[40] BL, Eg. MSS 225, pp. 292–9, 303–13.   [41] Walpole, *Memoirs*, IV, 212.
[42] Cobbett, *Parl. Hist.*, XVII, 173.

had not moved decisively to support the Bill. Consequently, in the immediate future the Company had no choice but to continue to rely on the wholly unsatisfactory and unregulated practice of granting contracts to individuals to raise troops for the Indian army. The episode highlighted the Company's difficulties in coming to terms with the need for reform, but it also illustrated just how important the support of the ministry was to the Company as it endeavoured to introduce new measures and procedures.

The directors encountered similar problems when they turned their attention to the reform of judicial practices and procedures in the territories under their jurisdiction. This issue was closely related to the regulation of the behaviour of Company servants and, as such, it must be seen as part of a broad strategy in which a concerted effort was made by the directors to impose their authority over their employees. As part of this strategy the Company sought between 1770 and 1772 to secure ministerial assistance for a reform of the administration of justice in Bengal. At best the support given was only half-hearted, and this played a significant part in the Company's eventual failure to come to terms with the difficult problem of administering justice to British subjects in its overseas territories. Once again, the ministry failed to provide the backing that was necessary to secure the passage of the Company's specific reform proposals through Parliament. However, there were a number of signs during this period which indicated that North's administration was preparing to give a more positive general lead in Company affairs. In fact, the winter of 1771–2 may be seen as the time when the Company began to lose control of its own destiny.

As things stood in Bengal in the 1760s, all civil and criminal cases involving British subjects were tried at the Mayor's Court in Calcutta.[43] The Court, first established in 1727, also had jurisdiction over Indians if they chose to submit civil suits to it for consideration and determination. However, although the Court had been further regulated by the Company's charter of 1753, many aspects of its activities remained ill-defined. Above the Mayor's Court, and acting as a court of appeal, stood the President and Council of Bengal, but this body also found that its jurisdiction and area of authority was open to question when it exercised judicial functions. The whole system was characterized by weaknesses and inconsistencies, and it was because of this that the directors sought reform reinforced by statute.

As a first step the Company secured in 1770 the enactment of a measure (10 Geo. III, c. 47) designed to eliminate some of the anomalies between judicial functions and practices in India and those in Britain.

---

[43] The Mayor was chosen on an annual basis by the twelve Aldermen of Fort William.

The Act, originally described as a measure 'for compelling persons dismissed the service of the East India Company to depart the East Indies, and for the better regulating the servants of the said Company and for other purposes',[44] declared that any Company servant found guilty of 'oppressing' any other British subject in India would be liable to prosecution in Britain. Punishments for those convicted of offences in India were also brought in line with punishments for similar offences at home.[45] However, the Act did not address any of the major issues related to the administration of justice in Bengal, and the following year the directors initiated a full review of the Company's judicial functions. The result of this activity was the introduction of the measure commonly known as the Judicature Bill into the Commons in March 1772.[46] This Bill failed to reach the statute book, but the reintroduction of major Indian issues into Parliament eventually prompted a second full-scale inquiry into the affairs of the East India Company.

The King's Speech at the beginning of the parliamentary session on 21 January 1772 contained a strong hint that a significant ministerial response to the problems of the East India Company would soon be forthcoming. George III spoke of parts of Britain's possessions 'so peculiarly liable to abuses and exposed to danger that the interposition of the legislature...may be necessary'.[47] William Vane seconded the Address of Thanks to the Speech, and he left observers in no doubt that the possessions referred to were those in India. He reminded the House of the many charges that had been brought against Company servants over the years, and he declared that the directors had still not managed to exert effective control over their representatives in Bengal. In conclusion he told the House that the 'malversation of the East India Company's servants called loudly for their interposition and that he trusted they would have an opportunity of displaying their legislative wisdom in adjusting these matters'.[48]

The Company took heed of these warnings and, less than a month later, on 19 February, the directors ordered that the Committee of Correspondence draw up a Bill for the better administration of justice in the East Indies.[49] The directors approved the Bill that was drafted, but a great deal of opposition was raised when the clauses were read to the proprietors on 4 March. One prominent proprietor, George Johnstone,

---

[44] The final version was entitled 'An Act for Better Regulating Persons Employed in the Service of the East India Company.' The Bill passed its final reading on 15 May 1770.
[45] The Act also served a number of other purposes, including the regulation of Company ballots and dividend payments.
[46] The full title was 'A Bill for the Better Regulation of the Affairs of the East India Company and of Their Servants in India, and for the Due Administration of Justice in Bengal'.   [47] Cobbett, *Parl. Hist.*, XVII, 233.   [48] *Ibid.*, XVII, 237.
[49] IOR, B/87, p. 469.

claimed that the measure was 'totally defective', and the General Court refused to endorse the directors' decision to lay the Bill before Parliament.[50] Instead, after 'many debates' it was resolved that it be recommended to the directors that they should apply to the Crown for a new charter of justice for Bengal, and for an Act to regulate the Company's affairs in India. However, it would appear that the directors chose to ignore this recommendation because, on 30 March, Laurence Sulivan, the director who had been principally involved in drafting the measure, gave notice of his intention to introduce the Judicature Bill into the House of Commons.

The opposition raised against the proposals in the Company's General Court suggested that the Bill would not enjoy an unhindered passage through Parliament. This was indeed the case and, following Sulivan's announcement in the House on 30 March, George Johnstone (MP for Cockermouth) again opposed the intended reforms by arguing that they were of 'no effect'. He was supported by Thomas Walpole, who observed that a majority of the Company's stockholders had already rejected the measure, and it soon became clear that many other Members were opposed to the introduction of the Bill without an inquiry into the Company's affairs. Charles Wolfran Cornwall best summed up this feeling when he observed during the debate that 'it is impossible to regulate well for the future without punishing the past'.[51]

The calls from MPs for another East India inquiry had been influenced to a large extent by knowledge of alleged crimes perpetrated by Company servants in India. These crimes had recently been brought to light in detailed book-length accounts of events in Bengal written by William Bolts and Alexander Dow.[52] The allegations had a profound effect upon public perception of British activity in India, even though Bolts's book in particular contained little more than a series of half-truths and false accusations. Both works were serialized in newspapers and periodicals in a manner that could not fail to increase hostility towards the Company. Excerpts from Bolts's book were, for example, printed in the *London Magazine* under the title of 'The nature and defects of the constitution of the East India Company', while the *London Evening Post* began a series of articles which catalogued the crimes and murders committed by Company servants in India.[53] Entrepreneurs

---

[50] *London Evening Post*, 5 Mar. 1772.   [51] BL, Eg. MSS 239, pp. 179, 181, 259.

[52] W. Bolts, *Considerations on Indian Affairs, Particularly Respecting the Present State of Bengal and its Dependencies* (1772); A. Dow, *The History of Hindostan* (3 vols., 1768–72), Bolts, who had served as a judge at the Mayor's Court at Fort William, had become involved in a series of disputes with the Bengal Council, and he had left India in April 1769 following the loss of his personal fortune. For full details see *William Bolts: A Dutch Adventurer under John Company* (Cambridge, 1920).

[53] *London Magazine* (1772), pp. 220–5; *London Evening Post*, 2 April 1772.

were swift to take advantage of the prevailing tide of public opinion: Samuel Foote's play *The Nabob* began a run at the Haymarket at the end of June, and a second edition of Bolts's book appeared later in the year.[54] All this, coupled with the fact that charges were brought against Clive and Harry Verelst by former Bengal servants, served to ensure that the Company continued to be viewed by many with deep suspicion and hostility. Ralph Leycester drew attention to this when he reported the latest Company news to Warren Hastings in March 1772:

> You will have heard from some of your correspondents of the clamour that has been raised this winter against Clive and his administration by Mr Petrie to the directors ... and Mr Bolts has lately published a large quarto on the same subjects which has raised the public indignation against the servants of the Company. He states striking facts against Clive and Verelst but he has I understand exaggerated and betrays a design to inflame. That prejudices his book very much ... However, it is swallowed very greedily by the public whose eyes are fixed on the correction of these abuses by the interposition of Parliament.[55]

The Company's problems had been well and truly placed in the public domain, and Horace Walpole was quite correct when he predicted to Sir Horace Mann on 12 February that 'the East Indies are going to be another spot of attention'.[56]

Finding itself under attack from several quarters, the Company was forced onto the defensive. In the Commons debate of 30 March Clive justified his conduct in Bengal at great length, while several MPs who had close links with the Company expressed strong doubts about the accuracy of the details in the recently published books.[57] Even so, there was almost universal agreement in the House that serious abuses had occurred in Bengal and, for many members, the main point of discussion centred upon exactly what form any inquiry into the Company's affairs should take. In particular, there was sharp disagreement over whether the inquiry should precede the passage of any legislation designed to improve the administration of justice in Bengal. Some argued that a lengthy diagnosis of the illness should be undertaken before a remedy was prescribed, while others, including North and Sulivan, declared that it was all too obvious where the major weaknesses in the Company's administration were to be found.[58] In the end a solution to the problem was offered by North, who suggested that the Company's Judicature Bill should address immediate questions, while a committee of inquiry

---

[54] *Public Advertizer*, 15, 18 Sept., 1772.   [55] BL, Add. MSS 29133, f. 72.
[56] *Walpole Corr.*, XXIII, 320–1.
[57] See, for example, the speeches of Sir George Colebrooke and Sir Thomas Rumbold as reported in BL, Eg. MSS, 239, pp. 246–7; and John Yorke to Lord Hardwicke, 30 Mar. 1772, BL, Add. MSS 35375, f. 82.   [58] BL, Add. MSS 35375, f. 81.

should be appointed to undertake a full review of the Company's overseas activities.[59] This was deemed to be acceptable by most of the Members present, and the Company, much to its dismay, found that, having taken the well-intentioned step of introducing a reform Bill into the House, it now seemed likely that it would soon be subjected to a second major inquiry into its affairs.

The demands for an inquiry were renewed on 13 April when the House next discussed Indian affairs. General John Burgoyne moved for the appointment of a Select Committee because it was too late in the session for a Committee of the Whole House to sit. While he denied that he held any particular hostility towards the Company, Burgoyne nevertheless recommended that the function of the Committee should be to 'present to Parliament a comprehensive view of the existence and extent of the evils under India government'.[60] This was a theme that was touched upon by many of the subsequent speakers in the debate, and several of them reflected upon the general effect of the Company's government on the native population. Among these were Sir William Meredith, who seconded Burgoyne's motion, and William Vane who called upon the House to 'make some attempt to rescue so many unhappy natives, industrious natives I may call them, of the country from the yoke of this government they now live under'.[61] Some doubt was expressed about the purpose of such an inquiry,[62] but in general there was little opposition to the motion. Even the Company's representatives in the House found that they could do nothing other than support the general demand for some sort of inquiry.

Much of the debate on 13 April centred upon what form the Committee should take, and an attempt was made to limit the scope of the inquiry. In particular, Edmund Burke and William Dowdeswell moved an amendment which was designed to have the inquiry 'confined to proper points'.[63] However, a majority of Members agreed with Conway who argued that 'no consideration [is] too great for Parliament'.[64] William Graves observed that because of the nature of the problem 'the larger the inquiry the better', while Meredith stated in blunt terms that any attempt to limit the scope of the committee 'was made very candidly with a view of defeating the whole inquiry'.[65] In total, four formal amendments were proposed, but all were defeated and

[59] BL, Eg. MSS 239, pp. 252–6. [60] Cobbett, *Parl. Hist.*, XVII, 456–8.
[61] BL, Eg. MSS 240, pp. 221, 225–6.
[62] See, for example, the speeches by Charles James Fox, Charles Cornwall, and Alexander Wedderburn: *ibid.*, 240, pp. 267–8, 281, 284, 285.
[63] *Ibid.*, 240, pp. 265–7, 284–92, 316, 354–355. [64] *Ibid.*, 240, p. 358.
[65] *Ibid.*, 240, pp. 358–9, 362.

Burgoyne's original motion was passed without a division: it was resolved that a Committee of thirty-one be appointed by ballot.[66]

One important feature of the long debate of 13 April was Lord North's speech, during the course of which he revealed and outlined the lengthy preparations he had undertaken in an attempt to come to terms with Indian affairs. He reported that

long before the beginning of the session I made it my business to consult all those from whom I thought I could receive information upon the very important question of the government of India...of which I do confess I have very confused ideas upon... and decided I will add to the Hon. Gentlemen that my consultations upon this subject have not been rare or accidental. I have endeavoured to make myself a master of the subject. My notion was at that time in order to effect the thing we desired there should have been several measures to accompany one another.[67]

He then outlined the measures that he had in mind. First, he indicated that three supervisors similar to those appointed in 1769 were necessary, as by now it was evident that the three original members of the Company's Commission had perished en route to India.[68] Second, he hinted at an extended degree of Crown influence in India itself by declaring that Parliament 'should arm them [the new supervisors] with power not only to represent the Company, but in some degrees [to act as] commissioners of state'. Finally, he proposed that a Bill should be introduced 'to regulate money matters, to extend and confirm the power of the India Company'.[69]

North's speech stemmed from an early realization that attempts to solve the long-standing problems of the Company could no longer be postponed by the ministry or Parliament. As early as October 1771 he had made this belief known to Clive, when he had written that 'the very critical and dangerous situation of our possessions in India will probably make it necessary to bring them under the consideration of Parliament during the next session'.[70] He had then taken part in a series of consultations with Clive, to whom he had been introduced by Solicitor-General Alexander Wedderburn.[71] The accepted view of Lord North as a somewhat indolent first minister who only responded to problems after they had reached crisis point stands in some need of correction as far as Indian affairs are concerned. On this occasion he prepared his ground in

[66] CJ, XXXIII, 691.   [67] BL, Eg. MSS 240, p. 246.
[68] The Aurora, on which the supervisors sailed in October 1769, had failed to arrive at its destination.   [69] BL, Eg. MSS 240, pp. 246–8.
[70] IOL, MSS Eur. G. 37, box 62, f. 51.
[71] Ibid., box 62, ff. 53, 78–9, 90. Since January 1770 Wedderburn had sat in the Commons as the Member for Bishop's Castle, Shropshire, a seat which was under Clive's control.

careful and methodical fashion long before the full crisis broke. By doing so, he was able to develop firm ideas on how best to solve the problems of the East India Company.

At the end of the debate on 13 April Laurence Sulivan formally introduced the Judicature Bill into the House.[72] The Bill contained a number of important proposed reforms. A Supreme Court consisting of a Chief Justice and three judges would be established at Calcutta, and this would perform all civil, criminal, and ecclesiastical functions for the entire Presidency of Bengal. The Court would have jurisdiction over all British subjects and Christians, and it would also determine cases brought against the former by Indians. The judges, who were to be nominated by the Company and approved by the Lord Chancellor, were to be barred from private trading and accepting gifts from the native population. Indeed, this important restriction was to be extended to include the Governor, Council, and all the other employees of the Company.

With public and parliamentary attention soon focusing upon the proceedings of Burgoyne's Select Committee, interest in the Judicature Bill waned. Although the Bill passed its second reading by 58 votes to 41 on 4 May,[73] wholehearted ministerial support for the measure was not forthcoming. This became quite clear a fortnight later on 18 May when the House went into the Committee on the Bill, and a number of prominent administration supporters participated in a sustained attack on the Company's proposals. The Bill's preamble was passed with no objections, but a number of dissenting voices were raised against the clause relating to the appointment of judges by the directors. In particular office-holder Welbore Ellis and the Attorney-General Edward Thurlow both argued that justice in all British possessions should flow directly from the Crown itself.[74]

Sulivan responded to this by stating that if a stand was made against the Bill on these grounds he would himself vote against the measure. After making this statement he was subjected to a characteristically savage attack from another member of the administration, the Solicitor-General Alexander Wedderburn. He criticized Sulivan's language as more befitting Calcutta than the House of Commons, and he condemned his proposed intention to vote against his own Bill. Depicting Sulivan as the 'dictator of Leadenhall Street', Wedderburn poured scorn on the Bill as 'the crude and unconnected production of a tavern meeting', and he argued that its introduction so late in the session was no more than

---

[72] BL, Add. MSS 35610, f. 198.   [73] CJ, XXXIII, 736.
[74] Cobbett, *Parl. Hist.*, XVII, 467–8. Cavendish did not report the proceedings.

a ploy to divert attention away from the real problems of the Company in Bengal.[75] Lord North did not openly endorse the attitude of his colleagues, but neither did he offer any support to Sulivan and the Company. He did, however, maintain that the Committee should continue with its task. Even so, a general lack of interest in the proceedings soon manifested itself when it was observed that a quorum of forty Members was not present in the House. In accordance with parliamentary practice the proceedings of the Committee had to be adjourned, and this proved to be the last action related to the Judicature Bill. The Committee did not sit again.[76]

The Judicature Bill represented a genuine attempt by the Company to address itself to problems related to its activities in India. Moreover, discussion of the Bill in the House of Commons had raised the important question of the wisdom of applying English law to a society which already possessed its own long-standing and well-established legal customs and notions of justice. This issue sharply divided the participants in the debates on the Bill. On 30 March Sulivan had declared that one of the main objects of his measure was to ensure that 'every Indian native may come to the pure fountain of English justice',[77] but others such as Edmund Burke argued that it was absurd to introduce English law to Bengal in a mistaken attempt 'to force a British happiness upon a banyan'.[78] 'You might as well', he declared, 'insist [that] in that burning climate every man is to put on red velvet because it is suitable to the month of March in England.' A similar point was made in India by Burke's future adversary Warren Hastings, the Governor of Bengal, who, at almost the same time as the Bill was being discussed in Parliament, was seeking to implement his own reform of judicial practices in Bengal. He had, unbeknown to those in London, established two new civil courts at Fort William.[79] When he wrote to Josias Du Pré on 8 October 1772 to report this, he regretted that a 'new judicature and a new code of laws are framing at home, on principles diametrically opposite to ours, which is little more than a renewal of the laws and forms established of old in the country with no variation than such as was necessary to give them their due effect, and such as the people understood and were likely to be pleased with'.[80]

Hastings returned to this theme a few months later when he argued,

---

[75] Ibid., XVII, 469–71.
[76] CJ, XXXIII, 770–1.
[77] BL, Eg. MSS 239, p. 183.
[78] Ibid., 239, pp. 267–8.
[79] For details of Hastings's reforms of 1772 see B.B. Misra, The Central Administration of the East India Company 1773–1834 (Manchester, 1959) pp. 229–32, and below pp. 113–15.
[80] Memoirs of the Life of the Right Honourable Warren Hastings, ed. Rev. G.R. Gleig (3 vols., 1841), I, 263.

in another letter to Du Pré, that necessity above anything else had demanded a reform of justice in Bengal. However, he was certain that his Council's actions would mean that 'we shall be crudely mauled at home, especially if the Parliament should lay hold of our code, for we have not a lawyer among us'.[81] Even so, he then made an extremely telling point when he asked, 'Is it not a contradiction of the common notions of equity and policy that the English gentlemen of Cumberland and Argyleshire [sic] should regulate the polity of a nation which they know only by the lakh which it has sent to Great Britain, and by the reduction which it has occasioned in their land tax?' Well-defined battlelines were being drawn up and, although some individual standpoints were to shift over the next decade or so, the parliamentary proceedings of 1772 may be seen as heralding the beginning of the long-running debate over the desirability of transferring anglicized notions of behaviour and conduct through the administration of justice to the Muslim and Hindu population of India.

Although assistance and encouragement had been forthcoming from the ministry during the early stages of the life of the Judicature Bill, that support evaporated when the Bill was introduced in Parliament. As with the recruiting Bills, the Company was then unable to steer its reforming measures through the Commons without the full weight of the ministry behind it. Sir George Colebrooke, ever suspicious of ministerial intentions, later identified this lack of support and legislative action as one of the principal reasons for the Company's failure to effect a general and thorough reform of its affairs between 1767 and 1772. He wrote in his memoirs that 'it looks indeed as if the Government refused to arm the Company with new and necessary powers adapted to its situation, merely to exhibit to the world its incapacity and to prepare mankind for those changes which the Court meditated from the beginning'.[82]

There is no evidence to support this imaginative theory, but ministers did seek to stave off intervention in the Company's affairs for as long as possible. Even so, there were definite signs by 1772 that the ministry was at last preparing to act. The cumulative effect of the Company's many problems could no longer be ignored and, most important of all, they now threatened to undermine the economic benefits derived from the possession of territory in India. To his credit, North recognized this earlier than most. It had become all too clear that the state could not expect to receive a regular financial payment from the Company if it was not prepared to assist in times of difficulty. Yet the final spur for government action was only forthcoming when the Company was

---

[81] *Ibid.*, I, 273.   [82] Colebrooke, *Retrospection*, II, 14.

plunged into a deep financial crisis in 1772. The Company's failure to reform its revenue and commercial systems eventually convinced the ministry that there was no alternative but to intervene in East Indian affairs, and assume at least partial responsibility for the problems of empire.

7   Attempts at reform (II): trade and revenue, 1767–1772

Concern about the conduct and behaviour of Company servants in Bengal was not the only aspect of Indian affairs to trouble ministers during the early months of 1772. The Company had experienced a series of financial difficulties, and this indicated that the economic benefits promised by the assumption of the *Diwani* were not being fully realized. On the contrary, the Company appeared to be locked into a deepening financial crisis. This crisis fully manifested itself during the second half of the year when the Company defaulted on customs payments and then failed to repay substantial loans to the Bank of England. Although these difficulties were undoubtedly exacerbated by the general European credit crisis of 1772, they also suggested a breakdown in the Anglo-Indian economic connexion, and the ministry, threatened by non-payment on a number of accounts, was forced into legislative action. As in 1767, financial considerations, above all else, prompted government intervention in the Company's affairs.

At first it had appeared that Clive's arrangements for the collection of revenue in Bengal would bear the expected fruit. In 1765 the Company already collected revenue in the districts of Burdwan, Chittagong, Midnapur, and the area known as the Twenty-Four Parganas; and this, which was intended to pay for the Company's armies, raised a net income of around £600,000 a year (see Table 2). Even though the economy of Eastern India was in decline by the mid-1760s, the addition of the Bengal, Bihar, and Orissa revenues served to quadruple this figure by the financial year 1766/7, the first full year of the Company's supervision of collection. 'Money', reported the Bengal Council to the directors as early as January 1766, 'is flowing into your treasury.'[1] However, this dramatic increase in the Company's income from revenue collection was not sustained. Income from the Bengal revenues peaked in the first full year of collection and declined steadily thereafter through

---

[1] *FWIHC*, IV, 379. The reasons for the recession in Bengal are discussed in D. Kumar (ed.), *The Cambridge Economic History of India* (2 vols., Cambridge, 1983), II: *c. 1757–c.1770*, 297–9.

Table 2. *Territorial revenues collected by the East India Company, 1761–1771*

May–April	Total net fig. (£s)	Net amount from Bengal and Bihar
1761–2	677,832	—
1762–3	635,199	—
1763–4	631,416	—
1764–5	606,132	—
1765–6	1,681,427	1,118,718
1766–7	2,550,094	1,817,649
1767–8	2,451,255	1,642,933
1768–9	2,402,191	1,761,713
1769–70	2,118,994	1,418,976
1770–1	2,009,988	1,266,613

Source: RCHC, IV, 60–1, 98–101

the years of the great famine of 1769–70 and into the early 1770s. The Bengal Council later produced figures in an attempt to show that in fact net revenue payments had not been affected by the famine, but they had to concede that this was only because collection had been 'violently kept up to its former standard'.[2]

Just as worrying for the directors was the fact that doubts were beginning to be expressed about the accuracy of the revenue assessments made by Clive at the time of the assumption of the *Diwani* in 1765. His optimistic assessments, which had caused so much excitement in London, were shown to have been quite erroneous. Harry Verelst, Clive's successor as Governor, reported to the directors in early 1768 that the calculations were based upon sums that had been raised 'in better times' and that they took no account of the cost of collection.[3] Indeed, the following year, when shortcomings in the revenue-collection system were beginning fully to manifest themselves, Verelst went one step further and told those at India House that 'the advantages of your late acquisitions have been exaggerated beyond all bounds'.[4] The directors responded to this disturbing news on 23 March 1770 when they declared to the Bengal Council that it was 'with equal surprise and concern that we find [the] revenues fall short of your first statements of

---

[2] RCHC, IV, 360. For a similar view see *Hastings Memoirs*, I, 249. It was estimated that the famine, which was caused by drought and crop failures in 1768 and 1769, cost the lives of approximately a third of the population of Bengal; *Cambridge Economic History of India*, II, 299–300.   [3] *FWIHC*, V, 469.   [4] *Ibid.*, V, 551.

them'.[5] It was clear to them that a thorough reappraisal of the Company's economic policy was necessary.

This general situation posed two particular problems for the directors: how could they arrest the decline in the level of their income from the Bengal revenues in deteriorating economic conditions; and, secondly, how could they effect the full transfer to Britain of what they had actually managed to collect? Because the former problem did not reveal itself to those in London until 1768, the directors were quite content to allow arrangements for revenue collection in Bengal to continue along the lines that had been laid down by Clive in the settlement of 1765. Instead, between 1766 and 1768 they devoted their efforts towards a reform and improvement of the Company's trading and commercial practices. They held this task to be imperative, for the amount of goods for sale imported into London had to be maximized. Only then would the Company be able to pay a substantial dividend to its shareholders and, after 1767, £400,000 a year to the government. With this in mind, all sorts of observers set about analyzing the level of profit the Company realized from its sales. They then attempted to calculate the proportion of the territorial revenues represented by these figures.[6]

One final factor played an important part in the directors' economic calculations. The production of a revenue surplus in Bengal was entirely dependent upon the Company's civil and military costs being kept to an absolute minimum. If overseas expenditure could not be strictly controlled then the revenues would serve no other purpose than to fund the manning and equipping of the Company's armed forces. This was by no means clear to all those who welcomed news of the assumption of the *Diwani* in 1765, but the former Governor of Bengal John Zephaniah Holwell was one informed observer who drew attention to the difficulties the Company faced as it attempted the task of combining the role of commercial agent and territorial proprietor. He wrote that

A trading and a fighting company is a two-headed monster in nature that cannot exist long, as the expense and inexperience of the latter must exceed, confound, and destroy every profit or advantage gained by the former. New *temporary* victories stimulate and push us on to grasp new acquisitions of territory. These call for a large increase in military force to defend them, and thus we shall go on grasping and expanding until we cram our hands so full that they become cramped and numbed, and we shall be obliged to quit and relinquish even that part which we might have held fast.[7]

---

[5] *Ibid.*, VI: (*Select and Secret*) *1770–2*, ed. B. Prasad (New Delhi, 1960), 42.
[6] See, for example, *Gentleman's Magazine*, 36 (1766), p. 443.
[7] Quoted in J.W. Kaye, *The Administration of the East India Company: A History of Indian Progress* (1853), p. 134.

At first the directors did little more than offer general encouragement to their servants as they attempted to divert as much of the revenue surplus as possible into the investment in goods for sale in London.[8] In doing so they sought an increase in the amount of the traditional goods, mainly textiles and saltpetre, that the Company exported from Bengal, but increasingly their attention focused on the development and expansion of the trade in silk. Some silk was exported as finished cloth which was made by weavers employed by the Company in Calcutta,[9] but most was shipped out in a raw state for use in the English textile industry.

The importance of this trade in raw silk was spelled out by the directors in March 1768 when they told the Bengal Council that 'it is the increase of this article of our investment that we chiefly depend [on] for bringing home our revenues, the importation being a national benefit and the consumption more unlimited than that of the manufactured goods'.[10] A year later Clive went as far as to describe raw silk as a 'great national object'.[11] Accordingly, the directors set in motion a number of schemes to improve both the level and quality of silk production in Bengal. The plantation and growth of mulberry bushes was encouraged, and wage increases were recommended for silk winders so that such workers would be better paid than a 'day labourer or common workman in any other business'. This, it was hoped, would 'induce the manufacturers of wrought silk to quit that branch and take to the winding of raw silk'.[12] Then, in the early 1770s, the directors sanctioned experiments with silk worms imported from China.[13] At the same time, experts in the textile trade, James Wiss, Pickering Robinson, and William Aubert, were appointed by the directors to oversee the Company's silk investment and production. They were charged with supervising the construction of new filatures at Kumarkhali and Kasimbazar in the style used at Novi di Modena in Italy, and a number of workers were recruited in Italy and Languedoc to help with the task of retraining Bengali craftsmen in new winding techniques. The general aim was to improve the overall quality of the Company's product by standardizing the thickness of the silk, and much stricter controls in the warehouses were imposed on the material destined for export to Britain.[14]

These innovations, which were not always welcomed by the Company's servants in Bengal, eventually had the desired effect. At first

---

[8] See above, pp. 13–14.
[9] This practice had begun in the early 1750s; *FWIHC*, XIV, 117–18. For a brief description of the Bengal silk industry see Marshall, *Bengal*, pp. 107–9.
[10] *FWIHC*, V, 80–1.   [11] Speech of 27 Feb. 1769; BL, Eg. MSS 218, p. 154.
[12] *FWIHC*, V, 175–6.   [13] *Ibid.*, XIV, lxxxi.   [14] *Ibid.*, VI, 14–16.

the new techniques proved to be prohibitively expensive,[15] and between 1772 and 1773 the value of silk exported by the Company from Bengal actually fell by almost a third. But, in the longer term, the innovations and reforms of 1770 proved to be a great success from the Company's point of view, and the purchase value of silk exported from Bengal more than doubled from £142,328 in 1769 to £318,406 in 1776.[16] Even so, this trend, and the fact that significant quantities of raw silk were imported into Britain from China, did not mean that the Company monopolized the supply of silk to the English market. They faced stiff competition from Italy. The directors recognized this and sought to secure favourable import conditions for the Company's silk in the hope that they could undercut their rivals' prices. In particular, they endeavoured in 1767 to obtain a reduction in the customs duty payable on all the calicoes, muslins, and silk (raw and finished) shipped into Britain by the Company.

This idea formed part of the general proposals the directors put to the ministry in the negotiations relating to the territorial revenues and, although in May it was reported that the matter was being considered by the Chancellor of the Exchequer, the Company were eventually told that the matter could not be dealt with during the course of the current parliamentary session.[17] In the event no reform of the duties was made by the ministry and, by the mid-1770s, the Company's raw silk imports only represented 21 per cent of the total value of the product shipped into Britain from all sources. The directors could derive some satisfaction from this figure because twenty years earlier the Company had held little more than a 16 per cent share of Britain's import trade in silk,[18] but it was not until the 1790s that Bengal became Britain's single greatest source of the product.

The increase in the exportation of raw silk from Bengal helped to sustain a steady overall growth in the value of the Company's direct shipments to Europe. Between May 1764 and May 1765 the value of Bengal cargoes sent to Britain was £276,772 at prime cost. By 1768/9 the value had risen to £658,341, while by 1770/1, despite a setback in 1769/70, it had reached £904,853.[19] On the face of things this represented a significant achievement by the Company.

The second major area of commercial concern for the directors during the late 1760s was the Company's trade with China and, in particular, the tea trade. Recent trends pointed to the fact that the trade with

[15] *Ibid.*, VI, 439–40.
[16] Figures from *Cambridge Economic History of India*, II, 819.
[17] IOR, B/83, pp. 118–19.
[18] R. Davis, 'English foreign trade, 1700–1774', *Economic History Review*, 2nd ser., XV (1962–3), 300–1.   [19] *RCHC*, IV, 60–9.

Canton was second in importance only to that with Bengal,[20] and it was clear that in tea the Company had a product that was much in demand in Britain despite the fact that their theoretical monopoly on sales was quite significantly undermined by the activities of smugglers. The logic of this situation seemed to be quite clear to the directors: as much of the Bengal revenue surplus as possible should be transferred to China to allow the Company's employees at Canton to increase the funding of the tea trade. They told the Bengal Council in November 1768 that 'the enlargement of the trade to China to its utmost extent is an object we have greatly at heart, not only from the advantages in prospect by gaining a superiority and thereby discouraging foreign Europeans from resorting to that market, but also from a national concern wherein the revenue is very materially affected'.[21]

The central problem was how best to effect the transfer of the revenue surplus to Canton, because few of the goods that the Company exported from Bengal were in sufficient demand in China to allow any profit made from their sale to be used for the purchase of large amounts of tea. The shipment of bullion to China carried with it the danger that much needed circulating specie would be withdrawn from the Bengal economy, thus exacerbating existing currency problems, but this was a risk that the directors were prepared to take. In November 1767 they ordered that specie worth 24 lakhs of rupees (about £300,000) should be sent to China,[22] even though at virtually the same time the Bengal Select Committee was warning that the exportation of treasure to China was already causing a 'scarcity of money', and that the 'effects of the considerable drain made from the silver currency' were already being felt.[23] The problems inherent in this policy became steadily more apparent over the next few years[24] but, in the short term, the injection of capital from Bengal did serve to boost the level of tea importation into Britain from China. The amount rose, albeit far from steadily, from 4,432,383 lbs in 1768 to 10,927,999 lbs in 1770, before peaking at 12,787,113 lbs in 1772.[25]

[20] Chaudhuri, *Trading World of Asia*, p. 510; trade figures for 1756–60.
[21] *FWIHC*, V, 136.
[22] *Ibid.*, V, 42. Two months later the Select Committee at Fort William were ordered to send £500,000 home in the form of specie because it was proving impossible to invest all of the revenue surplus in goods for export; *ibid.*, XIV, 17.
[23] *Ibid.*, XIV, 195; letter of 25 Sept. 1767.
[24] The Company tried to solve these problems in several different ways. Company servants in Bengal were encouraged to buy as much as possible of the silver that was shipped into India by the French, Dutch, and Danes, and in the early 1770s permission was granted for attempts to be made to discover new mineral sources in northern India; *ibid.*, V, 174; XIV, 239–40.
[25] B.W. Labaree, *The Boston Tea Party* (Oxford, 1964), p. 334. The level of tea importation had been low in 1767, but the average annual figure during the previous five years had been 7,477,767 lbs.

As with the silk trade, the directors recognized that there was little point in increasing the levels of tea importation if there were not sufficient outlets at home for the commodity. Consumption of the product had to be encouraged but, as things stood in 1766, a duty of 25 per cent on top of the Company's sale price for tea, and an 'inland' duty of 1s. a lb was payable upon all tea sold within Britain. No additional duty, however, was payable upon tea re-exported to America or anywhere else.[26] The Company, whose tea was significantly more expensive than that which could be bought by British merchants in Holland, sought throughout the negotiations with ministry in 1766 and 1767 to secure the removal or reduction of the tea duties so as to help increase the level of sales at India House. There had been rumours in April 1766 that an adjustment of the duties was imminent[27] and, in the autumn, Charles Townshend was reported to be considering schemes to help the Company sell more of its tea in the colonies.[28] Thus when the Chairman and Deputy Chairman waited upon ministers on 31 December 1766 'to know what they might expect in regard to a drawback upon tea', they found the administration already receptive to the idea of legislating in order to help the Company.[29] Accordingly, when the directors submitted formal proposals to the ministry on 8 January 1767, they asked for a reduction of the inland duty on tea so as to encourage legal consumption at home, and they requested a 'drawback' or rebate of at least 20 per cent on the customs duty payable on tea that was re-exported from Britain.[30]

After lengthy negotiations which lasted until the end of April, the Company was granted its requests: the inland duty of 1s. a lb was removed and a full drawback of the 25 per cent duty was applied to all tea exported to North America and Ireland. A formula was then agreed by which the Company would indemnify the government for any loss of revenue following the introduction of these measures.[31] However, this was not the end of the matter because as part of Townshend's plans to tax the colonies an import duty of 3d. a lb was to be levied upon all tea shipped into North America. Some of the Company's representatives complained bitterly that the Chancellor was giving to them with one hand while taking away with the other, but there is no doubt that the Company's tea was still far cheaper after the introduction of the

---

[26] Thomas, *Townshend Duties Crisis*, p. 18.
[27] *Lloyd's Evening Post*, 30 April 1766.
[28] Thomas, *Townshend Duties Crisis*, p. 19.   [29] IOR, B/82, p. 337.
[30] A copy of the proposals is printed in *Chatham Corr.*, III, 164–5.
[31] The proposals were discussed at a meeting between ministers and three directors on 28 April 1767 (IOR, B/83, p. 29) and they were adopted as a resolution by a Committee of the Whole House on 23 May; *CJ*, XXXI, 382. The proposals were finally enacted as 7 Geo. III, c. 56.

Table 3. *Exports from Britain by the East India Company, 1762–1772 (figures in £s)*

	Merchandize	Bullion	Total value
1762/3	488,596	56,856	545,453
1763/4	429,219	40,016	469,236
1764/5	445,327	345,404	790,732
1765/6	455,577	281,875	737,452
1766/7	449,075	54,968	504,043
1767/8	588,255	—	588,255
1768/9	555,429	162,583	718,012
1769/70	594,620	242,998	837,619
1770/1	529,878	302,625	832,503
1771/2	452,700	200,000	652,700

Source : RCHC, IV, 75. The figures cover the period from March to March.

Townshend duty than it had been before the Parliamentary session of 1766–7.[32] The short-term commercial benefits of the measure were soon plain for all to see: sales of tea for the home market almost doubled from 3,731,903 lbs in 1767 to 6,586,829 lbs in 1768, while sales for export rose from 430,020 lbs to 1,273,880 lbs during the same period.[33] What as yet could not be predicted, however, was how in the longer term the political repercussions of the decision to tax North America would affect the Company's hold on the tea market there.

The reshaping of the Company's commercial activities after 1765 had little effect upon the export of goods to Bengal. The value of the cargoes sent to the Presidency between 1767 and 1771 fell in the range between £120,000 and £160,000, figures which represented about 20 per cent of the Company's total exports. A significant increase occurred, however, in direct exports to Canton and, on several occasions, the annual value of cargoes sent there nearly touched £400,000 as the Company sought to increase the levels of capital available for tea purchases.[34] In overall terms, as Table 3 illustrates, the total value of the Company's exports ranged between £469,236 and £837,619 during the decade after 1762. These figures were slightly lower than those for the period 1749–54, but were broadly comparable with those for the earlier years of the century.[35]

The Company's export cargoes were made up of woollen goods, lead, copper, tin, iron, and bullion. In the past, large amounts of bullion had

[32] Thomas, *Townshend Duties Crisis*, pp. 27–9.
[33] Labaree, *Boston Tea Party*, p. 334.   [34] *RCHC*, IV, 60–9.
[35] *Ibid.*, IV, 75.

been exported by the Company to India in order to supply the means by which servants could purchase goods for shipment to Britain. Indeed, between 1708 and 1760 bullion had accounted for some 75 per cent of the value of all the Company's exports.[36] The transfer of gold and silver from Europe to Asia helped to balance Bengal's import and export trade, and it enabled one well-informed observer to remark that this was one of the sources of the 'prodigious ancient riches' of the province.[37] However, commercial conditions in the years after 1765 were such that the directors believed that there would no longer be any need for them to ship out as much bullion from Britain: investment needs would be met in the main by the revenue surplus. Indeed, ever since the Company had first become a territorial proprietor in the Twenty-Four Parganas in 1757 the directors had been seeking to scale down the level of the Company's bullion exports to India. The amount of bullion exported in 1766/7 was considerably less than that sent abroad the previous year and, in 1767/8, no shipments of gold or silver were made by the Company. The Company's export cargoes during the late 1760s thus in the main consisted of non-precious metals and manufactured goods, but this trend was not to last. Growing fears about the effects of the drain of specie from Bengal[38] forced the directors to resume bullion shipments and, in 1770/1, the value of this type of cargo rose above £300,000 for only the second time in fifteen years. The Company had found to its cost that it could not afford to abandon its long-established commercial practices in favour of a complete dependence on surpluses derived from revenue collection.

The administration closely monitored the Company's export trade during the course of its negotiations with the directors in 1769 for a renewal of the settlement agreed two years earlier. Indeed, there was considerable ministerial concern that the Company, now deriving most of its investment funds from within Bengal itself, might seek, deliberately or otherwise, to reduce the volume and value of its exported goods. This in the long term could inflict considerable damage on British industry. Ministers therefore sought guarantees from the Company that it would undertake to export a fixed amount of manufactured goods to India each year. At first the directors resisted this proposal and argued that trade 'must depend on the state of the markets abroad'.[39] Eventually, however following protracted discussions, the Company's negotiators, who were in broad agreement with the ministry over the terms of a new five-year settlement, capitulated on

[36] *Parliamentary Papers* (1812–13), VIII, 403.
[37] Verelst to the directors, 5 Apr. 1769, *FWIHC*, V, 547.   [38] *Ibid.*, V, 546–51.
[39] IOR, B/84, p. 352.

this point and agreed that in future the Company would annually export British goods to the value of the average over the previous five years.[40] As a result of this agreement, the value of the merchandize exported by the Company between 1771 and 1775 remained very close to the £475,000 mark.[41]

Although the Bengal Council reported throughout the late 1760s that the investment targets set by the directors were being met, if not exceeded,[42] by March 1768 concern was being expressed by Company officials at India House that revenue collections were not living up to expectations.[43] Accordingly, a review of revenue-collection practices and procedures was set in motion and, as a result of this, Clive's system was eventually abandoned in favour of much greater involvement in the process by Company servants. Yet opinion within the upper echelons of the Company was divided over the nature of the problem as well as the remedy. Many of those in London believed that if the methods employed to collect revenue could be improved there would be a significant increase in the amount entering the Company's treasury. In particular, they felt that the whole system needed to be more closely supervised by Company officials at local level.

Others, including most notably Harry Verelst, argued instead that the rapidly deteriorating condition of the Bengal economy was itself the single greatest cause of the Company's inability to realize a large revenue surplus. Verelst was, in particular, a harsh critic of the way in which bullion exports to Bengal had been systematically reduced by the Company since 1757, and he was the leading advocate of the 'drain of wealth' theory.[44] He produced detailed arguments which analyzed all aspects of the problem, and he left the directors in little doubt that their short-sightedness was one of the 'true sources' of Bengal's distress. He told them that 'a superficial or weak observer may estimate a country like an estate from its rent roll but the man of experience and reflection will easily see that its annual income must depend on the proportion of its produce which can be realized in specie'.[45] In seeking an immediate financial return from their new territories in 1765, the directors had forsaken the long-term view and had failed to realize the fundamental point that the Company's interests were now best served by promoting the general well-being of the Bengal economy. Thus Verelst argued that instead of immediately attempting to maximize revenue returns, 'when these lands came under our management we [should have] lowered the stated rents of those districts as an incitement to cultivation and

---

[40] *Ibid.*, B/84, pp. 42–3. For full details on the negotiations see Bowen, 'British politics and the East India Company', pp. 430–51.
[41] *Parliamentary Papers* (1812–13), VIII, 402.   [42] *FWIHC*, V, 389, 535.
[43] *Ibid.*, V, 24.   [44] See, for example, *ibid.*, V, 548–9.   [45] *Ibid.*, V, 551.

improvement'.[46] Similarly, he declared in 1769 that part of the revenue surplus should be 'employed on private security of the natives [and] in loans for the cultivation of waste lands by which method your possessions would in time become of real value to you'. The long-term benefit of such a policy would be that 'the country would be rendered more populous; the trade increased by an addition of the manufactures, and the means of realizing your property be more certain and less detrimental to the country or the native trades'.[47]

While Verelst's letters and dispatches must have made uncomfortable reading for those at India House, his proposed remedies were not taken up and implemented as Company policy. Instead, the directors remained preoccupied after 1767 with the exertion of a greater degree of Company control over all aspects of the Bengal revenue system. Their general attitude was most succinctly summed up in 1769 when they told the Bengal Council that 'with care and industry great improvements may be made in the *diwani* collections'.[48] They took as their model for improvement the districts of Burdwan, Midnapur, and Chittagong, where not only had levels of revenue collection increased since the mid-1760s, but also the total size of the native population had grown at the same time. The reason for this, so it was held, was that the entire revenue collection operation had been placed directly under the Company's control and management. This had led to the elimination of abuses which 'are still severely felt thro' all the provinces of Bengal and Bihar where the numerous tribes of Fougeders, Aumils, Sikdars etc. practice all the various modes of oppression which have been in use for so long as the Moorish government has subsisted'.[49] The general aim of the directors as far as the *Diwani* lands were concerned was, therefore, to seek the reduction of the 'number of idle sycophants between the tenants and the public treasury'.

By adopting this approach the directors convinced themselves that not only would they secure a better financial return from the territories under their jurisdiction, but that they would at the same time improve the lot of the oppressed native by introducing him to well-regulated, moderate collection procedures. This belief underpinned all the ensuing revenue reforms introduced by the Company. Thus, although reform was introduced in rather piecemeal fashion between 1768 and 1772, the general intention, as described by the Bengal Council in September 1772, was to 'render the accounts of the revenue simple and intelligible, to establish fixed rules for collection, to make the mode of them uniform in all parts of the province, and to provide for an equal administration of justice'.[50] Accordingly, native officials, including at the highest levels

---

[46] *Ibid.*, V, 468.   [47] *Ibid.*, V, 553.   [48] *Ibid.*, V, 211.
[49] *Ibid.*, V, 212.   [50] *RCHC*, IV, 302.

Naibs Muhammed Reza Khan and Shitab Roy, were replaced by Company servants. Many of these officials first operated at local level under the title of supervisor, but later became known as collectors. This change in nomenclature accompanied an important development in the role played by these individuals. As Warren Hastings explained to Josias Du Pré, 'They were originally what the word supervisor imports, simple lookers on, without trust or authority. They later became collectors, and ceased to be lookers on.'[51] A 'Committee of Circuit' and councils at Murshidabad and Patna were established to monitor revenue administration and, in 1772, the whole operation was placed under the direct supervision of a newly formed Revenue Board.

These were not just superficial administrative reforms. In 1772, in order to rationalize the whole system, the Council took the important step of moving the entire revenue administration from Murshidabad to Calcutta. At the same time, use was made of this opportunity to reform the *Khalsa* or Office of Revenue by reducing its large number of offices and native employees. This helped to end, not least in a geographical sense, the important distinction between the Company's commercial and administrative functions. This was a point that was not lost on those in Bengal, and they hoped that a consequence of the move of the revenue administration from Murshidabad would be 'the great increase of inhabitants and of wealth in Calcutta, which will not only add to the consumption of our most valuable manufactures from home, but will be the means of conveying to the natives a more intimate knowledge of our customs and manners, and of conciliating them to our policy and government'.[52] Yet only five years earlier the directors had firmly rejected such a move. 'We mean', they had told the Bengal Council in March 1767, 'to preserve the distinction in the forms entire, and that Fort William be the seat of commerce, and the administration of justice at Murshidabad, or at such place where the nabob's ministers reside.'[53] In view of this comment it is perhaps appropriate to remark that nothing better represented the ending of the old dual system than the directors' approval of the decision to reduce, if not eliminate, the importance of Murshidabad as a political and administrative centre. Calcutta had, in the words of Warren Hastings, become 'the capital of Bengal' by 1772.[54]

A second important reform was the abolition of the *punyah* ceremony held at Murshidabad each year when revenue assessments and settlements for each district were formalized between the Nawab and the principal revenue payers.[55] This was replaced in 1772 by a scheme

[51] *Hastings Memoirs*, I, 268. For details on the appointment and role of the supervisors see Misra, *Central Administration*, pp. 110–14.   [52] *RCHC*, IV, 304.
[53] *FWIHC*, V, 17.   [54] *Hastings Memoirs*, I, 263.
[55] For further details see Marshall, *Bengal*, pp. 59–61.

devised by the new Governor Warren Hastings, in which the Company fixed returns and granted revenue farms on five-year leases.[56] The Committee of Circuit toured the province selling these leases at public auctions, but the Bengal Council declared that they were not averse to the notion of the *zamindars* continuing with revenue collections in their traditional districts. Of course they were well aware that *zamindars* collected revenue as an hereditary right and that to interfere with this would create a whole host of legal and administrative problems. Nevertheless, the Council were still able to identify a number of advantages in leaving collections under the immediate supervision of *zamindars*. They told the directors that 'we believe that the people would be treated with more tenderness, the rents more improved, and the cultivation more likely to be encouraged; the zamindars less liable to failure or deficiencies than the farmer from the perpetual interest which the former hath in the country, and because his inheritance cannot be removed'.[57] To some extent, at least, ancient and familiar practices had been preserved.[58] Although this new system would itself soon fall into disrepute, those who engineered the transformation of revenue-collection practices in Bengal were well satisfied with their achievement. Warren Hastings could scarcely conceal his delight at the way in which the new system was working when he told Josias Du Pré at the beginning of 1773 that 'the officers are completely established, and the business in as good a train as could possibly be expected so soon after so great a revolution'.[59]

The reforms outlined briefly above represented some of the most important changes made in the British administration of Bengal in the eighteenth century, and they were to lead eventually to the Permanent Settlement of 1793. The attempt to extract a greater return from revenue collection had driven the Company inexorably down the path to greater involvement in the everyday life of Bengal. In marked contrast with the events surrounding the acquisition of the *Diwani* in 1765, the Company found by the late 1760s that its policy decisions were such that it had become a powerful agent for social and economic change in the province. No longer could it simply exercise a distant control and supervision from Fort William, and no longer could it leave the running of routine affairs to native officials. Yet, important as these reforms were, they were shaped and formulated in the main by the Company's officials in Bengal, and not by those in control of affairs in London.

Needless to say, neither the British government nor Parliament were

[56] For the directors' approval of this system see their private letter to Hastings, *Hastings Memoirs*, I, 256.   [57] *RCHC*, IV, 302.
[58] For a full discussion of the new arrangements and the ensuing debate see Marshall, *Bengal*, pp. 118–22.   [59] *Hastings Memoirs*, I, 271.

involved in the decision-making process in any way. Even the Company's directors offered only the broadest policy guidelines, and they were quite content to allow individuals such as Hastings to come to terms with the practical problems associated with general resolutions such as the famous one they passed in August 1772 which declared that the Company should now 'stand forth as Diwan' in Bengal.[60] In this respect those in Britain could only stand by and offer encouragement and very general advice, as Company servants struggled to adapt to the new roles demanded of them as revenue collectors and territorial administrators.

The Company's double-edged attempt to boost the level of silk and tea imports into Britain during the late 1760s appeared at first to be having the desired effect. The total value of the cargoes brought from Asia by the Company rose from £900,539 in 1763/4 to £1,640,598 in 1768/9: Bengal goods accounted for 45 per cent of the latter figure, and Chinese goods for 37 per cent.[61] Indeed, in July 1769 the directors resolved that 'the trade of the Company is so much increased as to render it absolutely necessary to add to the number of ships employed in the service'.[62] As a result of this decision, the number of ships used by the Company rose from 76 with a combined tonnage of 51,542 tons in 1768, to 87 with a combined tonnage of 61,656 tons in 1769.[63] This expansion of the East India trade was naturally reflected in an increase in the amount of income generated from the sale of goods at the Company's March and September auctions. The annual sum raised from these auctions rose from £2,575,819 in 1764/5 to £3,573,385 in 1769/70.[64] This offered considerable encouragement to the directors, as did the fact that the difference between the annual yield from the sales and the value of the Company's exported goods combined with payments to redeem bills of exchange drawn on the Company increased from £1,335,443 to £2,506,383 during the same period.[65] This steadily increasing balance of trade in favour of imported goods seemed to suggest that the attempts to secure the transfer of the territorial revenue surplus to Britain were meeting with some success by the end of the 1760s.

However, these figures conceal a number of trends which serve to modify the view that the Company's commercial activities were an unqualified success during these years. Most important of all, perhaps, the perceived decline of the Bengal economy and the Company's failure to exceed previous levels of revenue collection led Harry Verelst to inform the directors in April 1769 that investment in goods would have

[60] FWIHC, VI, 123.   [61] RCHC, IV, 60–9.   [62] IOR, B/84, p. 149.
[63] RCHC, IV, 259.   [64] Ibid., IV, 40–59.
[65] Ibid., IV, 75. The figure for exports includes goods and bullion.

to be reduced in future years.[66] Whether they agreed with this or not, by 1770 it had become clear to those in Britain that the level of the Company's importation of goods from Bengal would soon be diminishing.

A second important point was that much of the increased yield from sales during the late 1760s represented a taking up of the slack in the Company's commercial activities, which had been caused by the disruption to trade during the warfare and political upheaval in the years between 1756 and 1765. The volume of the Company's import trade was undergoing a significant expansion during the late 1760s, but the directors were seemingly incapable of coming to terms with the problem of generating an appropriate amount of income from the sales of goods. Indeed, the value of goods sold between 1765 and 1770 did not greatly exceed the amount realized between 1749 and 1754.[67] This is borne out by the fact that the value of the goods remaining unsold in the Company's London warehouses trebled from £1,005,056 in 1763 to £3,260,072 in 1772.[68] While goods were being shipped from Bengal and Canton in ever-increasing quantities, the Company was having little success in finding appropriate commercial outlets for them.

In more general terms, the Company also found that having forsaken its role as a traditional commercial organization in favour of that of a territorial power in Bengal, it was now incurring heavy additional expenditure which served to undermine its financial position by absorbing income derived from revenue collection. The decision to increase the Company's military presence in Bengal resulted, for example, in a doubling of military expenditure in the Presidency from £550,036 in 1764/5 to £1,093,006 in 1770/1. Civil expenses, including the rebuilding of Fort William,[69] rose even more dramatically, from £725,198 to £2,118,829 during the same period.[70] Such were the directors' concerns about this spiralling expenditure in Bengal that they recommended in March 1768 that in the church being built within the new fort at Calcutta 'simplicity should be preferred to rich and expensive ornament'.[71] All the dispatches sent from India House in the late 1760s contained lengthy strictures on the need to keep the Company's costs to an absolute minimum.

---

[66] *FWIHC*, V, 552.

[67] *RCHC*, IV, 40–59. The average annual value of sales of goods was £2,318,342 between 1749/50 and 1753/4, and £3,003,659 between 1765/6 and 1769/70.

[68] BL, Add. MSS 38397, f. 249. These figures were produced for ministerial man-of-business Charles Jenkinson by the Company's Deputy-Accountant Ransford Tookey in 1772 or 1773.

[69] The Company spent £1,601,967 on buildings and fortifications at Fort William between 1762 and 1772; *RCHC*, IV, 459.   [70] *Ibid.*, IV, 60–1.

[71] *FWIHC*, V, 84.

The increases in overseas expenditure served to offset much of the benefit derived from the territorial revenues, but the Company also found itself undertaking increased levels of financial commitment at home. Not only did ministerial interest in the territorial revenues cost the Company £400,000 a year in payments to the Treasury after 1767, but the wave of speculation begun by news of Clive's success eventually led to substantial increases in dividend payments to the stockholders. These increases, first implemented at Christmas 1766, saw the dividend rise from an average of 6 per cent a year during the first five years of the 1760s to $12\frac{1}{2}$ per cent in 1771. By midsummer 1772 these increases had cost the Company £814,493 above the sum they would have paid if the dividend had been maintained at 6 per cent.[72] Thus, although the surplus in the Company's annual balance of payments rose from £445,979 in 1765/6 to £1,060,930 in 1770/1, when the overall financial situation was calculated in early 1773 an accumulated deficit at home of £1,948,549 was reported.[73]

It is difficult to escape the conclusion that, as the Chairman of the directors, Sir George Colebrooke, later acknowledged,[74] the Company had incurred a net financial loss as a result of its assumption of the *Diwani*. In fact, the directors had begun to recognize this unpalatable truth as early as March 1768. Their general concern about the way in which the Company was failing to come to terms with its new role as a territorial proprietor prompted them to declare to the Bengal Council that if they were to suffer an unexpected disaster, such as a protracted war with an Indian power, they would find that the state of their finances was such that 'it will be found we have not altered our situation much to our advantage, but have only exchanged a certain profit in commerce for a precarious one in revenue'.[75] The Company's transition from trader to sovereign had been uncomfortable and, in many respects, unsuccessful.

---

[72] *RCHC*, IV, 40–59.
[73] *Ibid.*, IV, 18–30.
[74] Colebrooke, *Retrospection*, II, 18.
[75] *FWIHC*, V, 102.

8   The East India Company crisis of 1772

Individuals with a close interest in Indian affairs became deeply uneasy about the East India Company's general financial situation during the summer of 1771.[1] This concern was prompted by the realization that the Company's servants had far exceeded the limits that had been set in 1768 and 1769 on the submission of bills of exchange from Bengal to be drawn upon the Company in London. Furthermore, these bills had not been drawn up in compliance with the strict terms laid down by the directors. By July 1771 vast numbers of bills were arriving at India House.[2] Sir George Colebrooke later claimed that had he been a director at the time he would have refused to sanction acceptance of the bills,[3] but, on 31 July, the Committees of Accounts and Correspondence recommended that they be honoured 'as it was alleged that the credit of the Company might be hurt in the severest manner by refusing'.[4] As a result of this decision there was a fivefold increase in the value of the bills that the Company was liable to honour, from £296,562 in 1770/1 to £1,577,959 in 1771/2.[5]

In October 1769 the Bengal Council had decided that it was necessary for them to set up an exigency fund at Fort William because the sums accruing from the territorial revenues were not living up to their expectations, and the civil and military expenses of the Presidency were continuing to rise at an alarming rate. To attract the capital necessary for the establishment of such a fund, they decided that the 'only expedient within their reach is to open the treasury doors for remittances'.[6] It was for this reason that in 1769–70 the Council began to issue, in return for currency deposits, an increasing number of bills which were to be exchanged for cash in London either by Company servants returning home or by the representatives of those remaining in service in India.

[1] See, for example, Clive to Hastings, 1 Aug. 1772, BL, Add. MSS 29133, ff. 234–7.
[2] On 10 July a parcel of bills worth £747,195 arrived at India House; *RCHC*, IV, 378.
[3] Colebrooke, *Retrospection*, II, 105.
[4] *RCHC*, IV, 380. The Committee had, however, been informed that the Company was not legally bound to accept the bills if they had been drawn up in Bengal contrary to the directors' instructions.   [5] *Ibid.*, IV, 40–59.   [6] *Ibid.*, IV, 359.

For the many individuals involved in this practice such an arrangement served as a convenient way of transferring private fortunes back to Britain. Yet, in 1773, the parliamentary Secret Committee on East Indian affairs investigated this matter at great length and rejected the Bengal Council's claim that it had no alternative open to it as it sought to raise much needed capital. The Committee concluded that the Council should have instead borrowed money 'at interest' and thereby added to their bond debt in Bengal, and they observed that the exigency fund had never in fact been established at Fort William.[7]

During the late 1760s the directors had attempted to lay down firm guidelines for the Bengal Council by sending out to Calcutta detailed financial instructions which defined redemption terms for bills of exchange, and restricted the number of bills that could be drawn upon the Company. These instructions were ignored. In 1768 permission was given for the Council to grant bills worth £212,789 in 1770 and, although this limit was later extended to £228,577, a huge number of bills worth £1,063,067 were issued by the authorities at Fort William.[8] Bengal was not the only Presidency to exceed the limits set by the directors, but its excesses far outstripped those of Madras and Bombay. In November 1768, for example, the Council at Fort St George were restricted to issuing bills worth £30,000, a figure later increased to £50,000. They submitted bills worth £71,555 to India House in 1769/70, but the following year they complied with the instructions and took great care to limit the amount to £49,999.[9]

In spite of attempts by the Bengal Council to justify their action, the members of the parliamentary Secret Committee were later quite certain as to where the blame lay for this massive new burden upon the Company. They declared that 'in the bills drawn in the season 1770, the President and Council [of Fort William] departed from all the beforementioned instructions, by drawing them at different rates of exchange and on different terms'.[10] Moreover, they underlined the effect that this had on the financial situation of the Company at home when they observed that 'the present distress of the Company in England for want of cash is owing to the great quantity of bills drawn by the Company's Presidencies in the season 1770 and accepted in England between 1 March 1771 and 1 March 1772'.[11] When the desperate

---

[7] *Ibid.*, IV, 365. Verelst had argued during his governorship (which ended in December 1769) that any attempt to set up an emergency fund would serve only to exacerbate Bengal's economic problems by withdrawing specie from circulation; *FWIHC*, V, 468.

[8] *RCHC*, IV, 355–7. The bills were to be honoured over a three-year period. £372,873 became due in 1772, and £345,097 in 1773 and 1774.

[9] *Ibid.*, IV, 369. The bulk of the bills issued for redemption in 1769/70 were granted before the arrival of the instructions containing the restrictions.

[10] *Ibid.*, IV, 351. The new President was John Cartier.   [11] *Ibid.*, IV, 355.

economic position of the Company became public knowledge, this was a diagnosis that was accepted by most of those within India House itself.[12]

It was unfortunate for the directors that, just as these difficulties started to manifest themselves, the returns from the territorial revenues began to diminish. Moreover, a decline in the Company's commercial activities became apparent at the same time. As was shown in the previous chapter, the total value of the goods remaining unsold in the Company's warehouses had reached £3,260,072 by 1772, but equally worrying was the fact that annual income from sales of goods had fallen from £3,564,385 in 1769 to £3,254,124 in 1771.[13] As if to reflect that the Indian trade was entering a recession, it was estimated that in 1772 the Company was employing 26,360 tons of excess shipping, a figure which represented almost half of the combined tonnage of the fleet.[14] The following year the parliamentary Secret Committee came to the conclusion that 'many more ships are entertained in the service of the Company than are requisite for their trade' and, as part of a general cost-cutting exercise, they recommended a reduction of the fleet to 35,000 tons.[15] This stands in marked contrast to the directors' decision of only four years earlier to increase the number of ships in the Company's service in order to cope with the demands of a rapidly expanding trade. Nothing better symbolizes the Company's declining economic fortunes during this period than this call for a 43 per cent reduction in the size of the East India fleet.

Tea lay at the heart of all these problems. With an increasing number of ships consigned to Canton from India, the Company's representatives there were obliged to send them all home to London laden with large quantities of tea, mainly of the Bohea variety. In total some 44,141,190 lbs of tea found its way to Britain from China between 1768 and 1772, yet there was no great increase in the annual amount of tea sold by the Company.[16] On the contrary, as a result of illegal foreign competition, sales at home actually decreased between 1769 and 1773. Moreover, although the implementation of the terms of the Indemnity Act of 1767 and a reduction in the price of the Company's Bohea tea from 2s. 9d. a lb to 2s. 1d. a lb led to a threefold increase in the sale of tea for export between 1767 and 1769, this growth was not maintained thereafter and these sales also began to decline.[17] By the early 1770s the Company was

---

[12] See, for example, Rockingham to Dowdeswell, 30 Nov. 1772, WWM R1–1415 (b).
[13] *RCHC*, IV, 40–59.
[14] *Ibid*., IV, 259. The figures were produced by the Company's Surveyor of Shipping Gabriel Snodgrass.   [15] *Ibid*.   [16] Labaree, *Boston Tea Party*, p. 334.
[17] *Ibid*., pp. 13, 334. Sales of tea for export rose from 430,020 lbs in 1767 to 1,273,880 lbs in 1769, before falling to 1,146,255 lbs in 1772.

thus faced with an ever increasing surplus of tea stored in its warehouses. Although the amount had fallen from 13,500,000 lbs in 1767 to 8,800,000 lbs in 1768, it had more than doubled to 17,755,000 lbs by 1772.[18] If the price of tea bought at the Company's auctions in 1772 is taken as 2s. 3¾d. per lb,[19] it may be calculated that the sale value of the tea stored in the Company's warehouses that year was £2,052,922. This figure represents approximately 63 per cent of the total value of all the unsold goods, and clearly the tea trade was the area of the Company's greatest commercial failing during the early 1770s. How had this situation arisen, and why was the Company unable to sustain the expansion of its tea sales after 1769?

The introduction and retention of the Townshend Duties Act of 1767 had served to offset many of the advantages the Company derived from the Indemnity Act. The imposition of the 3d. a lb duty on all tea imported into North America reduced the commercial benefits that had been granted to the Company by the withdrawal of the import duty on tea destined to be re-exported from Britain. Indeed, it was observed in the House of Commons in March 1770, during a debate on a motion to repeal all of the Townshend duties, that the introduction of the measures in 1767 had been 'anti-commercial'. Thomas Pownall quoted the Governor of Massachusetts Thomas Hutchinson's estimate that the Townshend Duties Act bestowed a 25 per cent commercial advantage upon the Company's foreign competitors.[20] However, even more important was the fact that the imposition of the duties had provoked an angry response from many Americans and, although opposition to the Act gained ground only slowly, by October 1769 Boston merchants had agreed to a boycott of all British imports and manufactures.[21] Although it proved impossible to enforce this general boycott, tea was singled out for special attention. A campaign directed against tea gained ground in 1770 and this resulted in a dramatic fall in the amount of the commodity imported into the colonies from Britain. In 1767 868,792 lbs of tea had been shipped from Britain to North America, but by 1770 the figure had fallen to only 108,629 lbs.[22] The actions of merchants in New York, Philadelphia, Boston, and Charleston thus played a large part in

[18] *Ibid.*, p. 334. T. Shearer, 'Crisis and change in the development of the East India Company's affairs, 1760–1773', unpublished D.Phil. thesis, Oxford University, 1976, p. 111 calculates the tea surplus to be 13,013,031 lbs, but this is some 4½ million lbs short of the true figure. Labaree's figure is based upon BL, Add. MSS 8133B, ff. 326–7, and is supported by evidence in BL, Add. MSS 38397, ff. 224–5.
[19] Labaree, *Boston Tea Party*, p. 383.
[20] Simmons and Thomas, *Proceedings and Debates*, III, 218.
[21] Thomas, *Townshend Duties Crisis*, pp. 150–2.
[22] Labaree, *Boston Tea Party*, p. 331.

increasing the commercial pressures upon the Company. Problems of empire in the West exacerbated problems of empire in the East; and vice versa.

Further pressure came from the financial burden imposed upon the Company by the Indemnity Act. Under the terms of the Act the Company was obliged to compensate the government for any loss of revenue sustained through the reduction of import duties on tea. This cost the Company £299,200 between 1768 and March 1772.[23] Moreover, when the Act expired in 1772 the Company incurred further losses by agreeing to indemnify those merchants who had purchased tea between 1767 and 1772, had continued to store it in the Company's warehouses, and were now liable to pay the reimposed inland duty of 1s. a lb.[24] This decision cost the Company an additional £560,049 by March 1773.[25] Sir George Colebrooke was thus not far wide of the mark when he later calculated that the Indemnity Act had cost the Company a million pounds.[26]

The ministry and Parliament were obliged to act twice in 1772 on the question of tea duties, firstly as a consequence of disputes between the Company and the Treasury over interpretation of the Indemnity Act, and then, secondly, when the Act expired in July. The differences between the Company and the Treasury centred on the amount of compensation to be paid to the government in order to make up the shortfall in revenue caused by the reduction of the customs duties on tea. A complicated system of calculation led to protracted wrangling each year as the estimates of this sum presented by the directors inevitably differed from the figure worked out by Treasury officials.[27] Such disputes had led the Company to prepare a draft Bill in December 1769 'in order to prevent any further litigation between the government and the Company'.[28] This measure proposed the repeal of the Indemnity Act and the removal of the Townshend Duty on tea 'without which the Company see no possibility of finding a market for teas in America'. The Company offered to make good any deficiency in the average total duties paid on tea before July 1769, a figure calculated to be £723,865 a year.

[23] *RCHC*, IV, 40–9.
[24] This decision was taken on 1 July; IOR, B/88, p. 96. The value of tea owned by buyers but stored in the Company's warehouses had risen from £892,400 in 1762 to £5,395,880 in 1772; *RCHC*, IV, 58.
[25] This figure, based on Company sources, is cited by Shearer, 'Crisis and change', p. 108.
[26] Colebrooke, *Retrospection*, II, 18. This figure was also presented to the House of Lords by the Company's Deputy-Secretary Richard Holt in December 1772; *Public Advertiser*, 25 Dec. 1772.
[27] See, for example, IOR, B/85, pp. 250, 252, 315, 370, 380 and 413.
[28] *Ibid.*, B/85, 330–1.

In future there was to be a drawback of 12 per cent on all teas sold by the Company, plus an inland duty of 6d. a lb on all black and singlo teas.

The Chairman of the Company, Sir George Colebrooke, met with Lord North to discuss these proposals and he offered that 'if he [North] had any objection to repeal the tea duty to satisfy America, the East India Company should petition to give him an opportunity to take it off at the request of that body'.[29] North declined this offer but, in betraying an attitude that he revealed to the House of Commons three months later, he admitted that 'if he were disposed to repeal the law he had rather do it at the desire of the India Company than that of America'.[30] The Company's bid to lessen the burden imposed by the legislation of 1767 failed and the tea duty was retained, although in March 1770 all the other Townshend Duties were repealed. The disputes over compensation payments to the Treasury continued and no further action was taken until 1772.

In January 1772 the directors sanctioned the drafting of another Bill to explain and amend the Indemnity Act of 1767. The Bill was drawn up by the Company's Solicitor Thomas Nuthall and the Company's Counsel Charles Sayer. It was approved by the directors on 29 January and then, after the proposals had been sent to the Treasury, a copy was submitted to the House of Commons. North addressed the House on the subject, sketched the problems that had arisen between the Company and the Treasury, and reported that as the existing act was 'perplexed', the directors had offered in lieu of government estimates to make compensation payments up to a sum determined to be the average of all the tea duties paid each year before 1767.[31] He then offered to introduce a Bill for explaining and amending the Act of 1767. Under the terms of this Bill the Company would be liable to pay the Treasury £117,314 in compensation for the year 1771/2 instead of the £240,552 that had been demanded under the old method of calculation. North was seconded by Laurence Sulivan who observed that the Company had been the losers under the old Act and, although opposition was forthcoming from 'Spanish' Charles Townshend (MP for Yarmouth) who objected to the measure on principle, it was ordered that a Bill be brought into the House.[32] The Bill was presented on 17 February, and thereafter it had an unhindered passage through the Commons and the Lords.[33] It received the royal assent on 1 April and was enacted as 12 Geo. III, c.

[29] Colebrooke, *Retrospection*, I, 174.
[30] *Ibid.* For North's speech to the Commons on 5 March see Simmons and Thomas, *Proceedings and Debates*, III, 210–16.
[31] Simmons and Thomas, *Proceedings and Debates*, III, 407–8. When the Act was eventually entered on the statute book the sum was calculated to be £718,966 p.a.
[32] The more famous Charles Townshend who had given his name to the Duties Act had died in 1767.   [33] *CJ*, XXXIII, 479, 545; *LJ*, XXXIII, 291.

7.: a source of constant friction between the ministry and the Company had been removed.

Although the disputes related to the Indemnity Act were solved to the apparent satisfaction of all the parties concerned, the solution outlined above was in fact only a temporary one because the Act was scheduled to expire on 5 July 1772. The ministry was therefore obliged to introduce more legislation to regulate the Company's tea trade. North himself reopened the issue on 13 May when a motion was made to establish a Committee to consider the continuation of the drawback on the import duty of tea brought to Britain for re-exportation to America and Ireland. He observed that if the drawback was removed foreign competitors would gain a considerable advantage over the Company. He therefore proposed a drawback of three-fifths of the tea duty so that the Company 'shall be able [to sell] to the American market in competition with foreigners'. When the House went into the Committee the next day it was resolved that such a drawback should be allowed for a period of five years, and several other resolutions were made about the colonial sugar and cord trade. These measures were incorporated in a Bill which met with little or no opposition in either House, and royal assent was eventually granted on 3 June. The Drawback Bill was enacted as 12 Geo. III, c. 60.[34]

The problems related to the Company's stockpile of tea can be seen to have been ever-present between 1767 and 1772, yet government measures intended to bestow commercial advantages upon the Company proved ineffective in the long term. The failure of these measures was exacerbated by political developments in America; by the continued importation of huge amounts of tea from Canton; and, after some initial success, by the failure of the Company to increase its domestic sales. By 1772 the tea problem had reached, literally, mountainous proportions. The Company, at a time of acute financial difficulties in other areas, found itself with some £2 million worth of much needed capital tied up in tea which was lying unsold in its London warehouses.

Any response by the directors to general economic problems was, as noted above, conditioned by an overriding concern to maintain the Company's credit. The annual dividend had reached its highest permitted level of $12\frac{1}{2}$ per cent in March 1771, but without revealing the nature and full extent of the Company's difficulties the directors could not sanction any reduction in payments to the stockholders. To do so would damage public confidence in the Company and would undoubtedly have a detrimental effect upon stock prices. The consequences of this were all too well known to the directors in a personal as well as a

---

[34] Simmons and Thomas, *Proceedings and Debates*, III, 442–3, 446.

corporate capacity. In the autumn of 1771 a small group of them, including Sir George Colebrooke, Henry Crabb Boulton, and Sir James Cockburn, had become involved in a speculative scheme which depended upon the price of India stock being kept high and, as the parliamentary Secret Committee was later to discover, this played no small part in clouding their financial judgement.[35] Thus, when the Quarterly General Court met on 25 September 1771 the proprietors were quite content to endorse the directors' recommendation that the dividend should be maintained at $6\frac{1}{4}$ per cent for the forthcoming half year.[36]

In his memoirs Colebrooke later admitted that his judgement had been flawed, and he wrote that 'the least penetration would have enabled me to foresee the want of cash and therefore the impending distresses of the Company occasioned by the Bengal drafts'.[37] This was an opinion endorsed by a Committee of twenty-five proprietors appointed under the chairmanship of Herbert Mackworth (MP for Cardiff) in December 1772 to examine the state of the Company's affairs. Taking a medium-to long-term view of the financial situation, the Committee reported that 'it evidently appears that, notwithstanding the balances in favour of the Company upon the annual statements of their affairs... the profits of the Company have for several years past been insufficient to support the increased dividend and the heavy payments made to government which have, in great measure, occasioned the large debt now due from the Company'.[38] Yet, while in retrospect the weakness of the Company's financial position appeared to be all too clear, the directors in March 1772 repeated their personal and collective misjudgements of the previous autumn by recommending a further six-month continuation of the dividend at $6\frac{1}{4}$ per cent. Mistake had followed mistake in the financial year 1771/2, and the general quality of decision-making at India House left much to be desired during this critical period in the development of the Company's affairs.

With difficulties mounting abroad, trade stagnating, and the directors and proprietors continuing in their blind pursuit of a high dividend, it was unfortunate that just as the full extent of the Company's problems became clear the City of London was shaken by a major credit crisis. The crisis began with the collapse of the banking firm of Neale, James,

[35] Bowen, 'British politics and the East India Company', pp. 511–22.
[36] This was opposed by one director, John Manship, who questioned the accuracy of the financial analysis of the Company's affairs upon which the decision was based; RCHC, IV, 381–3.   [37] Colebrooke, Retrospection, II, 15.
[38] Report from the Committee of Proprietors, Appointed 1 December 1772...to Enquire into the Present State and Condition of the Company's Affairs (1773), p. 5.

Fordyce and Downe which ceased trading on 8 June 1772 and was later declared to be bankrupt. Other banks were forced to stop payment. Ten firms closed within a fortnight; Glyn and Halifax stopped payment on 22 June; and, three days later, the prestigious Scottish banking house of Douglas, Heron and Company, otherwise known as the Ayr Bank, also closed its doors.[39] The Bank of England intervened to stem the closures and this saved many houses from going out of business. However, it was reported by a reliable source that the Bank itself was under threat of closure.[40] The rescue attempts had placed a severe strain on the Bank, and reserves had become very low by August. When, in the same month, the East India Company requested an extension of credit and a loan to cover its immediate deficit and payments, the Bank was unable to offer much help.

An important long-standing feature of the Company's credit arrangements had been dependence upon the Bank to ease liquidity problems after each March and September sale of goods. While awaiting final settlement of accounts by merchants after the sales, the Company borrowed from the Bank and undertook to repay the sum before the next sale. This was an established pattern[41] but, in 1772, circumstances conspired to disrupt the normal method of procedure. Not only had the Company overestimated the income from the March sales in all its cash projections, but in July those projections were themselves found to be far from accurate.[42] The Company was faced with an immediate cash crisis. When Laurence Sulivan wrote to Warren Hastings in April 1773 he recalled the pattern of events of the previous year: 'our domestic distresses came fast upon us – a general gloom springing from immense bankruptcy had brought public credit almost to stagnate, affected our sales in a deep degree and brought the Bank of England (our single resource) to be severely cautious.'[43]

In order to alleviate this situation and meet immediate commitments, the Company's Committee of Treasury applied to the Bank on 15 July for a loan of £400,000 for two months. This was granted, but when a fortnight later the Committee asked for a further £300,000 the Bank

[39] Sir J. Clapham, *The Bank of England* (2 vols., Cambridge, 1944), I, 242–8; H. Hamilton, 'The failure of the Ayr Bank, 1772', *Economic History Review*, 2nd ser., VIII (1955–6), 405–17; R.B. Sheridan, 'The British credit crisis of 1772 and the American colonies', *Journal of Economic History*, XX (1960), pp. 161–86. For the European dimension of the crisis see F.C. Spooner, *Risks at Sea: Amsterdam Insurance and maritime Europe, 1766–1812* (Cambridge, 1983), pp. 83–96.
[40] David Hume to Adam Smith, 27 June 1772, *The Correspondence of Adam Smith* eds. E.C. Mossner and I.S. Ross (Oxford, 1977), p. 162.
[41] For details of the pattern of borrowing between 1769 and 1772 see BL, Add. MSS 38397, f. 241.   [42] *RCHC*, IV, 399–400.
[43] BL, Add. MSS, 29133, f. 534.

refused to comply with the request and would only advance £200,000.[44] Instead of granting the loan in the usual manner the Bank, wary of overcommitment, requested security for the advance and, when this was not forthcoming, they limited the amount that they were prepared to release to the Company.[45] With this traditional source of credit now restricted the Company looked elsewhere for assistance. The directors turned to the ministry and, with payment of unrated customs duties worth £203,619 due on 5 August, they asked Lord North if the payment could be postponed until 1 October. This request was granted and during the course of the meeting North was made fully aware of the difficulties under which the Company was now labouring. He was shown a cash estimate 'whereby it appeared that the sum of near one million sterling would be necessary to be borrowed to carry on the circulation of the Company's affairs'.[46]

In spite of these measures, the financial pressure upon the Company did not ease and the directors began to consider other alternatives. But, even though the Company was hard-pressed, Laurence Sulivan 'conceived that these were difficulties which could be surmounted without resorting to the aid of Parliament'.[47] The Chairman, Sir George Colebrooke, now acknowledged that the dividend was intolerably high, and he recognized that if it was reduced to 6 per cent a year the Company would, under the terms of the agreement of 1769 with the state, be discharged from its payments of £400,000 a year to the Treasury.[48] However, there were serious and obvious risks involved in following such a course of action. Any reduction in the dividend would cause panic among the proprietors, which in turn would lower the price of Company stock in the financial markets. Even so, the directors decided to take a calculated risk and adopt this measure in the hope of easing the crippling burdens upon the Company.

Treading a careful path, the directors determined not to seek the proprietors' immediate approval for a reduction in the dividend but, on 22 September, they resolved instead to recommend that a decision on future levels of payment be postponed. They justified this on the grounds that they had commenced 'a treaty' with the ministry and the outcome of this should be awaited before any significant reduction in dividend was made,[49] but clearly they also hoped to limit the amount of damage that might be made to the Company's standing in the City as a consequence of this public declaration that all was not well at India House. The following day at the General Court the proprietors accepted the directors' recommendation, but many references were made to the

[44] RCHC, IV, 400.
[46] RCHC, IV, 400.
[48] Ibid., II, 18.
[45] Clapham, Bank of England, I, 244.
[47] Colebrooke, Retrospection, II, 17.
[49] IOR, B/87, pp. 176–7.

confident assertions that had been voiced the previous year about the Company's flourishing financial position.[50] A great deal of criticism was levelled at Colebrooke, and a group of prominent stockholders offered to provide whatever sum was required for relief of the immediate cash shortage. This offer was not taken up by the directors, who were able to derive a small amount of satisfaction from the fact that the postponement of the dividend recommendation did not have a dramatic adverse effect on Company stock prices. Instead, their action served merely to continue the steady downward trend that had been evident since August and, on 17 September, the price of India stock fell below 200 for the first time since July 1771.[51] The General Court of 23 September thus served only to confirm the worst fears of the proprietors who had for several weeks been subjected to all manner of press speculation about the parlous state of the Company's affairs.

In spite of the General Court's acceptance of the decision to postpone a dividend recommendation, continued hostility was directed against Colebrooke and his associates for their actions the previous year, and they were condemned from all quarters for having endorsed flawed cash estimates in an attempt to keep up stock prices in support of their own speculative activities. It was rumoured that they had profited by some £200,000 from their 'bulling' of the market,[52] but there is no evidence to support such an extravagant claim. However, the accusations directed against Colebrooke rendered his position as Chairman almost untenable at the very time when the Company needed firm direction and decisive leadership. Edmund Burke depicted Colebrooke to Rockingham on 27 October as 'wholly without authority in the Company, baffled in all his attempts; under imputations, all of which he cannot remove',[53] and Sulivan later recalled the general situation in the following way:

Upon lowering our dividend, together with the great fall of stock, a general clamour arose against the leading directors of 1771 and 1772. The October 1771 Court, Purling's accounts and weak declaration, and Sir George Colebrooke's etc. stock purchases were all remembered. The sufferers were violent in the extreme and it must be acknowledged (tho' I believe the Parties innocent of any sinister views) that appearances were very unfavourable – Sir George Colebrooke by misfortunes retreated.[54]

Yet the decision to postpone a recommendation of the level of future dividend payment had little immediate effect upon the Company's financial situation, because any decision taken at the September

---

[50] *London Evening Post*, 24 Sept. 1772.
[51] Stock prices as recorded in *London Magazine*.
[52] *London Evening Post*, 10, 18 Oct. 1772.   [53] *Burke Corr.*, II, 354.
[54] Letter to Hastings of 28 April 1773, BL, Add. MSS 29133, f. 534.

Quarterly Court related only to payments covering the half-year from the following Christmas. Thus, while the directors struggled to find a permanent solution to the Company's problems, short-term relief was still necessary. With this in mind, and following a further postponement of customs duty payments on 24 September, the half-yearly payment of £200,000 to government as part of the agreement related to the territorial revenues was postponed in late September at the request of the directors.[55] As a consequence of these applications to the ministry, the Company then submitted detailed financial proposals to Lord North in October. They asked that the accumulated debt to the government, which was calculated to reach £1.2 million by August 1773, be extinguished through the repayment of part of the public debt to the Company;[56] and, secondly, a request was made that the Company be empowered to raise money on bond.[57] These proposals received short shrift from North who rejected both requests on the grounds that they would 'be inconsistent with parliamentary faith and weaken the security which the creditors of the Company enjoy'. Instead North took the opportunity at a meeting with Colebrooke and Sulivan on 28 October to request 'the accounts which had been desired that a more proper method of assisting the Company might be considered before the meeting of Parliament'.[58]

It had been anticipated that Parliament would not meet before Christmas, but in the early weeks of October North decided that the affairs of the Company required attention as soon as possible. He hinted at this when he wrote to his father on 5 October and reported that apart from John Wilkes's possible election as Lord Mayor of London 'we have other political matters under consideration which are very unpleasant and I fear that we must call the Parliament together before Christmas'. 'In short', he concluded in characteristic fashion, 'there are vexations enough in my office to make me melancholy amidst all the honours I receive.'[59] The matter was discussed in cabinet on 12 October, two days after the Earl of Rochford had complained to Lord Gower that 'it is the damned East India Company that will call us together [before Christmas]'.[60] It was resolved that Parliament should reconvene on 26 November, and this was reported at once in the press where it was well understood that the 'cause of this early meeting is the embarrassed state

[55] IOR, B/88, p. 183; London Evening Post, 1 Oct. 1772.
[56] The Company's entire paid-up share capital of £3.2 million had been lent to the state at 5% interest in 1708, and a further £1 million had been advanced at 3% in 1744.
[57] IOR, B/88, pp. 220–1.   [58] Ibid.
[59] E. Hughes (ed.), 'Lord North's correspondence, 1766–1783', English Historical Review, LXII (1947) p. 223. The honour of which he wrote was his election as Chancellor of Oxford University the previous day.   [60] PRO, 30/29/1/14, f. 667.

of the Company's affairs'.[61] Horace Walpole, a consistent and forceful critic of the Company, interpreted this development as a sure sign that ministerial intervention in East Indian affairs could no longer be avoided. He wrote to Sir Horace Mann on 4 November that 'the iniquities of our East India Company and its crew of monsters seem to be drawing towards a conclusion, at least to be falling on their own heads. They have involved themselves in such difficulties that the Parliament is forced to meet earlier than was intended in order to assist or correct them.'[62]

The opening of Parliament in November drew together several strands related to the various problems confronting the East India Company. Throughout the proceedings the ministry laboured under the generally held suspicion that its actions were motivated by a simple desire to extend its web of patronage to India. In the press it was assumed that North was seeking to transfer British military and administrative functions on the subcontinent to the Crown,[63] and this was also a view held by Edmund Burke, who told William Dowdeswell on 27 October that 'next to the grand object of the destruction of Wilkes, the leading object in the politics of the court is to seize upon the East India patronage of offices'.[64] However, there is no evidence to support this theory and, as on previous occasions, financial concern above all else must be held to have prompted ministerial and parliamentary action. Even so, new important dimensions were being added to the general problem because the intervention of 1772–3 took place against a backcloth provided by Burgoyne's Select Committee, and renewed anxieties about the nature and direction of the Company's activities in Bengal. When Parliament met it seemed expedient and very necessary to review the operational, administrative, and commercial problems of the Company as well as the more immediate financial crisis.

By November 1772 it was acknowledged on all sides that the Company could no longer cope with the burden it had created for itself in Bengal. A new form of partnership with the state was required if the nation as a whole was to derive any form of benefit at all from British activity in India. The importance of these issues was at last being recognized by politicians, for the Company's near-complete financial collapse had brought home to them just how precarious the position in Bengal had become. Moreover, it now seemed more than likely that any permanent setback in Bengal would affect and undermine Britain's world standing and general strategic position. The back-bench MP William Burrell made this important connexion when he spoke in the debate on the King's Speech on 26 November. Referring to the

---

[61] *London Evening Post*, 15 Oct. 1772.   [62] *Walpole Corr.*, XXIII, 441.
[63] *London Evening Post*, 8, 15 Oct. 1772.   [64] *Burke Corr.*, II, 351.

distressed state of the East India Company's affairs, he declared: 'Sir, let no gentleman think this is a trivial question of ministry or opposition. No sir, it is [the] state of Empire; perhaps upon it depends whether Great Britain shall be the first country in the world, or ruined or undone.'[65] The ministry had to grasp the nettle of the Indian problem before it was too late.

[65] BL, Eg. MSS 242, p. 22.

9   Response to crisis (I): high politics and the
      committees of inquiry, 1772–1773

By 1772 it had long been understood that the three supervisors, Forde,
Scrafton, and Vansittart, who had sailed for India aboard the *Aurora* in
October 1769 had met with misfortune during the course of their
journey. They had arrived safely at the Cape of Good Hope, from where
Vansittart had sent several letters to Laurence Sulivan,[1] but nothing
further was heard from the frigate and it was assumed that she had
foundered in rough seas. This tragic loss of the supervisors was a great
blow to the directors' hopes of enforcing discipline and instilling a sense
of responsibility into the Company's servants in India. Sir George
Colebrooke later calculated the loss to the Company in the following
way:

Had the supervisors arrived safe... certain it is that a great part of the
misconduct of the Company's servants had been corrected and many bad
measures prevented; the great load of bills which involved the Company in
distress had not been drawn, or a proportional investment had been made as they
carried out the Company's instructions, for the carrying of which into execution
the directors relied on their abilities and integrity... in a word they could not but
have remedied many evils...[2]

Yet although the unfortunate loss of the supervisors was universally
regarded in such terms, and although Sir John Lindsay's term of
appointment as Commander-in-Chief in the Gulf was little short of
disastrous,[3] no attempts were made to appoint a new Commission until
August 1772.

    In February it had been rumoured that the Company would appoint
new supervisors before the end of the year,[4] and Lord North had
declared in the Commons in April that he favoured such a course of
action,[5] but no immediate response was forthcoming from the directors.

---

[1] Bodl., MS Eng. hist. b. 190, f. 7.   [2] Colebrooke, *Retrospection*, I, 158.
[3] Gurney, 'The debts of the Nawab of Arcot', pp. 112–22. Lindsay was replaced by
    Admiral Robert Harland in April 1771.
[4] *London Evening Post*, 8 Feb. 1772.   [5] See above p. 98.

The *London Evening Post* was in fact accurate in its report that consideration of the issue had been postponed until after the beginning of a parliamentary inquiry into the Company's affairs.[6] Such a development was not really surprising for, by the end of April, the general sense of outrage that had been provoked by the recently published revelations about corruption and abuse in India was being channelled into, and focused upon, Burgoyne's parliamentary Committee. Accordingly, there was little point in the directors developing any new or long-term policy initiatives until the final direction and form of these deliberations was known.

Burgoyne's Select Committee of thirty-one was elected by ballot on 15 April, and this led to the establishment of a broadly based Committee which, in theory, represented all shades of opinion. Prominent figures within the Company such as Clive, George Johnstone, Henry Strachey, and Robert Gregory were elected, together with eleven others who were India stockholders. They served alongside members of the administration such as Attorney-General Edward Thurlow and Solicitor-General Alexander Wedderburn, prominent government supporters such as Welbore Ellis and Charles Fox, and opposition MPs such as Sir William Meredith, Rose Fuller, and Barlow Trecothick.[7] Constituted in order to examine the 'nature, state, and condition of the East India Company and of British affairs in India', the Committee began its task by first considering the historical perspective, and it settled down to a detailed reconstruction of the Company's affairs since 1757. As Burgoyne later told the Commons when he submitted his first progress report, the business had been arranged under five broad headings.[8] First, the charters and treaties with Indian princes were read; second, the commissions and appointments of Company servants were examined; third, the general history of the Company was considered; fourth and fifth, disputes with foreign companies and the conduct of the directors at home were studied in detail.

The nature of this initial sub-division of the subject matter at once lent a retrospective slant to the Committee's proceedings, and this occasioned some dispute during the first few meetings. Horace Walpole later recalled these disagreements over the role and functions of the Committee when he wrote: 'The Select Committee for Indian affairs began with great warmth. Governor Johnson [*sic*], Lord Clive's great enemy, called witnesses against his corruption. Lord Clive said he thought this inquiry had been to regulate those affairs, but found it was

---

[6] *London Evening Post*, 20 Feb. 1772.   [7] *CJ*, XXXIII, 699, 703–4.
[8] *Ibid.*, XXXIII, 792.

for accusation. Sir Gilbert Elliot replied 'they could not regulate without going to the bottom of abuses.'[9] This set the tone for the remainder of the Committee's work. Conditioned by prevailing concern about abuses, the Committee was diverted from the very beginning into a protracted study of British crimes and misdemeanours in Bengal. It provided an opportunity for the airing of private grievances, and it served as a convenient platform for accusation, defence, and counter-accusation. While this served at first to capture public attention, it nevertheless deflected the Committee from its intended purpose of examining the Company's corporate affairs.

Although it opened amidst great publicity and carried great expectations, interest in the Committee soon waned when it entered into the details of individual activity in India. Indeed, Horace Walpole had predicted with some accuracy and characteristic cynicism that this would happen. He wrote to his friend Sir Horace Mann on 21 April before the Committee had begun to examine witnesses:

There is a select committee appointed to examine into those grievances – but I expect nothing from it. People will be very eager and very important at first. The criminals will puzzle and weary them: the idle will grow tired with the discussion and the persevering will probably be bribed to drop or perplex the pursuit. Should you wonder if the most guilty, who are the most rich, should obtain a verdict of applause.[10]

Subsequent events were to bear out much of this assessment.

The Committee sat on nineteen days between 27 April and 25 May, but on no occasion did attendance rise above half of the elected members. Indeed, attendance averaged only 40.4 per cent over the whole period.[11] The main burden of participation fell upon six individuals, all of whom attended on more than fifteen of the nineteen days: Burgoyne who chaired the Committee on each day it sat, Frederick Vane, Barlow Trecothick, Henry Strachey, George Johnstone, and Rose Fuller. Attendance among the other twenty-five members was uneven, and six of them did not attend at all.[12] By the third week of May attendance had declined to the point that the Committee's quorum of seven was only just achieved on two occasions. Even so, the

---

[9] *The Last Journals of Horace Walpole during the Reign of George III from 1771 to 1783,* ed. A.F. Steuart (2 vols., 1910), I, 87. [10] *Walpole Corr.,* XXIII, 401.

[11] Figures derived from *The Genuine Minutes of the Select Committee Appointed by the House of Commons, Assembled at Westminster in the Fifth Session of the Thirteenth Parliament of Great Britain to Enquire into East India Affairs* (1773).

[12] The six non-attenders were Solicitor-General Alexander Wedderburn, Lord Howe, Charles James Fox, Constantine Phipps, Robert Gregory, and Sir George Savile.

Committee reported to the Commons on 26 May. Burgoyne presented two reports, the first of which reconstructed events prior to the loss of Calcutta to Siraj-ud-duala in 1756, and the second of which was related to a petition from an Armenian, Gregore Cojamaul, complaining about the conduct of several of the Company's servants.[13] A fortnight later, with no further progress made by the Committee, the House adjourned for the summer recess and Indian affairs were left in a state of suspension. Little constructive progress had been made, and it appears that the production of a lengthy historical narrative was regarded as sufficient justification for the Committee's detailed investigations. Certainly no attempt had been made as yet to analyze, and offer solutions to, the Company's problems in India.

During the recess the attention of the directors was once more focused upon Bengal. No one with any knowledge at all of Indian affairs could fail to recognize the direct causal link between the submission of bills of exchange from Fort William and the Company's acute cash crisis in Britain. Equally, no one could deny that more effective means of control over the Company's servants were required to prevent the same thing happening again. Such was the nature of the crisis that it soon became obvious that the directors could not afford to wait for the Select Committee to produce answers to the Company's problems. Although a formal decision to appoint supervisors 'with extraordinary powers' was taken after 'much debate' at the Court of Directors on 5 August,[14] it seems that these appointments had been discussed in detail some time earlier. Indeed, on or before 4 August Edmund Burke had been offered, but had declined to accept, an appointment as one of the supervisors.[15]

The appointment of supervisors occupied the minds of stockholders and directors alike until the opening of Parliament at the end of November. When he later recalled the traumatic events of 1772, Laurence Sulivan considered that all had passed off as well as could be expected until 'the supervision came to be agitated'.[16] These difficulties stemmed from the directors' failure to persuade any 'conspicuous character' to serve on the Commission. Not only did Burke refuse to accept an appointment, but so also did Charles Wolfran Cornwall, Sir Jeffrey Amherst, Isaac Barré, Sir Richard Sutton, and even Laurence Sulivan.[17] Sir George Colebrooke later recalled that it was he who had proposed Burke as a supervisor, 'to which Lord North gave his consent,

---

[13] The first two reports were printed in *CJ*, XXXIII, 792–944. The later reports were printed separately.   [14] IOR, B/88, p. 129.
[15] *Burke Corr.*, II, 320, 323.
[16] Sulivan to Hastings, 28 April 1773; BL, Add. MSS 29133, f. 533.
[17] *Ibid.*; *London Evening Post*, 5 Sept. 1772.

probably to get rid of an opponent'.[18] This interesting statement gives some indication that North was monitoring Indian affairs reasonably closely during the summer of 1772, but it also suggests that there was an element of close liaison between the First Lord of the Treasury and the Chairman of the Company. This helped to give rise to the popular belief that Colebrooke had become little more than a tool of the ministry. The *London Evening Post* denounced this supposed association in September: 'The greatest cordiality imaginable passes between the Premier at the Treasury and the Little Premier at Leadenhall Street on this occasion; the latter obliging himself to carry every government mandate through the Proprietary.'[19]

The directors were forced to seek other candidates. When the issue was first raised it was thought that, as in 1769, only three supervisors would be appointed. However, it was later decided that six supervisors would be sent from Britain to join three already resident in India, one of whom would be the Governor of Bengal, Warren Hastings. Robert Monckton had long been considered a suitable candidate,[20] and Colebrooke championed the cause of Andrew Stuart, a Scot and 'a gentleman now well known as the principal actor in the Douglas case'.[21] It would appear that others, including Sir Adam Ferguson and Adam Smith, were also recommended to the directors, the latter by the MP William Pulteney.[22] A final list of candidates was eventually drafted by Colebrooke and Sulivan, and this was then submitted to their fellow directors for formal approval. Included on this list were Hastings, Monckton, Stuart, Edward Wheler, Sir Elijah Impey, and Andrew Langlois. However, when the directors met to consider this list on 23 October, the situation was further complicated when a number of the individuals present put forward their own names as candidates for the Commission.[23]

With the number of candidates now exceeding the number of places available on the Commission, it was decided that a ballot should be held to determine the appointments. The outcome represented a significant setback for Colebrooke and Sulivan who failed to secure the election of three of their preferred candidates: Impey, Stuart, and Langlois. The

[18] Colebrooke, *Retrospection*, I, 99.
[19] Issue of 22 Sept. See also *Burke Corr.*, II, 354 for a later expression of this view.
[20] Monckton was a distinguished soldier who had taken part in the assault led by General Wolfe on Quebec in 1759, and in 1762 he had commanded the troops who captured the island of Martinique.
[21] Sulivan to Hastings, 28 April 1773, BL, Add. MSS 29133, f. 533. Stuart, a lawyer, had defended the Duke of Hamilton in the infamous Douglas case of 1769.
[22] Smith to Pulteney, 3 Sept. 1771, *Smith Corr.*, pp. 163–4.
[23] An account of this meeting is to be found in *London Evening Post*, 29 Oct. 1772.

six successful candidates included four incumbent directors, Wheler, Peter Lascelles, William Devaynes, and George Cuming; Daniel Wier who had been a director the previous year, and Monckton.[24] Contemporaries interpreted this result as a further erosion of Colebrooke's authority, and Edmund Burke, who took a close interest in the matter, reported to John Stewart on 20 October that the Chairman had received a 'rude shock'.[25] Burke also held a poor opinion of the abilities of those who had been elected to serve on the Commission.[26] The weakness of Colebrooke's position was underlined when the proprietors later endorsed the directors' choice of supervisors. Indeed, the Chairman chose not to offer the General Court any justification for his original choice of candidates. Instead, he and Sulivan contented themselves with 'making no opposition, satisfied that such a commission would never be endorsed [by the ministry]'.[27] 'India affairs are in a strange confusion', wrote the Duke of Richmond to Rockingham on 2 November.[28]

The supervisors and the nature of their task were discussed at three General Courts on 29 October, 12 and 17 November.[29] Attention focused upon the Commission in general and there was little debate about the appointees, apart from George Dempster's objection 'to all the commissioners being called from behind the bar, as in an affair like this the persons of the first consequence in every kind of knowledge should be solicited for this purpose'.[30] Colebrooke and Sulivan steadfastly maintained their silence and refused to be drawn into any dispute. Nevertheless, their conduct during the events related to the appointment of the supervisors prompted heated exchanges in the press, and one correspondent in the *Public Advertiser* of 11 November wrote of the 'grossest and most illiberal attacks' made upon their characters. Colebrooke in particular suffered a great deal of abuse and misrepresentation in several newspapers in the days before the important General Court of 12 November.[31] Eventually, however, a majority of stockholders sanctioned, albeit by a small majority, both the appointments and the Commission itself.[32]

Yet, despite overcoming all these difficulties, the way was still not clear for the directors to send their representatives to India because the

---

[24] IOR, B/88, p. 214.   [25] *Burke Corr.*, II, 358.   [26] *Ibid.*, II, 355.
[27] Sulivan to Hastings, 28 April 1773, BL, Add. MSS 29133, f. 533.
[28] WWM, R1–1411.   [29] IOR, B/88, pp. 227–30, 248–9, 256–62.
[30] *London Evening Post*, 29 Oct. 1772.
[31] See, for example, the letters of PHILO-MOGUL and DION in the *Public Advertiser* of 11 November. In the same issue a vigorous defence of Sulivan and Colebrooke was mounted by ANGLO-INDIANUS and TRIUMPHE.
[32] IOR, B/88, p. 290. The appointments were approved on 29 November by 209 votes to 188.

ministry now declared its hand and refused to grant formal approval of the Commission. The Southern Secretary, the Earl of Rochford, had met with Colebrooke in mid-October and asked whether the Company intended to dispatch supervisors to India. If so, he enquired, would the Commander-in-Chief of the King's naval forces in the region have a 'voice' in their deliberations?[33] It was this very issue that had precipitated the lengthy dispute between Lord Weymouth and the directors in 1769, and its resurrection now by Rochford boded ill for future relations between the ministry and the Company.

In the weeks prior to the opening of Parliament preparations were made on all sides for what was believed would be a long and difficult session. The Company, wracked by internal division, searched for solutions to a variety of problems; the parliamentary opposition, most notably the Rockinghams, discussed tactics and attempted to define their position on Indian affairs; and key figures in the ministry briefed themselves on the state of the Company and the nature of British activity in Bengal. The eventual outcome of all this activity was that the political initiative passed to the ministry and allowed them, and not the Company, to determine how the Indian problem would be tackled.

The debate among the supporters and associates of Lord Rockingham was conditioned by the underlying weakness of their position in the House of Commons. In general terms they considered the possibility of seceding from Parliament as a form of protest against the ministry[34] but, at the same time, they devoted a considerable amount of thought to the problem of what line they should adopt on Company affairs. Rockingham himself clung to the faintest of hopes that once a course of action had been determined it would serve as a rallying point, as it had done in 1767, for other members of the opposition. In particular, Rockingham hoped to attract the support of Chatham who, quite correctly, he thought had never developed 'any fixed plan or idea' on the subject of the Company. He believed that Chatham 'will wait a little longer either to see *what our* ideas may be, or till he thinks he sees which way the public in general may incline'.[35] In either case it was necessary for the Rockinghams to take a lead, for nobody else in the ranks of the opposition was prepared to do so.

The debate among the Rockinghams centred upon three main figures: Rockingham himself, Edmund Burke, and William Dowdeswell. The last served as the principal source of ideas and policy on Company matters. An indication of this early reliance upon Dowdeswell's

[33] *Ibid.*, B/88, 202.
[34] F. O'Gorman, *The Rise of Party : The Rockingham Whigs, 1760–1782* (1975), pp. 291–2.
[35] Rockingham to Burke, 24, 27, 28 Oct. 1772, *Burke Corr.*, II, 346.

judgement was forthcoming on 7 November when Burke admitted a lack of knowledge on these issues and empowered his colleague to 'decide for me as you please'.[36] But if Burke had not yet developed any thoughts on Company or Indian affairs he was not alone: few, if any, politicians had thought the matter through and developed any coherent or overall policy related to the issues at hand. The Rockinghams were in urgent need of advice and they sought this from their contacts inside India House, although they were dismayed to discover little unity of purpose between themselves and the beleaguered Company.

Colebrooke, who for many years had been a staunch supporter of Rockingham in Parliament, was not involved in any of the discussions, a circumstance which served to reinforce the belief that he had been won over by the ministry. Burke commented upon Colebrooke's conduct to Dowdeswell in early November: 'Sir G. Colebrooke is not in our hands; nor has he ever consulted with Lord Rockingham or any of his friends upon one step he has taken, or which he is to take.' He added, 'it is true he did not refuse to send me copies of such papers as I should desire. But he showed so little willingness in the business that I have not yet thought fit to trouble him.' He concluded that the Rockinghams might well have to look elsewhere for information.[37] Thus, while Burke kept in touch with Colebrooke, discussions were also conducted with Robert Gregory who had close links with Rockingham. From these discussions, and a constant exchange of letters, there emerged a rudimentary policy with which the Rockinghams hoped to galvanize the opposition into action in order to counter the ministry's alleged designs upon the Company.

In general terms the Rockinghams maintained their opposition to ministerial measures by utilizing the arguments they had employed in 1767 and 1769; they stressed the need to preserve the sanctity of chartered rights, and the need to secure the independence and autonomy of the Company. Having established a particular position during the first parliamentary inquiry, some of the Rockinghams felt honour-bound to maintain a consistent line of thought and action. Dowdeswell, for example, argued in such terms towards the end of November when he outlined the reasons for not compelling the Company to lower the level of dividend payments: 'it is wrong for us in *consistency* to take upon us to meddle and direct in the interior management of the Company's affairs and that *we* have always declared against Parliament so frequently interfering etc. etc.'.[38] On the other hand, Burke believed that the Rockinghams should not consider themselves to be under any obligation to adhere to any previous statements or declarations. He explained why

[36] *Ibid.*, II, 366.   [37] *Ibid.*, II, 365–6.
[38] *Ibid.*, II, 381. Views of Dowdeswell as reported to Rockingham by Burke.

in a statement of his general attitude towards the Company and its problems:

I am not governed in my present opinions by any idea of our being tied down to a servile adherence to the maxims which we supported in 1767. Since it is obvious that we have no interest one way or another in the point, we might be allowed, without any suspicion of deserting our principles, to alter an opinion upon six years experience, if six years experience had given us reason to change it. But the fact is that we never denied, on the contrary, we always urged it, to be the province and duty of Parliament to superintend the affairs of this Company as well as every other matter of public concern; but we considered it as the duty of Parliament to see that the Company did not abuse its charter privileges, or misgovern its asiatic possessions; but we thought it abominable to declare their dividends in the House of Commons; and to seize their revenues into the hands of the Crown. These were our opinions then; and I see no sort of reason for altering them since that time.[39]

In spite of all the time and energy devoted to the problems of the East India Company by the Rockinghams, little more than the broadest of policy guidelines emerged from their discussions. They inclined towards support for a government loan to the Company and they sought to avoid a reduction of the dividend; but in general they took refuge in the same statements and pronouncements that had characterized their earlier parliamentary interventions on the Company's behalf. Yet, with some of the Rockinghams unsure of what line to follow on Indian affairs, and with a considerable amount of disagreement over the proposed secession from Parliament, there was never any real prospect of effective opposition being mounted against the ministry in the House of Commons. On 29 October Burke had observed to Rockingham that 'the Company by its dissension...has played the whole game for the King's friends',[40] but he may well have added that the opposition had also played their own part in conceding the initiative to the ministry.

Ministers were not slow to take advantage of the confusion within the ranks of the opposition and the Company, and they spent much time

---

[39] Burke to Rockingham, 23 Nov. 1772, *ibid.*, II, 385. In a recent article Elofson has argued that the Rockinghams were unanimous in their opposition to the extension of state control and patronage over the Company; that they felt it 'was their responsibility to support the principle to which they had committed themselves in the past'; and that 'none of them ever suggested that they should modify their central policy in the least to accommodate public sentiments'; W.B. Elofson, 'The Rockingham Whigs in transition: the East India Company issue 1772–1773', *English Historical Review*, CIV (1989), 958, 967, 978. Burke's views outlined above indicate that the issue was not as straightforward as Elofson might have us believe and, in fact, a vigorous debate took place among the Rockinghamite leadership over how they might adapt their long-held stance on East Indian issues in the light of recent developments in the Company's affairs. For a detailed discussion of these Rockinghamite debates see Bowen, 'British politics and the East India Company', pp. 549–58.   [40] *Burke Corr.*, II, 355.

preparing for the opening of Parliament. To this end they availed themselves of as much information as possible about the financial condition of the Company. Large numbers of accounts and estimates were ordered to be sent from India House to the Treasury, where they were examined by John Robinson and Charles Jenkinson.[41] Indeed, it was to these two industrious individuals, neither of whom initially had any specialist knowledge of either India or the Company, that North entrusted the development of ministerial strategy. This, however, was not recognized at the time and it was generally believed, as the *London Evening Post* observed on 8 December, that 'Lord Mansfield, the delegate of Lord Bute, is the minister in all the business relating to the East India Company.' This was little more than a further manifestation of the belief that Bute still exercised a powerful influence over the King and his ministers.[42] There is no evidence whatsoever to support such a view but, for almost a year, North's reputation had suffered from the popular belief that he was little more than a prisoner of the more extreme elements within his cabinet, and this was held to be particularly the case in an East Indian context. John Macpherson commented upon this when he wrote to Warren Hastings from Madras on 12 October in order to pass on the latest news from Britain and, although he wrote of events that had taken place earlier in the year, his assessment of the political situation would still have been endorsed by many domestic commentators in October or November 1772. He wrote that 'The cabinet are not unanimous as to India measures. Ld. North is afraid to meddle without doing so effectually. The Bedford people and Grafton wish him to interfere – that he might stand the danger of breaking the ice and they reap the advantage, and then tumble him from his seat.'[43]

Such criticism was to continue throughout 1773[44] but, on this occasion, North's reputation was further sullied by a general assumption among commentators that he was unwilling to confront the problems of the Company and decide a course of action for his ministry. Only a fortnight before the opening of Parliament, Burke complained of North's 'procrastinating disposition', and he observed to Rockingham on 11 November that 'the ministers have nothing very precisely determined with relation to Indian affairs'.[45] The ever hostile *London Evening Post* condemned North's supposed inactivity and his failure to deal with the problem at an earlier date. His public assertions at the beginning of the year that he would tackle the East India problem were

[41] IOR, B/88, p. 234.
[42] This belief was wholeheartedly endorsed by Burke; *Burke Corr.*, II, 369.
[43] BL, Add. MSS 29133, f. 261.   [44] *London Evening Post*, 13, 16 Feb. 1773.
[45] *Burke Corr.*, II, 369.

now recalled, and it was generally assumed that characteristic idleness had prevailed.[46]

Before the opening of Parliament on 26 November John Robinson gave the Company ample time and opportunity to prepare financial proposals, but the directors failed to take advantage of his offer.[47] Furthermore, while the General Court met on each of the two days preceding the opening of Parliament, and while the urgency of the situation was acknowledged by all, no initiative was forthcoming from the stockholders.[48] Yet the ministry itself also approached the opening of Parliament without any fixed plans or established policy on Indian affairs. As Horace Walpole later indicated, no-one knew what was intended: 'Whatever was the measure in embryo, they [the ministry] set out prudently with determining to lay open to the public the abuses committed by the Company or their servants.'[49] North was prepared to bide his time while a solution to the Company's problems was found, and it was with this in mind that ministers were to propose the establishment of a secret parliamentary committee to supplement the work of Burgoyne's Select Committee. The *London Evening Post* predicted this course of action two days before the opening of Parliament in such accurate terms as to suggest a disclosure of information from a source close to the ministry: 'The first thing is India. A new committee is to be appointed to enquire into the state of the Company affairs. Upon the report of this committee a bill will be brought in after Christmas.'[50]

The ministry's last-minute preparations centred upon how best to introduce the Indian business into the House, and particular attention was focused upon the content of the Speech from the Throne. North insisted that the Speech be 'softened' but, lest this be interpreted as a sign of weakness, the King stepped in to strengthen the resolve of his first minister. In a manner that was to become commonplace during the last years of the ministry, the King wrote to North on the eve of the opening of Parliament stating that 'I know I may depend upon your remaining stiff in treating with the Company; 'till now the conduct you have held towards the directors is much to your honour, but any wavering now would be disgraceful to you and destruction to the public.'[51] Demonstrating a close interest in Company affairs, the King wrote again to North the following day, after the Address had been passed without a division. This letter illustrates the direction in which

---

[46] *London Evening Post*, 5 Dec. 1772.   [47] IOR, B/88, pp. 272–3.
[48] *Ibid.*, B/88, pp. 279, 282; *London Evening Post*, 26 Nov. 1772.
[49] Walpole, *Last Journals*, I, 160,   [50] *London Evening Post*, 24 Nov. 1772.
[51] *The Correspondence of George III from 1760 to 1783*, ed. Sir J. Fortescue (6 vols., 1927), II, no. 1157.

George III expected events to follow, and it also confirms that North had not yet determined any firm course of action:

I cannot omit reminding you that though I trust when the Company finds the committee has laid the state before the house, that it cannot avoid coming into such an agreement as may be thought secure for its creditors and equitable for the public and proprietors; but that if this should not happen that you will be prepared with a plan for conducting those affairs; if you form it yourself it will be just, and there are men of ability in Parliament who will certainly support it well in the house; but if you are open to their ideas nothing will be done for everyone will have schemes incompatible with those of the others you may consult.[52]

Two points are worth stressing about this letter. Firstly, the priority, as perceived by the King and his ministers, was undoubtedly that the Company's financial problems should be resolved as soon as possible. In other words the East India business was still seen as representing a domestic political and financial problem rather than a problem of empire: at this stage of the proceedings there was little discussion of the reform and regulation of the Company's overseas affairs. Secondly, and to the King's slight anger, North was prepared to await the outcome of the Committee's deliberations before applying any remedy to the Company's ills. Clearly, it was anticipated that it would take some time to decide upon the measures necessary to enable the Company to overcome its liquidity difficulties.

The King's Speech was read to Parliament on 26 November. The reasons for meeting before Christmas were explained and members were invited to make 'such provisions for the common benefit and security of all the various interests concerned [in the Company], as you shall find best adapted to the exigencies of the case'.[53] The general content of the Speech reflected the restrained approach favoured by North, but when the Address of Thanks was proposed and seconded by administration supporters Richard Fitzpatrick (a nephew of Lord Gower) and Dr William Burrell, there was a marked change of tone. Shelburne noted to Chatham that both held a 'very hostile language' towards the Company, while Burke observed that although the speech of Fitzpatrick was 'decent; and let no more of the court cat out of the bag, than that the Company were to have no dividend...Dr Burrell bullied–threatened directors, servants, proprietors, and the charter itself'.[54] Then, perhaps recalling the damage that had been inflicted upon Chatham's policy by William Beckford's wild opening speech six years earlier, North rose

---

[52] *Ibid.*, II, no. 1158.   [53] *CJ*, XXXIV, 3.
[54] Shelburne to Chatham, 26 Nov. 1772, *Chatham Corr.*, IV, 228; Burke to Rockingham, 26 Nov. 1772, *Burke Corr.*, II, 388.

and in 'terms of moderation' moved for the immediate establishment of a thirteen-man Secret Committee of inquiry to examine the affairs of the Company.[55] The justification he offered for this particular course of action was that it was necessary to preserve the secrets of the Company from both the public and foreign powers. The House also needed information before Christmas, and North was in no doubt that 'a Secret Committee will come much sooner to the report than the Select Committee where every member of the House may be admitted, [and] where every member of the House may examine books'. Even so, he warned that this new inquiry would last for as much of the session as was necessary for the Committee to establish 'a sufficient, plain, clear, and methodical account of the present situation of the Company'.[56]

Opposition to North's motion was forthcoming from William Hussey, Sir Joseph Mawbey, Governor Johnstone, and Herbert Mackworth, the last of whom claimed that he had a 'hundred objections' to the establishment of a Secret Committee.[57] However, the main objections came, not surprisingly, from an aggrieved Burgoyne who believed that any Secret Committee would supplant the functions of his own Committee. He mounted an impassioned defence of the Select Committee's work, and he declared that it was well capable of covering the required ground on the timescale desired by North. He underlined this confidence in his own Committee by announcing that the following day he would move for its immediate reappointment. North was undoubtedly annoyed by Burgoyne's speech and, in response to it, he stressed the importance of the Secret Committee's work by remarking rather sharply that its task would be somewhat greater than 'inquiring into the proceedings of Change Alley'.[58] Horace Walpole captured the warmth of North's speech when he later recalled that 'he treated his [Burgoyne's] opposition with contempt; said he did not mean to defeat the former committee – that he did not intend to inquire into petty larceny, but he looked upon the proposed Secret Committee as the commencement of a great inquiry'.[59] Burgoyne was taken aback by this and he announced in rather meek terms that he had not intended to obstruct the Secret Committee in any way. North's forceful intervention ensured that his motion as well as the Address of Thanks were both passed without a division.

The following day, as announced, Burgoyne moved for the reappointment of the Select Committee and, although there was little debate on

[55] *Chatham Corr.*, IV, 228.   [56] BL, Eg. MSS 242, pp. 26, 27–8, 31.
[57] *Ibid.*, 242, pp. 27, 28–30, 34–45. Most of the objections centred on the fact that the Committee was not open.   [58] *Ibid.*, 242, p. 58.
[59] Walpole, *Last Journals*, I, 161.

his motion, Henry Seymour expressed the general concern that there would be a clash of interests between two committees of inquiry.[60] However, Burgoyne overrode all objections; his motion was passed; and the Committee was reappointed under the same terms of reference that it had been granted the previous April.[61] Most observers were of the opinion that the re-establishment of the Select Committee was to provide little more than a window dressing; its role was to be no more than a public relations exercise designed to demonstrate that the misdemeanours of the Company's Bengal servants were being taken seriously. It was understood that the important business related to Company affairs would be undertaken by the small Secret Committee. Soame Jenyns gave expression to this belief when he reported to Lord Hardwicke on 1 December that the function of the Secret Committee 'must be to re-establish the credit of the Company and bring them under the management and direction of the government, but in what manner I don't know, and the other committee will proceed to find out misdemeanours and accusations'.[62] Edmund Burke later made a similar, albeit more colourful, observation in the House when he compared the functions of the two Committees and depicted the Select Committee as 'contrived for state, [holding] out a fair face to the public, the other for business. The first the great wife, the grand, stately, Juno fit to decorate the persons of great men, the other an easy wife to be left fit for secret business'.[63]

The thirteen members of the Secret Committee were elected by ballot on 28 November, and the result was announced two days later.[64] The outcome reflected the success of the ministry in marshalling support and votes for its candidates for the Committee, and, as Horace Walpole observed, 'the persons were all ministerial'.[65] They included notable officeholders such as Charles Jenkinson, Hans Stanley, and the Paymaster-General Richard Rigby. Also elected were William Burrell and Richard Fitzpatrick, both of whom had demonstrated a strong degree of hostility towards the Company only a few days earlier; and several of the other members of the Committee also had ministerial connexions.[66] On the day of the ballot the Serjeant-at-Arms had requested attendance in the House from members who were going about other business in Westminster Hall and the immediate vicinity, but the election had not aroused much interest, and Thomas Harley had been elected at the head

---

[60] BL, Eg. MSS 242, pp. 35–6.　　　　[61] CJ, XXXIV, 6.
[62] BL, Add. MSS 35631, f. 115.　　　　[63] BL, Eg. MSS 242, p. 94.
[64] CJ, XXXIV, 9, 11.　　　　[65] Walpole, Last Journals, I, 160.
[66] The remaining members of the Committee were Richard Jackson, Thomas Harley, Thomas Gilbert, Lord Frederick Campbell, Lord Viscount Palmerston, Nathaniel Ryder, Thomas Walpole, and John Eames.

of the poll with only 120 votes. Yet, although the administration had encountered only apathy and ineffective opposition at the time of the ballot, there was general outrage when the final composition of the Committee became known, and the press was quite content to portray the whole episode as another ministerial 'job'.[67]

Unlike the Select Committee, and although Fitzpatrick, Jackson, Rigby, Ryder, Stanley, and Walpole were all stockholders, none of the members of the Secret Committee had any active interest in Company politics, and none of them had ever been to India. In view of this, it was perhaps to be hoped that the Committee, despite its lack of specialist knowledge, would be freed from preconceptions about the nature of the problems inherent within the Company's framework of operations, and would therefore be able to provide an objective analysis of the situation. The first priority, however, was to examine in detail all aspects of the Company's affairs both at home and abroad. Accordingly, the Committee was given a quorum of five, was empowered to send for whatever witnesses and papers it required, and was granted permission to meet wherever and whenever it was thought necessary. Needless to say, the ministry set the agenda for the Committee's work, and the first task, reflecting concern about one aspect of the Company's recent activities, was an examination of the events surrounding the appointment of the Supervisory Commission. The Committee set to work at once, and in stark contrast with Burgoyne's Committee it produced its first report within a week. This swift despatch of business was noted in the press: 'The Secret Committee...sat yesterday at the Company's house in Leadenhall Street; this is the first time any parliamentary committee has sat in the City since the reign of George I and there is much reason to suppose that the cause must be very extraordinary to produce so remarkable [an] effect.'[68]

The proprietors responded at once to these developments. An unsuccessful attempt was made to petition the Commons against the activities of the Secret Committee,[69] and the General Court established their own Committee of inquiry 'to take into their most serious consideration the present state and condition of the East India Company's affairs'.[70] This measure was proposed to the General Court by Herbert Mackworth on 1 December. Mackworth had only recently made his first appearance at the Court and it is unclear why he took it

[67] *Public Advertiser*, 2 Dec. 1772; *London Evening Post*, 5 Dec. 1772.
[68] *General Evening Post*, 5 Dec. 1772. The Committee sat in a room next to the General Court Room at India House.
[69] *London Evening Post*, 3, 5 Dec. 1772. The petition, drafted by George Johnstone and eight others, was eventually rejected by 137 votes to 107 on 7 December.
[70] IOR, B/88, pp. 299–305.

upon himself to move for the Committee. Nevertheless, he was eventually appointed as chairman of a twenty-five-man Committee which comprised many of the leading personalities in the General Court such as George Johnstone and the outspoken lawyer Keane Fitzgerald. The Committee, which included eight MPs among its number,[71] was given powers to order papers and accounts, and to examine witnesses. By the middle of December, therefore, three Committees were engaged in the difficult task of analyzing Company affairs. Never before had the activities of the British in India been subjected to such a thorough scrutiny and examination.

The parliamentary Secret Committee produced its first report on 7 December and, as instructed, it dealt with the Company's intended plan of sending supervisors to Bengal. Lord John Cavendish reported this to Rockingham when he observed on 9 December that 'the town and the two Houses are not so full as usual, and ministry seem well disposed to take that advantage and carry on the business the quicker'.[72] The report was only fourteen pages long and, as the Chairman of the Committee Thomas Harley commented when he presented it to the House, it provided 'nothing more than a historical account' of the events surrounding the appointment of the Supervisory Commission. The report itself contained no recommendations, but Harley took the House by surprise when he moved that a Bill be introduced to 'restrain', for a limited time, the Company from sending out commissioners to Bengal. This move was justified by the high cost of the entire operation to the Company, and no attempt was made to undermine either the legality or purpose of the Commission. Harley argued that such a step was necessary because it was an 'extraordinary circumstance' that at a time when the Company was in such a weak financial position it should undertake the 'enormous expense' of a Commission which, it was calculated, had already cost £60,000 to establish.[73]

This unforeseen development led to a protracted dispute which eventually lasted ten days or so, during the course of which not only the measure itself, but also the manner in which it had been introduced into the House were attacked. George Dempster complained of the 'unparliamentary manner' in which Harley had made his motion, and he eventually went as far as to denounce the Secret Committee as unconstitutional.[74] Many speakers in the debate on 7 December considered the ministry's measures to be unnecessary, as the Company did not intend to send out the supervisors until after the Secret

[71] In terms of membership there was little overlap between the parliamentary committees and the Company's committee. Only Henry Strachey served on Burgoyne's Select Committee and Mackworth's Company Committee.   [72] WWM, R1–1417.
[73] BL, Eg. MSS 242, p. 59.   [74] Ibid., 242, p. 61.

Committee had completed its work, but Harley declared that this had not been made clear to the Committee. The motion was supported in characteristically vigorous fashion by the Solicitor-General Alexander Wedderburn, who enraged many listeners by implying that the directors could not be trusted to abide by any parliamentary decision not to send the supervisors. 'A frigate is ready', he told the House, 'they may take the step if you do not prevent it.'[75]

The opposition protested against this slur on the character of the directors, and they denounced the interference of Parliament in the internal affairs of the Company. This forced North to stand up and calm the proceedings and, adopting a conciliatory tone that was lacking in many of his colleagues' pronouncements, he explained that the intended measure 'was not an act of blame, of censure, of punishment, merely an act of prevention'.[76] This had the desired effect and then, as the debate came to a close, Edmund Burke rose to address the House with a speech that was regarded by various commentators as 'wonderful', 'very vehement and very brilliant', and of 'exquisite wit and eloquence'.[77] Yet, as usual, this was to no avail. Although Burke attacked the ministry on the familiar grounds that it had disregarded and infringed upon chartered rights,[78] the administration was secure in the knowledge that it possessed a large and unassailable majority. This indeed proved to be the case when the previous question was moved and the House voted by 114 votes to 45 that the main question be put. This was done and it was resolved that the Restraining Bill be introduced.

In spite of a vigorous rearguard action by both the Company and the Rockinghams,[79] the Bill eventually passed its final reading on 18 December by the overwhelming margin of 153 votes to 20, a result that was described with good reason as a 'mortifying division' by Rockinghamite spokesman William Dowdeswell.[80] Stalwart supporters of Rockingham such as Lord George Germain, Sir William Meredith, and 'Old' Thomas Townshend voted in favour of the measure, while others, including Thomas Townshend junior, Charles Wolfran Cornwall, and James Townsend, were absent from the House at the time of the division.[81] Burke could find no comfort in any aspect of this crushing blow to the opposition, and when he wrote to Dowdeswell in January

---

[75] *Ibid.*, 242, pp. 76–8. [76] *Ibid.*, 242, p. 89.
[77] Lord John Cavendish to Rockingham, 9 Dec. 1772, WWM, R1–1417; Joseph Yorke to Lord Hardwicke, 8 Dec. 1772, BL, Add. MSS 35375, ff. 70–1; Walpole, *Last Journals*, I, 162. [78] BL, Eg. MSS 242, pp. 93–101.
[79] The Company petitioned against the Bill on 14 December and, four days later, the Company's Counsel Elijah Impey and James Adair addressed the House on the urgent need for supervisors to be sent to Bengal; *London Evening Post*, 19 Dec. 1772.
[80] Dowdeswell to Rockingham, 20 Dec. 1772, WWM, R1–1419.
[81] *Burke Corr.*, II, 406; BL, Add. MSS 35631, f. 116; WWM, R1–1419.

1773 he came to the gloomy but quite realistic conclusion that 'in truth, the battle for power is over; nothing now remains but to preserve consistency and dignity'.[82] So far, Company affairs were not providing the opposition with a rod with which they could beat Lord North's administration. If anything, the ministry was gaining strength and confidence from their handling of the business. The Restraining Bill had passed through the Commons in only eleven days, and it met with little opposition in the Lords.[83] The measure passed onto the statute book as 13 Geo. III, c. 9, and the Company was prevented from sending supervisors to India for six months. However, in reality the restraint covered a rather longer period of time because, as the *Public Advertiser* observed on Christmas Eve, the Act 'carries beyond it the season in which the ships can sail so as to make their passage'.

With the preliminary business related to the supervisors completed in swift and efficient fashion, the ministry was now able to proceed to the heart of the East India Company's problems. While the Restraining Bill had not been a central issue, it had been of the greatest importance in the sense that its passage had illustrated how the main Indian business would be conducted. The focus of policy-making was to be found in the Secret Committee, and it was quite clear that unless the Company and the opposition presented a united front against the ministry's large majority in the Commons they stood little chance of defeating any of North's legislative proposals. There had been some speculation that Charles Cornwall was forming an East Indian plan of campaign upon which the opposition 'might concur', but this had not come to anything by the end of December.[84] It was with this worrying general situation in the back of his mind that Rockingham wrote to Burke in order to express the fear that the ministry, spurred on by its successful handling of the issue to date, might seek an early opportunity to press home the advantage. 'I fear', he declared on 5 January 1773, 'the Select and Secret Committee will be very alert when Parliament meets again, and that the ministry will hurry on, least time should give the opportunity for some cool reflexions, and least reason and justice should have any weight.'[85] Lord North had managed firmly to seize the initiative, and there was now the very real danger that the pace of political events might soon leave the Rockinghams and the Company far behind.

---

[82] *Burke Corr.*, II, 403.
[83] A *Protest* was entered by Richmond and four other peers, but this represented no more than token resistance.
[84] Dowdeswell to Rockingham, 20 Dec. 1772, WWM, R1–1419.
[85] *Burke Corr.*, II, 402.

10 Response to crisis (II): trade, finance and reform

With the attention of Parliament and the public focused on the passage of the Restraining Bill in late December 1772, the reduction of the Company's dividend to 6 per cent passed almost unnoticed. Indeed, the issue excited little interest among the proprietors. When the question was put to the vote on 29 December only 143 of them participated in the ballot and, of these, only 12 voted against the measure.[1] This confirmed Burke's opinion, offered to Rockingham on 23 November, that the proprietors, unable to perceive any other way of relieving the Company's distress, were now prepared to make individual financial sacrifices.[2] This would have been unthinkable only a few months earlier, but their action now helped to reduce the Company's annual expenditure. Dividend payments would fall by £208,000 a year and, under the terms of the agreement of 1769, the Company was no longer obliged to make an annual payment of £400,000 to the Treasury. Moreover, the anticipated and much feared stock crash did not occur. With some of the immediate pressure eased, the Company now turned its attention towards framing a long-term solution to its financial problems.

Towards the end of December a number of proprietors submitted proposals to the General Court designed to alleviate the Company's financial distress.[3] One scheme in particular, submitted by Robert Herries, attracted the immediate attention of the directors. Herries's plan centred upon the large amount of capital tied up in the unsold goods lying in the Company's warehouses. In an attempt to release this large source of revenue he proposed that the Company itself should export tea to the Continent. He believed that with ministerial assistance in the form of a drawback on export duties the Company would be well placed against foreign competitors. Even if the tea was sold at a loss, the Company would free itself from the burden of storing a deteriorating commodity in its London warehouses. In optimistic terms Herries

---

[1] IOR, B/88, p. 362.   [2] *Burke Corr.*, II, 384–5.
[3] See, for example, IOR, B/88, p. 360, and Labaree, *Boston Tea Party*, p. 66. For press comment see *Public Advertiser*, 17, 18 Dec. 1772.

estimated that if the Company sold 11,500,000 lbs of its tea surplus an income of £1,425,000 could be generated.[4]

The directors discussed Herries's proposal during the first week of January 1773, but the issue was complicated by the fact that under existing legislative arrangements the Company was only permitted to dispose of its imported goods at sales 'by inch of candle'. For the Company itself to act as an export agent a licence would have to be granted by the government. Consequently, on 6 January the directors empowered their Chairman Sir George Colebrooke to enquire of Lord North whether the ministry would approve of an application to Parliament requesting permission for the Company to export duty-free tea to the Continent. They further requested permission to 'make the experiment' of sending a small quantity of tea for sale to Holland.[5] A debate on the matter in the General Court the following day prompted agreement that efforts should be made to reduce the tea stockpile, but there were differences over how such a reduction should be effected. George Johnstone favoured disposal of the tea on the Continent, but William Crichton argued that this would do little more than 'glut' the European market.[6] Instead, he declared that the price in London should be reduced so as to 'thereby encourage foreigners to take it off our hands'. He also added a further dimension to the discussion by advancing the proposal that Parliament should be asked to remove the Townshend Duty of 3d. per lb payable on tea imported into North America. This idea was well received by the proprietors, who endorsed the proposal and empowered the directors to seek removal of the Townshend Duty as well as permission to export duty-free tea to foreign markets.

The directors now sounded out mercantile opinion on the Continent about the viability of the Company's proposals. A letter was dispatched to Hope and Company of Amsterdam on 8 January, asking whether or not the Herries plan would capture a significant part of the European tea market for the Company. The reply was read to the Court of Directors on 20 January, but it offered little encouragement to the Company since the Hopes advised against the implementation of such a project. They observed that if the continental market was flooded with low-price British imports it would serve further to encourage the smuggling of the tea back into Britain. Illegal cheap imports would then be placed in direct competition with tea sold at a more expensive price at the Company's London sales.[7] This confirmed the worst fears of the

---

[4] Labaree, *Boston Tea Party*, pp. 66–7.   [5] IOR, B/88, p. 379.
[6] *London Evening Post*, 9 Jan. 1773. 'Orator' Crichton was a West India merchant who made more speeches at India House between 1769 and 1773 than any other stockholder (see Table 1).   [7] Labaree, *Boston Tea Party*, pp. 68–9.

directors and, thereafter, they directed their efforts towards gaining access on favourable terms to the North American market.

The reduction of the tea surplus was only one part of a strategy designed to extricate the Company from its financial distress. Tea sales alone could not ease the cash-flow problems, and some other form of assistance from government was deemed necessary. This was the essence of a decision taken by the directors on 14 January, when they resolved to request from the ministry a loan of £1,500,000 to be repaid over four years at 4 per cent interest. The directors lost no time in approaching the ministry, and North promised that the administration would consider the proposals as soon as possible.[8] However, in the meantime he 'did not give hopes' that the Townshend Duty would be repealed, or that the duty-free exportation of tea to the Continent would be permitted if the Company chose to pursue that particular course of action. On the other hand, in order to assist with short-term difficulties, North expressed a willingness to allow the Company to petition for an extension of the payment of £214,300 customs duties which were to fall due on 27 January.[9]

A detailed written ministerial response to the Company's requests was made known to the full Court of Directors on 26 January, and North availed himself of this opportunity to define the administration's general attitude towards the Company and its problems. In contrast to 1769, when he had handled the East Indian business for the ministry in the House of Commons, he now addressed himself to reform of the Company, as well as to more immediate economic problems. He linked the two issues and made it quite clear that in return for financial assistance from the state, the ministry expected a thorough reform of the Company to be implemented.[10] North also reintroduced the thorny issue of the right to the Company's territorial revenues and possessions. He asked whether the directors had a proposal to offer on that subject, and whether it would 'be expedient to offer it at the same time to the consideration of Parliament'. Colebrooke recognized the implications of North's letter and, in a realistic assessment of the situation, he indicated to Laurence Sulivan on 24 January that the minister was proceeding along the lines that had been used by the ministry to secure agreements in 1767 and 1769. This time, however, there was a new dimension:

My Lord North's plan is to get the East India Company to come to Parliament with regulations – it will then be said *violenti non sit injura*. But the difficulty, the impossibility is the settling of a plan of regulations to suit the Court of Directors,

---

[8] IOR, B/88, pp. 402–3.
[9] A memorial to the Treasury on this subject was drafted by the directors on 20 January; *ibid.*, B/88, pp. 406–7.   [10] *Ibid.*, B/88, pp. 414–15.

Proprietors, and Parliament. We want their money, they want power, at least a check on our power.[11]

The directors began to draft a set of proposals which took due notice of the ministry's sentiments. The proposals were then presented to the General Court on 9 February, after it had been announced to the proprietors that plans to export tea to Europe had been abandoned.[12] However, stiff opposition was encountered after the Rockinghams, through the activities of James Adair, had taken a leading part in co-ordinating measures against the directors.[13] George Johnstone and William Crichton were particularly severe on the inadequacy of the proposals placed before them: they 'objected to the generality of the directors' proposals; they said they were such as disgraced a great Company in point of insignificance, as nothing of consequence was pointed out for Parliament to proceed upon'.[14]

Although no formal decisions were taken at the Court, the directors had no choice but to acknowledge the popular opposition to their proposals and they undertook to reconsider their course of action. As a result of this, when new proposals were submitted to the proprietors three days later, several clauses in the original plan had been amended or deleted altogether. The directors, as had been originally desired, requested a loan of £1,500,000 from government, repayable over four years at 4 per cent interest. Secondly, the Company would restrict itself to a 6 per cent dividend payment until an unspecified amount of the loan had been discharged. The dividend would then be raised to 8 per cent, and when the loan had been entirely repaid any surplus profits would be divided between the state and the Company; threequarters going to the former and one quarter to the latter. Thirdly, new regulations for the administration of justice in Bengal would be drafted by the Company. Fourthly, all important Company accounts would in future be laid before Parliament on an annual basis. Fifthly, in future, Company tea would be exported to America free of all duties, and deposits on the purchase of Bohea tea from the Company would be increased from £2 to £4 per chest. Finally, it was proposed that the Company should apply for the release from the 'heavy penal interest' inflicted upon it by the non-payment of monies due to the state as a result of the Indemnity Act and the agreement of 1769.[15]

None of these alterations satisfied the proprietors and, indeed, it was argued by some that it was far too early for the Company to submit any

---

[11] Bodl., MS Eng. hist., b. 237, f. 33. The letter can be dated from internal evidence.
[12] IOR, B/88, pp. 442, 443, 445–7.
[13] Adair to Rockingham, 6 Feb. 1773, WWM, R1–1425.
[14] *London Evening Post*, 11 Feb. 1773.
[15] IOR, B/88, pp. 450–1, 454. The original proposals submitted to the Court on 9 February are to be found at *ibid.*, B/88, pp. 445–7.

proposals at all. Once again there were signs of a co-ordinated campaign of opposition against the directors, and two Rockingham supporters, the Duke of Richmond and James Adair, were prominent in the lengthy debate on the proposals.[16] The former warned of the duplicity of ministers, while the latter reminded the proprietors that 'Parliament in 1767, in the course of a few months, passed two acts relative to the Company, the most repugnant to each other of any, perhaps in the records of history'. After some confusion and procedural wrangling, a motion made by George Johnstone was then passed by 151 votes to 45, empowering four named individuals, Colebrooke, Sulivan, Edward Wheler, and Robert Gregory, to meet with Lord North. They were instructed to express the good faith of the General Court, but they were also to inform him that 'with respect to the territorial revenues and acquisitions, the General Court do not think they are enabled to make any propositions on that head until they shall be acquainted with the whole of the arrangements that may be intended for regulating the affairs of the East India Company'.[17]

This latest development represented a significant tactical error on the part of the proprietors.[18] Their reluctance to offer any proposals to the ministry left North with no alternative but to refer the matter to Parliament. As he wrote to the directors on 16 February, 'the formation of any such plan, if it be not suggested by the Company's own experience and the thorough knowledge of their present situation, cannot with propriety take its rise anywhere but Parliament'.[19] The implication of this was quite clear: if the Company refused to submit proposals of its own then Parliament would proceed and form its own regulations. In view of events the previous December it was unlikely that this would provide regulations to the Company's liking. Some contemporaries recognized that the proprietors had made a grave mistake which left the Company vulnerable to the designs of the ministry. On 13 February a former director of the Company, Charles Raymond, wrote to Rockingham: 'The East India Company have thrown themselves into the hands of government and I know not how they can properly extricate themselves.'[20] Nevertheless, the directors did attempt to head-off the ministry by drafting a petition to the House of Commons in which they incorporated the proposals that had been submitted to the General Court a few days earlier.[21]

North's uncompromising attitude had the desired effect. When his letter of 16 February was read to the General Court the following day there was a marked change of attitude among the proprietors. After a

[16] *London Evening Post*, 13 Feb. 1773.   [17] IOR, B/88, pp. 464–5.
[18] Sutherland, *East India Company*, p. 250.   [19] IOR, B/88, p. 472.
[20] WWM, R1–1426.   [21] IOR, B/88, pp. 470–1.

long debate on procedural matters and a short discussion of North's letter and the directors' petition, a motion was passed declaring that proposals should be made to the ministry in order 'to obtain the assistance immediately necessary for the relief of the Company's present distress'.[22] Over the next week the proprietors first approved by 405 votes to 199 an application to Parliament for a loan under the terms already specified, and they then made a number of minor amendments to the directors' draft petition. The atmosphere at the Court throughout this period was tense. The proceedings received extensive coverage in the press, and one observer was moved to describe the debate of 25 February as 'the most important, as well as the longest for many years'.[23] Indeed, for a time events at India House eclipsed those at Westminster as the political nation focused its attention on the deliberations taking place at the General Court.

The petition incorporating the directors' proposals was put to a ballot at the General Court on 1 March. Like the motion for the loan, it received overwhelming support and was accepted by 377 votes to 84.[24] Few alterations had been made to the proposals that had first been put before the Court on 12 February, but all references to the Townshend Duty were omitted. No specific proposals were forthcoming on the administration of justice in Bengal, but the directors pledged that they would consider the matter as soon as possible. Most attention, however, had been focused on the issue of dividend payments, but the clause related to this matter in the petition did not differ much from that which had been included in the original proposals. The reason for this was that the proprietors had been led to believe by Sir George Colebrooke that the Company had the full support of Lord North for this clause, and, largely because of this they had, as the ballot figures demonstrated, no hesitation in approving the contents of the petition. Unfortunately, North later refused to accept the clause related to dividend payments. He was adamant that he had never undertaken any such commitment,[25] and Colebrooke paid the full price for his mishandling of the whole affair. In fact, following hard on the heels of the scandal related to his stockjobbing activities the previous year, this episode marked the end of Colebrooke's political career in the East India Company. Although he claimed that he had been deceived by Lord North,[26] he had no choice other than to withdraw from India House politics at the first available

---

[22] *Ibid.*, B/88, pp. 472–6. The motion was made by Herbert Mackworth; *London Evening Post*, 18 Feb. 1773.

[23] *London Evening Post*, 25 Feb. 1773. The amendments are to be found in IOR, B/88, pp. 485–6, 494–5.   [24] IOR, B/88, p. 508.

[25] Cobbett, *Parl. Hist.*, XVII, 812.   [26] Colebrooke, *Retrospection*, II, 27.

opportunity. He declined to stand for re-election to the Court of Directors in April 1773 and, as Augustus Keppel remarked to Rockingham on 15 March, he ended his time as Chairman of the Company 'pelted at and much disavowed by everybody'.[27]

The Company's petition was submitted to the House of Commons on 2 March, and a copy was also sent to Lord North. The minister replied to the directors two days later and, while he did not make any comment on the content of the petition, he did nevertheless urge that any reform of its internal and overseas affairs that the Company had under consideration should be submitted to Parliament as soon as possible.[28] The ministry considered the directors' proposals to be incomplete, and indeed this was the case. The Company's petition dealt with financial matters alone: reform and regulation had not yet been discussed in any detail. Under considerable pressure from the ministry, the Company was now obliged to move on and consider this difficult subject. However, many observers felt that as some form of proposal had been forthcoming from India House there was in fact little work left to be done. The *London Evening Post* captured this mood on 2 March when it reported that 'it is confidently believed that Government and the East India Company have compromised matters and that nothing remains but to have the sanction of Parliament'. This proved to be false optimism, and, in fact, at this stage of the proceedings the business was only half complete: the Company's liquidity problem was in the process of being solved, but as yet no progress had been made with the problems of empire.

While the Company and the ministry had been involved in protracted negotiations during the early months of 1773, the Secret Committee had been tackling its task in a brisk and efficient manner. The second report from the Committee had been presented on 17 December 1772 and it had contained a financial analysis which distinguished the Company's debts, credits, and assets in London from those in India, China, and 'floating on sea'.[29] The third report, presented by Thomas Harley on 9 February, complemented the second by extending the financial analysis to include a detailed examination of the profits the Company derived from its trade and territorial revenues. These two important reports served as the core of the Committee's work: they presented an accurate and up-to-date picture of the Company's financial situation, and they identified recent trends in trading and revenue patterns. But, while the

---

[27] WWM, R1–1428.   [28] IOR, B/88, p. 511.

[29] Chatham expressed wholehearted approval of the work of the Committee following the presentation of the second report; Chatham to Shelburne, 22 Jan. 1773, *Chatham Corr.*, IV, 241.

reports provided copious documentation supported by relevant stat-istical detail, the Committee made no recommendations. In short, the reports served as briefing documents for those MPs (and latter-day historians) with an interest in the Company's affairs. Those hoping to find the genesis of reform within the reports were to be disappointed. The reports looked backwards not forwards, providing a complete economic analysis of the Company's affairs over the previous decade or so.

It was recognized by most observers that the Secret Committee was conducting its business in a 'more masterly manner' than the Select Committee,[30] but it was the latter which captured the attention of the public. Although Burgoyne's Committee had not made any further reports (and was not to do so until 8 April), the evidence presented to it in December 1772 contained allegations which proved to be of far greater interest than the Secret Committee's rather 'jejune and dry' reports.[31] This interest had been heightened after further evidence of the misdemeanours of Company servants had been forthcoming when Counsel in support of the Company's petition against the Restraining Bill had been heard in the Commons on 18 December. In reinforcing their claim that supervisors were essential for the regulation of the Company's affairs in Bengal, the Counsel, James Adair and Elijah Impey, had questioned a number of witnesses, including the Examiner of the Company's records Samuel Wilkes and the Company's Ac-countant John Hoole. During the course of this questioning serious charges of corruption were levelled against a number of Company servants, including Francis Sykes, the former Resident at the Nawab's Durbar, who now sat in the House as the Member for Shaftesbury.[32] This brought gasps of astonishment and anger from the House, and Horace Walpole, in the absence of any other news, could write of nothing in late December 'but new horrors coming out every day against our East India Company and their servants'.[33] Sensational revelations such as these meant that public interest during the first quarter of 1773 was focused almost entirely on past events in Bengal, rather than on the current financial distress of the Company.

The Commons returned to the Company's proposals on 9 March, when the House resolved itself into a Committee of the Whole House in order to consider the petition submitted by the directors a week earlier.

[30] View expressed by John Caillaud to Warren Hastings, 15 Mar. 1773, BL, Add. MSS 29133, f. 446.
[31] Joseph Yorke to Lord Hardwicke, 8 Dec. 1772, BL, Add. MSS 35375, f. 70. See, for example, the evidence of Stanlake Batson, Randolph Marriott, and Samuel Wilkes as recorded in NLW, Clive MSS 1712, ff. 56–9.
[32] London Evening Post, 19 Dec. 1772.
[33] Walpole to Sir Horace Mann, 22 Dec. 1772, Walpole Corr., XXIII, 451–2.

From these proceedings emerged a series of resolutions which served to provide the framework for the eventual settlement between the state and the Company. The scope of the business before the Committee was limited to financial matters by Lord North in the opening speech of the day for two important reasons: the Secret Committee had so far only dealt with economic matters, and the Company had not yet presented any proposals related to reform in India.

North then turned his attention to the financial assistance which the ministry was prepared to offer and, using figures incorporated in the second report of the Secret Committee, he calculated that the Company would be £1,300,376 in debt by September 1774. He proposed that the state advance a similar sum to the Company but, because this would place an additional burden upon the nation's finances, North sought to justify this course of action at some length to the House. In doing so, he defined his own view of the nature of the relationship between the state and the Company:

If my maxim is true, and the opinion of many and learned men [is] that the East India Company could acquire nothing by conquest but for the state, then the public has been entitled to these conquests and, having agreed with the Company to let them remain in possession on certain conditions, was as well entitled to £400,000 as any gentleman to his land. The Company in that respect are farmers to the public.

On these grounds North advanced the argument that while the ministry was not 'in point of justice' to assist the Company, 'in point of policy' there were good reasons for doing so. The East Indian trade and revenues could, if properly managed, bring great wealth to the nation, and this alone was sufficient reason for the state to offer financial assistance to the Company during times of distress. North moved that £1,400,000 should be advanced to the Company at once, but he added the important qualification that the loan would only be made if a thorough reform of the Company's affairs was undertaken. He concluded his long speech by returning to this theme: 'I should be of the opinion that unless some promising plan is laid before the House [by the Company] ... our granting the loan should die in this House and never go into the other.' This placed the Company under considerable pressure, because the directors now had to produce regulatory proposals as soon as possible. Unlike previous ministers, North was seeking reform of the Company's affairs in return for the state's financial aid.[34]

William Dowdeswell and Edmund Burke mounted a double-fronted attack against North's speech and resolutions. Dowdeswell, taking the

[34] For North's speech see BL, Eg. MSS 244, pp. 279–91.

broad ground, concentrated on the issue of the right to the territorial revenues,[35] but Burke was rather more particular in his criticism of North. He devoted his attention to the manner in which North sought to obtain reform proposals from the Company, and he desired to know whether the directors were obliged to submit regulations to the ministry before or after state relief had been applied to their debts.[36] North defended his position by arguing that because Parliament was obliged to frame new regulatory measures, it was in the Company's best interest to submit detailed proposals as soon as possible. This represented a less hostile tone than that expressed in his opening speech, but North's sentiments remained unchanged: 'Parliament should not grant this loan till it has formed a plan of regulation... I should think it more becoming of the Company, better for the Company, to offer their opinion to Parliament.'[37] Eventually, despite an amendment moved by Burke, North's resolutions were agreed to by the House. This meant that the outline of the financial settlement was in place and the onus was now placed upon the Company to draft suitable regulations. The King was delighted with the proceedings and he wrote to North that the day's events were 'so favourable a commencement of the East Indian business that I cannot help expressing the pleasure it gives me'. He also hoped that 'with a constant inspection of those affairs, Parliament may yet avert the ruin to which the Company has nearly been plunged into by the ill conduct of its directors and rapine of its servants'.[38]

North's important statement and the resolutions passed in the Commons on 9 March did not serve to concentrate all Company minds on the issue of reform. While an open Committee of Correspondence was delegated to draft regulations,[39] the proprietors remained pre-occupied with their own dividend payments. Because of this, when the Committee of the Whole House next met on 23 March to discuss outstanding matters related to the Company's petition of 2 March, North's primary concern was to end speculation about future levels of payment to the proprietors. As one government speaker and member of the Secret Committee, Charles Jenkinson, remarked during the course of the proceedings, the 'fixing' of the dividend was now the most important business before the House.[40] North pointed to the 'unreasonable' nature of the Company's dividend proposals, and he made two motions: that payments be restricted to 6 per cent while the loan was

---

[35] *Ibid.*, 244, pp. 297–8.   [36] *Ibid.*, 244, pp. 299–300.
[37] *Ibid.*, 244, pp. 300–1.
[38] George III to North, 9 Mar. 1773, *George III Corr.*, II, no. 1205.
[39] IOR, B/88, p. 528, The Committee was open to all directors.
[40] BL, Eg. MSS 245, p. 74.

outstanding and that they then be restricted to 7 per cent until the Company's bond debt was reduced to £1,500,000. He argued that it was a waste of time demonstrating the absurdity of the Company applying for a loan 'to enable the proprietors to squander the money they borrowed in dividends among themselves'. He was 'amazed' that the Company could advance such a proposal, and he concluded by pointing out that 'the Company can have no cause for complaint...By advancing them the money [it] enables them to make any dividend at all.'[41] North reported to the King that his motions prompted 'conversation in general and not debate on the question', and Horace Walpole later recalled that 'Burke almost alone' opposed the measures.[42] It came as no surprise, therefore, when both motions were passed without divisions.

The second important stage of the settlement was now effectively in place, and North prepared to tackle the all-important issue of the right to the territorial revenues. The need to do so was immediate, because the compromise incorporated in the agreement renewed in 1769 was scheduled to expire in 1774. North received enthusiastic support from the King who once more endeavoured to strengthen the resolve of his minister, and Shelburne reported to Chatham a mood of quiet optimism within the cabinet at the end of March.[43] Even so, it had long been rumoured that North had in fact abandoned the idea of declaring the Crown's rights to the Bengal revenues.[44] The press gave expression to the belief that while the more extreme members of the administration such as Lord Mansfield, Lord Rochford, and Sir Gilbert Elliot desired an immediate declaration in favour of the Crown, North stood against such a measure because 'he foresees it will occasion more trouble and business than he is able to manage'.[45] This was another example of an attack on North's supposed indolence, but it helped to foster the belief that the ministry was divided at this critical moment in the development of East Indian policy.

The popular view was that the ministry was close to the point of collapse, and that moves were afoot to replace North with those who took a hard line against the Company.[46] However, there is no evidence to support this theory and, despite the fact that he had suffered an

[41] Ibid., 245, pp. 51–66.
[42] North to George III, 23 Mar. 1773, George III Corr., II, no. 1212; Walpole, Last Journals, I, 181.
[43] George III to North, 23 Mar. 1773, George III Corr., II, no. 1211; Shelburne to Chatham, 30 Mar. 1773, Chatham Corr., IV, 254.
[44] See, for example, Shelburne to Chatham, 17 Jan. 1773, Chatham Corr., IV, 238.
[45] London Evening Post, 13 Feb. 1773. See also ibid., 16 Feb.
[46] Burke to Rockingham, 26 Mar. 1773, Burke Corr., II, 426; Walpole, Last Journals, I, 180.

embarrassing defeat in the Commons on the issue of rates of pay for naval captains,[47] North remained in firm control of affairs with the full support of the King. His almost single-handed direction of the East Indian legislation through the Commons was proceeding unhindered, with only a minimum of resistance being offered by a divided opposition. There could not have been a more favourable situation in which to secure a declaration of right in favour of the Crown, but no such attempt was made. North instead shied away from redefining the legal and practical relationship between the state, the Company, and the territorial possessions in Bengal and, like other ministers before him, he sought a compromise on the issue.

The compromise was secured on 5 April in the Committee of the Whole House on East Indian affairs when North moved that 'it is the opinion of the committee that it may be for the mutual benefit of the public and the Company that the territorial possessions lately obtained in India shall, under proper restrictions, remain in the possession of the East India Company [for a period] not exceeding six years'.[48] The revenues would not be shared until the bond debt had been reduced to £1,500,000, but thereafter threequarters of the profits would be paid to the state, the remainder being used by the Company to pay outstanding debts and to fund 'extraordinary exigencies'.

North sought to justify this arrangement which, as he pointed out, was similar in outline to those established in 1767 and 1769. He reiterated his belief that the right to the revenues and territories lay with the Crown, but said that as far as a matter of policy went it was now 'better to continue the territorial revenues in the hands of the Company and under their management under certain conditions'. He drew attention to the practical difficulties involved in the Crown managing the revenues,[49] and he reaffirmed his view that it had been judicious and prudent for the public in the recent past to 'receive the payment [of £400,000 per annum] in consideration of permitting the possession to remain in the hands of the Company'. 'In the present circumstances', he told the House, 'till you can take possession I think it not right to come to a direct decision on the question of right.' North then outlined his reasons for limiting the Company's continued possession of the territories to six years, conceding in the process that the whole scheme was an 'experiment' and that 'our regulation must be novel'. On these grounds

---

[47] North had opposed the referral of a petition from naval captains to a committee, but when the matter was put to a vote on 9 February he was defeated by 154 votes to 45.
[48] This, and the following quotations from the speech, are taken from BL, Eg. MSS 245, pp. 248–9.
[49] These difficulties had been mentioned in the fourth report of the Secret Committee.

alone it was not wise to 'entrust the Company with those possessions for a longer time'. It was also convenient because the Company's charter would expire in 1780 and the whole experiment could then be reviewed. Apart from violent speeches from Dowdeswell and Burke,[50] the opposition offered nothing at all in response to North. The proceedings were brought to an abrupt close when Burke stormed out of the chamber declaring that he had 'done with' the Indian business,[51] and only an hour and a quarter after North had first risen to speak his motion was passed without a division.

The package of measures related to the Company's financial position was completed three weeks later on 26 April when the final parts of the petition of 2 March were considered by the Committee of the Whole House. The chamber was fuller than usual because North had moved for a call of the House on this day,[52] a development which arose from the lack of interest that was being shown by MPs in the East Indian business.[53] The only clauses in the petition that had not yet been discussed were those relating to the exportation of tea, and North had little hesitation in agreeing to the Company's requests. Most importantly, the Company was granted a licence to export tea to North America, together with a rebate on the British import duty and an exemption from the inland duty on such tea. William Dowdeswell drew attention to the fact that no mention had been made of any repeal of the duty on tea imported into America[54] and, although the Company had not formally asked for this important concession, the ensuing debate centred on this point. Dowdeswell argued that the retention of the Townshend Duty did not help the Company in any way, and he asserted that the Americans would not accept the idea in such circumstances.

In reply North again indicated his unwillingness to give up the duty. He argued that if the Company was successful in exporting large quantities of tea to America the revenue accruing from the duty would be greatly increased. This prompted a protracted discussion of how much revenue had been, and could be, raised from the duty but, in the end, North conceded that there were also political considerations to be taken into account. He told the House that 'unless I find it absolutely necessary to take off the duty I shall be very unwilling to touch that string'.[55] The attempt to procure the removal of the tea duty ended and

---

[50] BL, Eg. MSS 245, pp. 261–5; *General Evening Post*, 8 Apr. 1773.
[51] BL, Eg. MSS 245, p. 269.
[52] He had done this on 7 April and, at the same time, he had moved to have three Members added to the Secret Committee; *CJ*, XXXIV, 271.
[53] On 13 April the *London Evening Post* estimated that only 60–80 members had been present in the House during debates on Indian affairs.
[54] BL, Eg. MSS 246, p. 4.   [55] *Ibid.*, 246, p. 16.

North secured the Committee's approval for the measures.[56] The consequences of this decision were in fact to have a profound effect upon the future course of British imperial history because, as has recently been pointed out, the debate of 26 April provided the last opportunity before the Boston Tea Party to secure an alteration to the ministry's policy on American taxation.[57] The fate of the thirteen colonies was effectively sealed in a debate related to economic problems which had stemmed from British activity in India and the Far East.

The details of the financial settlement between the ministry and the Company had now been firmly established. All the resolutions of the Committee of the Whole House were agreed to on 27 April: those which related to the exportation of tea were incorporated in one Bill, and the remainder were formed into a separate Bill which became known as the East India Loan Bill. The Company had been granted much of what it had requested, but this still only represented one side of the bargain, and attention now focused upon what the Company would produce by way of regulatory proposals and reforms.

While the outlines of the financial settlement were being shaped in the House of Commons, the Company had been making slow progress with the drafting of its regulatory measures. Indeed the proposals framed by the Committee of Correspondence were not placed before the pro-prietors for approval until 25 March. Two sets of regulations were put forward: one comprehensive plan, and a series of proposals for 'the more due administration of justice without such Supreme Court as is proposed in the first mentioned regulations'.[58] Laurence Sulivan later sketched for Warren Hastings the difficult conditions under which the measures had been formulated. 'Parliament', he wrote on 28 April 1773, 'was calling with impatience for our reforms, the Court of Directors and General Court meeting upon the subject for months past, and so divided from their ignorance that all was chaos.'[59] After the proposals had been read to the proprietors on 25 March it was decided that, in order to simplify the task before them, the question of reform in India should be separated from reform of the Company at home. With this in mind a committee of thirteen proprietors was set up to examine the latter issue.[60]

Proposals related to reform in India were read to the General Court a week later. Two 'new modelled' sets of proposals were discussed and

[56] For an account of the debate see Labaree, *Boston Tea Party*, pp. 70–3, and Thomas, *Townshend Duties Crisis*, pp. 252–3.

[57] Thomas, *Townshend Duties Crisis*, p. 254.   [58] IOR, B/88, p. 550.

[59] BL, Add. MSS 29133, f. 535.

[60] IOR, B/88, p. 561. It was reported that the directors had suggested this course of action in order to ease their heavy workload; *London Evening Post*, 30 Mar. 1773.

an important motion was made: 'that it is the opinion of this Court that it will be more expedient to alter and amend the constitution and jurisdiction of the present courts of justice in the East Indies than to establish any new court or courts of justice there'.[61] It was not until 21 April that this motion was resolved in the affirmative, the grounds being that it was 'less difficult and expensive' to amend existing regulations than it was to create a whole new judicial framework.[62] A week later Sulivan explained the thought behind this decision to Warren Hastings:

It was proposed to annihilate the Court of Appeals and the Mayor's Court, allowing the Council to act as common justices of the peace – a supreme court of judicature to be created for Bengal – all judicial [sic] independent of the Company, named (I believe) by the Crown: but upon reading and discussing your regulations [of 1772]... the General Court have passed a unanimous vote to abide by their old system of Mayor's Court with some regulation.[63]

The recent arrival of news of Hastings's reforms satisfied the proprietors that attention was being paid to judicial problems by the men on the spot who were best placed to offer sensible solutions. It remained to be seen, however, whether the ministry would be so easily pleased or whether they would seek a complete overhaul of British judicial practice in Bengal.

The proprietors continued to discuss the administration of justice throughout the last week of April, but a blow was struck against their progress on 30 April when the new Chairman, Henry Crabb Boulton, formally informed the General Court of the resolutions related to the Tea and Loan Bills that had been passed in the House of Commons three days earlier. The response of the proprietors was immediate. They drafted a petition in which they protested that the dividend restriction was unfair, and that the clause related to possession of territories was 'arbitrary'. Echoing much of what Edmund Burke had said in the House, the proprietors complained that such a decision 'may be construed into a conclusive decision against the Company respecting those territorial possessions to which they insist they have an undoubted right, a right against which no decision exists, nor any formal claim has been made.'[64]

The pressure upon the Company increased when the petition was presented to the House on 3 May and North took the opportunity to announce that he had not yet received any regulatory proposals from the directors. He declared that he could wait no longer and he was in fact ready to make recommendations of his own.[65] This was a development

[61] IOR, B/88, p. 568.
[62] Ibid., B/89, p. 19.
[63] BL, Add. MSS 29133, f. 535.
[64] IOR, B/89, pp. 69–72.
[65] BL, Eg. MSS 246, p. 32.

that John Caillaud had forecast to Warren Hastings at the end of March when he had reported that the Company had formed a 'very general loose, and futile' plan of regulation. 'They may have saved themselves the trouble', he had added, 'as I believe administration intend settling all those matters for them.'[66]

Caillaud claimed that his assessment of the situation was based upon inside information which illustrated that the ministry had long been contemplating its own plan of reform. Indeed, on 15 March he had reported to Hastings that he had seen a draft ministerial document which proposed the establishment of a Council of four to assist Hastings in a new appointment as Governor-General.[67] The Company had not been formally involved in any negotiations surrounding the development of this ministerial policy, although it may well have been the case that some directors with close links to the administration had offered advice on a private basis. In general, however, the directors knew little more than what was reported in the press. 'The leading men in the direction', wrote Caillaud to Hastings, 'are quite in the dark as to the intentions of the minister.'[68] It came as a great surprise, therefore, when on 3 May North declared the outline of his plan of reform of the Company's affairs.

In his speech to the House on 3 May North mentioned a few of the principal features that he felt should be incorporated in any regulating Bill. He identified two major flaws in the Company's structure at home, both of which required an immediate remedy. First, he proposed that the directors should enjoy a longer term of office and, secondly, he proposed further alterations to the voting qualifications in the General Court 'so that it will not be worthwhile in [future] by splitting and alley-jobbing the endeavour to form a party in order to overturn the directors'. In future proprietors would have to have been in possession of stock for a year before being deemed eligible to vote at the Court. Furthermore, on this point he also advocated increasing the minimum voting qualification from £500 to £1,000. He advanced the opinion that many of the Company's problems stemmed from the large number of £500 proprietors: perhaps he had the troublesome William Crichton in mind.

North then moved on to a consideration of the Company's affairs in India. He identified the need for one overriding reform: 'that there must be some superiority lodged in one of their Presidents in India in certain cases over others'. North proposed that the Governor of Bengal should be given the 'superintending power' over all the Company's possessions

<hr />

[66] BL, Add. MSS 29133, f. 495.   [67] Ibid., 29133, f. 443.   [68] Ibid.

in India. Furthermore, he proposed the concentration of power in only a few hands. A council of four with 'extraordinary powers' would be chosen, and North was of the opinion that Hastings ought to be at their head. A new Supreme Court was to be established in Bengal with a chief justice and three justices appointed by the Crown. It was to have local 'jurisdiction civil and criminal there; likewise a personal jurisdiction with all His Majesty's British subjects within the provinces of Bengal'. All other cases, at the discretion of the Council, would be referred to the Mayor's Court in Calcutta.[69]

The ensuing debate centred not upon North's propositions, but upon Lord Clive's attempts to clear his name in the face of charges that had been laid against him in the third and fourth reports of the Select Committee.[70] Claiming that 'mismanagement abroad was founded upon mismanagement at home', Clive attacked those men like Sulivan and the Select Committee who were attempting to 'mark' him and treat him like a 'sheep stealer'.[71] This served to divert attention away from all that North had said, and it was only towards the end of the proceedings that the debate was brought back to the main business of the day when Lord George Germain asked whether or not North's proposals had been made with the consent of Company. North replied that the propositions had been made in the belief that the Company accepted the terms of the settlement that had already been laid down by Parliament. Although this threat of resistance from the Company was raised near the end of the debate, North's proposals were accepted without a division and, the following day, leave was given to bring into the House the Bill which became known as the Regulating Bill.[72] The King was again well satisfied with the course that the business in the House had taken. Late on the same day, he expressed to North approval of the measures, but he hinted that additional reforms might be necessary in future years in order to counter new abuses in Bengal.[73]

These developments in the House of Commons outraged the proprietors, and a mood of defiance characterized General Court proceedings on 4 and 6 May as individuals began to consider alternative methods of relieving the Company's financial distress; methods, above all, that would not result in the imposition of unacceptable ministerial reforms in return for assistance. A plan was drafted by Lockhart Gordon, one of the Company's Counsel, and this centred upon the

---

[69] All the following references to North's speech are taken from BL, Eg. MSS 246, pp. 32–44.   [70] These reports had been presented on 8 and 21 April.
[71] Cobbett, *Parl. Hist.*, XVII, 852–3.
[72] *CJ*, XXXIV, 297. Among those deputed to draft the Bill were North himself and John Robinson.   [73] *George III Corr.*, II, no. 1237.

Company raising £1,500,000 by subscription. The plan was circulated through the General Court, and the *London Evening Post* reported on 15 May that a subscription had been opened at once with considerable success, 'an eminent baronet and a public spirited merchant proposed subscribing £150,000'. But, despite these public gestures of defiance and independence, discussion of the Company's own regulatory proposals continued and was completed on 10 May. A set of thirty-nine articles related to reform in India was agreed to, and it was resolved that the directors should present them to the Commons, together with a petition containing the assurance that the Court would now proceed at once to a consideration of regulating measures for the Company's affairs in Britain.[74]

Up to this point, Lord North had remained in firm control of the shape and direction of the Indian business in the House of Commons. Between 9 March and 3 May he established the necessary framework for the future regulation of the Company's affairs and the reflation of its finances. His task was made easy by two important factors: the numerical weakness of the parliamentary opposition, and the able assistance provided by the penetrating analyses of the Company's affairs presented in the Secret Committee's reports. Although these reports contained no formal recommendations, there is little doubt that the financial settlement and regulatory proposals were framed by North and leading members of the Committee such as Charles Jenkinson and Richard Rigby. Indeed, firm evidence points to the fact that North met from time to time with members of the Secret Committee in Downing Street and, while the propriety of this troubled the individuals concerned, it did allow ministerial policy and strategy to be co-ordinated.[75] The picture of North that emerges at this time, therefore, is not the one presented so often in the press. He was not an indolent and weak-willed individual following a course determined by stronger members of the cabinet. On the contrary, what can be discerned is North, often alone, shouldering an incredibly heavy ministerial burden in the House of Commons, and often delighting in those aspects of policy he enjoyed most: financial details, and the development of economic and commercial strategy.

[74] IOR, B/89, p. 112.
[75] Richard Rigby to Charles Jenkinson, 21 Mar. 1773, BL, Add. MSS 38398, ff. 38–9

11 The final act? The passage of Lord North's East India legislation, 1773

In May 1773 there was a break in the long-established pattern of proposal and counter-proposal between the Company and the ministry. General Burgoyne, true to his word, decided to act upon the findings of his own parliamentary committee. His much publicized intervention not only served to deflect public opinion and parliamentary attention away from the subject of regulation and reform, but it also forced the Company and the administration into positions of irreconcilable hostility and suspicion. Whether Lord North favoured such a diversion at this point is doubtful, but he had little choice in the matter: public opinion demanded that errant Company servants be brought to justice, and Burgoyne took full advantage of this prevailing hostility towards nabobs to press home his attack.

North was in a difficult position because he could not afford to ignore the views of his cabinet colleagues, many of whom it was reported were calling for positive action to be taken against those who had committed offences in India.[1] Indeed, Charles Cornwall warned Charles Jenkinson that the ministry would be 'irreparably disgraced' by inaction or prevarication on the matter, and he suggested that the only solution was to 'lay hold of Burgoyne and make him the instrument of bringing forward such a scheme as was in his judgement most proper'.[2] This offered North the means of escape from an awkward situation. The position of Clive, a government supporter and close associate of the Solicitor-General Alexander Wedderburn, was bound to provide the focus for any parliamentary attack upon the nabobs. Because of his close links with the accused, North could not play a part in such an attack, yet he could not offer a defence of Clive without bringing the ministry into disrepute. However, public and parliamentary opinion might be satisfied by an attack on the nabobs by Burgoyne, while the ministry could abandon Clive and retreat quietly to the sidelines.

It was unfortunate for North that Burgoyne's actions served to

---

[1] *London Evening Post*, 4 May 1773; Walpole, *Last Journals*, I, 199.
[2] Undated letter, BL, Add. MSS 38207, f. 359.

disrupt his carefully laid plans to effect a settlement with the East India Company. When Burgoyne proceeded with his attack on Company servants he did not satisfy himself with a simple and limited condemnation of individual activities in India. Instead, he broadened the base of his attack in such a way that it threatened the very nature and form of the relationship between the state and the Company. In particular, he upset the delicate compromise that North had settled with regard to the right to the territorial acquisitions and revenues in Bengal. North had been careful to avoid any definitive declaration of right, but Burgoyne took it upon himself to decide the issue once and for all in favour of the state. This, Horace Walpole later proclaimed, was the 'capital point, the point of sovereignty; a question eagerly contended for, denied by the East India Company, claimed and ambitioned by the Crown, staved off by Lord North, and that ought to be settled on the most mature deliberation'.[3] But mature deliberation was not forthcoming and an attempt was made by Burgoyne to settle the 'capital point' in a day.

Before proceeding in the House of Commons to any specific allegations of misbehaviour, Burgoyne sought to establish guidelines for the conduct of British activity in India. This he did on 10 May when, following the order of the day to consider the various reports of the Secret and Select Committees, he made three motions, all of which were seconded by the Rockinghamite spokesman Sir William Meredith. They were as follows:

That all acquisitions made under the influence of a military force, or by treaty with foreign princes, do of right belong to the state.
That to appropriate acquisitions so made to the private emolument of persons entrusted with any civil or military power is illegal.
[After some amendment] That very great sums of money and other valuable property have been acquired in Bengal from princes and others of that country by persons entrusted with military and civil powers of the state by means of such powers; which sums have been appropriated to the use of such persons.[4]

Burgoyne disclaimed any role as a prosecuting counsel but, in support of his resolutions, he presented a chronological account of the major crimes perpetrated by Company servants. The debate that followed was heated, the tone being set by a vigorous defence of Clive by Alexander Wedderburn.[5] Most importantly, he advanced the argument that Burgoyne's motions contradicted and endangered the ministry's entire East India policy. The appeals for restraint made by Wedderburn attracted considerable support and, as Horace Walpole noted, 'the tone

---

[3] Walpole, *Last Journals*, I, 199–200.   [4] *CJ*, XXXIV, 308.
[5] This, and the following quotations, are taken from Walpole, *Last Journals*, I, 200–1.

of the House ran irresistibly for temper and delay'. Even so, the Attorney-General Edward Thurlow called for immediate punitive action against the accused and this 'in a moment revived and heightened the odium against Lord Clive'. Because of this, it came as no surprise that when Burgoyne's three motions were put they were all passed in the affirmative. Walpole described the scene in the House at the time of the vote:

> It happened too that the House was exceedingly crowded. It would have been unpopular to exclude many who might have been proprietors of India stock, and unpolite, as many ladies were present too. Yet the heat was intolerable, and the younger men, who had gone away to dinner and returned flushed with wine, growing impatient as the interesting part of the debate was over, they roared impetuously for the question. There was no question ready but Burgoyne's for Wedderburn's [motion for an adjournment] was not attended to; and thus, without almost a negative Burgoyne's momentous resolution, that had been abandoned, was before eleven at night, voted as the general sense of the House of Commons. In so tumultuous manner was the sovereignty of three imperial vast provinces transferred from the East India Company to the Crown! So rashly did one house of Parliament decide.

Walpole overstated the case. Sovereignty was not transferred from the Company to the Crown by this vote. Acceptance of Burgoyne's resolutions represented no more than an expression of parliamentary opinion, but the vote was nevertheless greeted with almost universal public approval.[6]

After Burgoyne's motions had been passed, the House resolved to consider the Committee reports the following Friday. 'The hounds go out again on Friday', was the historian Edward Gibbon's comment to J.B. Holroyd on 11 May.[7] However, in the event, the business was postponed until Wednesday 19 May, and only then could Burgoyne make any additional motions. The proceedings that day were described by one observer as being 'dull and tedious', and this was not surprising, since they were concerned in the main with points of order related to parliamentary practice on such occasions.

The general level of interest and excitement was only raised when Clive spoke in his own defence. As Sir John Hynde Cotton remarked to Lord Hardwicke, the former Governor of Bengal outlined 'in a very decent manly manner the services he had done the India Company'.[8] Such a defence was very necessary for, in his opening speech, Burgoyne had declared that when the House had finished considering the reports,

[6] Lloyd Kenyon jnr. to Lloyd Kenyon, 11 May 1773, *HMC Fourteenth Report, Appendix. Part IV : Kenyon MSS* (1894), p. 504.
[7] *The Letters of Edward Gibbon*, ed. J.E. Norton (3 vols., 1956), I, 366.
[8] BL, Add. MSS 35611, f. 91.

he would make a motion declaring that Clive had illegally acquired £234,000 at the time of the revolution of 1757 in Bengal. Clive was the only individual to be mentioned in the motion, and John Yorke reported to Lord Hardwicke that the business was 'irregular and episodic' with Burgoyne's attack being 'very heavy, unedifying and unsatisfactory'.[9] Clive's friends launched a vigorous attack upon the unfair nature of the motion, 'because it left no room for stating his merits and circumstances upon which he acted'.[10] In the end it was resolved that a number of witnesses should attend the House and, after a division of 119 votes to 81, it was ordered that their attendance should be on 21 May when the reports of the Committee would be taken into final consideration. The scene was now set for one of the great parliamentary debates of the eighteenth century, the day which Horace Walpole described as determining the 'fate of this every way great criminal'.[11]

The proceedings on 21 May began with a lengthy examination of a former member of the Bengal Council, Richard Becher, on the circumstances surrounding events in 1757.[12] This was punctuated by repeated clashes between Wedderburn and Burgoyne over the admissibility of such evidence. After numerous digressions, Clive's own evidence was then read to the House. Clive himself made a short speech and, after ending it with the dramatic plea 'leave me my honour, take away my fortune', he left the House 'with a pretty general "hear, hear"'.[13] Burgoyne then made his motion as follows:

That it appears to this House that Clive...through the influence of the powers with which he was entrusted as a member of the Select Committee and Commander-in-Chief British forces, did obtain and possess himself of...£234,000; and that in doing so the said Robert Lord Clive abused the powers with which he was entrusted, to the evil example of the servants of the public.[14]

Burgoyne's motion occasioned an impassioned debate which cut across the usual dividing line between ministry and opposition. Edmund Burke wrote to Charles O'Hara on 22 May and pointed to the divided nature of the ministry, upon whom North had been unwilling or unable to impose any discipline or unity: 'He [North] had let his sheep wander

---

[9] BL, Add. MSS 35375, f. 87.   [10] Ibid., f. 88.

[11] Walpole, Last Journals, I, 231.

[12] BL, Eg. MSS 247, pp. 73–100. Becher refused to answer any questions that might implicate himself.

[13] Ibid., 247, pp. 131–4. Clive did not deny that he had received presents. He claimed that he had a right to them, and he pointed to the approval he had received from the directors for his actions. He also reminded the House that he had been granted numerous rewards and honours by the Crown in recognition of his achievements in 1757.

[14] CJ, XXXIV, 330.

on the common in the morning, but he could not get them together in the fold at night. He is not a good shepherd and the flock has no regard for his voice.'[15] Thus while some ministerial supporters such as Jeremiah Dyson, Edward Thurlow, and, surprisingly, North himself spoke for the motion,[16] Clive's defence was again ably mounted by Alexander Wedderburn. The Rockinghams, with whom Wedderburn had been in contact, supported Clive and a particularly effective speech was made in his favour by Lord George Germain.[17] On the other hand, the followers of Chatham, most notably Isaac Barré, were forceful in their condemnation of Clive, and they were in general identified with the hostile stance adopted by the Bedfordites.

The debate lasted long into the night, and a majority of speakers was opposed to Burgoyne's motion and sympathetic towards Clive. This was confirmed when amendments moved by ministerial supporters Hans Stanley and Rose Fuller were put to the vote. First, upon Stanley's amendment, the motion was divided into two parts after '£234,000'. Then, at Fuller's prompting, the words 'through the influence of the powers with which he was entrusted as a member of the Select Committee and Commander-in-Chief British forces' were deleted. A division took place upon the question that these words should stand as part of the motion, and the result was that the words were removed by 155 votes to 95. As Burke remarked to Charles O'Hara, these amendments entirely altered the tone of Burgoyne's motion: the 'proposition was reduced to a simple stating of the fact that my Lord Clive had received presents'.[18] The House next proceeded to vote on the first part of the main question and it was resolved in the affirmative. However, the second part of the question was passed in the negative and Clive was therefore cleared of any criminal behaviour. Even so, this was not the end of the matter, for Wedderburn sought to press home Clive's advantage. He made the motion that 'Robert Clive did at the same time render great and meritorious service to this country.' This was also resolved in the affirmative, and the House adjourned at five o'clock in the morning.[19]

Unable to obtain a censure of Clive, Burgoyne did not seek to press charges against any other individuals. The expected condemnation and humiliation of other much abused Company servants was not forthcoming, and it was generally assumed that Clive and his associates had

---

[15] *Burke Corr.*, II, 435.
[16] A report of North's speech is to be found at BL, Eg. MSS pp. 189–209. He made two points: Clive's merits should not be permitted to provide cover for other criminals; and it was undoubtedly an abuse to receive presents when in 'public authority'.
[17] Burke to O'Hara, 22 May, *Burke Corr.*, II, 433; Walpole, *Last Journals*, I, 233.
[18] *Burke Corr.*, II, 434–5.   [19] *CJ*, XXXIV, 331.

bought their way out of trouble.[20] This was nonsense: Clive owed his escape to his own forceful defence of his conduct, and to well-established methods of parliamentary management. Wedderburn was the key figure in this. He mounted an effective defence of his patron in speech after speech, and he managed to assemble a powerful coalition in support of Clive. Indeed, so successful was this campaign that it seems that Clive's reputation was enhanced at the very time when it was assumed, and by some eagerly anticipated, that he would be humiliated.[21]

With the high drama of the proceedings against Clive now at an end, attention focused once more upon the passage of the ministry's legislative proposals. The General Court had proceeded with the drafting of its regulations, but opposition to the ministry had been heightened by the acceptance in the House of North's resolutions of 3 May, and of Burgoyne's resolutions on 10 May. When the proprietors met on 12 May they had been overtaken by events. They were now obliged in particular to consider the implications of the resolutions passed in relation to the position of the Company's territorial acquisitions. A heated debate took place, during which the Duke of Richmond played a leading part 'with his usual friendly interference'.[22] First, the petition related to the Company's regulatory proposals was approved, and then a series of seven strongly worded resolutions were drafted and incorporated in a second petition. The general sentiments of the proprietors were expressed in the first of these resolutions. They declared their dislike of the resolutions passed in the House of Commons and they desired to have them altered. It was stated 'in the most respectful manner' that the proprietors would refuse 'the loan and the agreement respecting the territorial acquisitions rather than accede to them upon the whole of the terms proposed'.[23] A number of those present considered the petition to be unnecessarily provocative and advised caution, but they were swept aside by a strong tide of anti-ministerial sentiment.

The decision on the petition, when it was eventually taken on 14 May, represented an endorsement of the opposition to the ministry by 319 votes to 149. The anti-ministerial London Evening Post depicted the vote as a 'necessary act of self-defence on behalf of the Company', and it commended the proprietors for their independent spirit and action in

[20] Walpole, Last Journals, I, 234.
[21] Burke to O'Hara, 22 May, Burke Corr., II, 435.
[22] London Evening Post, 15 May 1773.
[23] IOR, B/89, pp. 117–18. The rest of the petition concentrated upon the dividend issue. By way of a compromise the proprietors offered to limit increases to 1 % a year above 8 % after the bond debt had been reduced to £1,500,000. The petition had been drawn up at a meeting at the Crown and Anchor tavern; General Evening Post, 15 May 1773.

the face of intimidation from the ministry.[24] Widespread canvassing had taken place, and a campaign orchestrated by Richmond and George Johnstone had convinced many ordinary proprietors that the very independence of the Company was threatened by the ministry's actions.[25] They had taken great care to represent the ministerial legislation as an assault on chartered rights and the individual property of the proprietors. This was a difficult charge for ministers to refute, and it served to widen the breach between the Company and the administration. The Earl of Rochford reported the ballot result to the King, who recognized the setback that the ministry had received. Nevertheless, the King exhorted North to proceed with 'redoubled zeal' and he advocated the adoption of a hard line towards the Company. He suggested that if the Company would not accept the loan they should be prevented from making any dividends for three years, so that 'they must then come on their knees for what they now seem to spurn'.[26]

The hopes for an amicable settlement were now dashed, and North was obliged to press on with the business in the face of the proprietors' unequivocal opposition to his measures. He was, of course, in a position of great strength. The ministry's unchallenged supremacy in Parliament was such that he remained secure in the knowledge that his legislation could be guided through the House with little or no opposition. This was no better illustrated than when the Regulating Bill received unopposed and largely unnoticed first and second readings on 18 and 21 May, days on which the House was preoccupied with the findings of the Select Committee.

Even so, the proprietors met on 21 May to consider how best to mount an effective campaign against the ministry. The previous day the Court had discussed the future regulation of the Company's home affairs[27] and, although a report containing twenty-seven articles of reform had been read by the Committee appointed to draft the proposals, such considerations were now put to one side. The directors declared that the Company's situation was critical, a circumstance that was underlined by the release of the latest financial figures.[28] The Duke of Richmond then told the proprietors that they had to make a simple choice: 'They were reduced to one of two situations, one of which they must unavoidably fix on. The first was to lie at the mercy of administration; the latter to resist,

---

[24] Issue of 15 May.
[25] See, for example, the printed text of the question to be balloted on sent to Robert Orme; IOL, Tract 404, no. 14.
[26] George III to North, 15 May 1773, *George III Corr.*, III, no. 1245.
[27] IOR, B/89, pp. 160–4.
[28] *Ibid.*, B/89, pp. 166, 168–70. It was reported that there was a current cash deficit of £200,000, and that the Company's total debt would rise to £1,749,700 by September.

like Englishmen, every illegal attack upon their chartered rights and privileges.'[29] It came as no great surprise when the proprietors chose the latter course of action. A committee of seven proprietors and seven directors was appointed to consider ways of opposing the parts of the ministry's strategy which appeared to be 'subversive of the charter rights' of the Company. Three days later the Committee reported back to the proprietors with a draft petition, and that was approved by 445 votes to 14 at a ballot on 26 May, the majority of 431 being the largest in the Company's history to date.[30] The petition attacked the Regulating Bill as unconstitutional and defective, and it portrayed the intended legislation as 'tending to destroy the liberties of the subject from an immense addition of power it must give to the influence of the Crown'.[31]

While the Committee of fourteen co-ordinated the campaign of opposition against the Regulating Bill, consideration of the Company's own reform measures was suspended.[32] All energies were devoted to a vigorous and sustained denunciation of the ministry's measures and, moving beyond the confines of Leadenhall Street, the Company sought support from other chartered bodies.[33] Alderman John Kirkman, who had been an India stockholder for less than three months,[34] requested a meeting of the Court of Common Council to enable the Company to state its case. When this took place on 28 May he went through the Regulating Bill clause by clause and, according to one report, 'proved uncontestably that the bill was no less injurious to the rights of every corporate body in the Kingdom from its principle than a direct and immediate attack on the privileges of the East India Company'.[35] Kirkman then moved that a petition be sent to Parliament drawing attention to the Common Council's deep concern at the implications of the Regulating Bill. He was seconded by John Wilkes, who observed that the Bill 'was founded on the principle of iniquity and robbery, as well as the barefaced violation of public faith and therefore ought to be opposed by every corporation in the kingdom, as well as every elector in it'.[36] The motion was then carried unanimously. With powerful extra-parliamentary allies such as these the Company could make life uncomfortable for the ministry, even though it could not offer a direct challenge to its supremacy in Parliament. But, even so, some observers detected more than a hint of desperation about the Company's actions;

[29] General Evening Post, 25 May 1773.   [30] IOR, B/89, pp. 169–74.
[31] The petition is printed in CJ, XXXIV, 346.
[32] IOR, B/89, p. 193. This decision was taken at the General Court of 27 May.
[33] The initiative for this came from the Duke of Richmond; General Evening Post, 27 May 1773.   [34] List of Proprietors, p. 37.
[35] Gentleman's Magazine (1773), p. 253.
[36] London Evening Post, 29 May 1773.

a desperation that was born out of a realization of their weak and hopeless political position.[37]

The petition from the Common Council was presented to the Commons on the day that it was drafted, 28 May, and, at the same time, the House received the Company's petition against the Regulating Bill.[38] The Company's Chairman, Henry Crabb Boulton, asked that Counsel be heard in support of the petition in the Committee of the Whole House, which was scheduled to discuss the Regulating Bill the same day. This request was granted, but only after the Speaker, Sir Fletcher Norton, had declared his opinion that because the Committee stage was for the detailed consideration of legislation, 'the House would hardly hear them against the principle of the Bills'.[39] The Counsel, James Adair and James Mansfield, heeded this warning and presented the Company's objections in speeches which lasted for an hour and a half.[40] Their detailed objections were founded upon three heads: first, that the Bill would disfranchise 1,246 proprietors; second, that vesting power in a Governor-General and Council was impracticable; and, thirdly, that the appointment of the Bengal Supreme Court judges by the Crown would present the ministry with 'full and absolute power over the possessions of the Company'.

The ensuing debate centred upon the first clause of the Bill, that related to the Company's annual election. Both William Dowdeswell and George Dempster defended the existing system, the former declaring in no uncertain terms that the only reason for the introduction of new regulations was that they would facilitate ministerial control over the Company.[41] Administration speakers responded to this in vigorous fashion,[42] but the most remarkable development of the debate, perhaps of the entire session, occurred when North rose to speak. Abandoning his customary caution, he made an extraordinary declaration. He identified the major flaw in the Company's structure as being the inability of the Court of Directors to cope with their responsibilities. He then stated that 'I have a direct, declared, open purpose of conveying the whole power [and] management of the East India Company either directly or indirectly to the Crown, and this cause is given as the first instance: Sir, the directors cannot govern their concerns as it is now [sic].' In these circumstances North had no hesitation in proposing the transfer of responsibility for the administration of these important possessions to the Crown. In case anyone had misunderstood him, he

[37] John Yorke to Lord Hardwicke, 28 May 1773, BL, Add. MSS 35375, f. 83.
[38] CJ, XXXIV, 343, 346–7.   [39] BL, Eg. MSS 249, pp. 56–7.
[40] Ibid., 249, pp. 58–69.   [41] Ibid., 249, pp. 69–79.
[42] See, for example, the speech of Welbore Ellis; ibid., 249, pp. 79–83.

concluded his short speech by repeating his view that the Company's territory would be 'better administered by the Crown that is so ill administered by directors so incapable of governing it'.[43]

North's statement supplied plenty of ammunition to all those who had long identified the ministry's main purpose in the East India business as being the transfer of power and patronage to the Crown. Dowdeswell reiterated all these familiar arguments,[44] but North found powerful support from within the Company itself where Clive and Sulivan had been advocating such a reform for some years. Fresh from his triumph in the House a week earlier, Clive was now free to return to his favourite role as self-appointed advisor to the House on Company affairs. He restated his views on the flawed nature of the Company's constitution, and he pressed for a Direction that was elected for a three-year term of office.[45] Such was the weight of opinion in favour of change that few speakers chose to defend the old system, and although Dowdeswell fought a determined rearguard action, it was apparent that he was flying in the face of prevailing opinion. This was demonstrated when the clause was agreed to without a division, after an amendment had been made to the effect that in the interests of continuity in Company decision-making only six directors should stand for re-election each year.[46]

The Committee then proceeded to a consideration of future voters' qualifications, a clause upon which there was far less agreement in the House. Objections were founded upon two main arguments: the Bill if enacted would deprive existing proprietors of their rights, and it would not serve its intended purpose of putting an end to stock splitting.[47] North stood firm, although he did propose a slight amendment which would allow a longer period for proprietors to acquire additional stock before the new regulations came into effect.[48] The question was then put that the qualification for voters at the General Court should be raised from £500 to £1,000, and this was resolved in the affirmative by 179 votes to 56, figures which represented a comfortable majority in view of the determined resistance that had been mounted against the ministry during the debate on this controversial issue.[49]

The Committee on the Regulating Bill sat again on 2 June, and the day's proceedings were dominated by the subject of future Crown

---

[43] *Ibid.*, 249, pp. 84–6.   [44] *Ibid.*, 249, pp. 98–9.

[45] *Ibid.*, 249, pp. 99–100.

[46] John Yorke to Lord Hardwicke, 29 May 1773, BL, Add. MSS 35375, f. 85.

[47] See, for example, the speeches of Sir Richard Sutton, George Johnstone, George Dempster, Herbert Mackworth, and William Dowdeswell; BL, Eg. MSS, 249, pp. 110–12, 115–19.

[48] *Ibid.*, 249, p. 109. He proposed that the regulations should come into effect in October 1773.   [49] *Ibid.*, 249, p. 125.

appointments of judges and Council members in Bengal.[50] By now even the most committed MPs were tiring of the whole business, and there was little to excite the opposition and provoke meaningful debate.[51] Dempster, Dowdeswell, and Johnstone did, as ever, maintain a stubborn resistance to the ministry but this was little more than a forlorn gesture. Few significant amendments were made to the clauses and North's proposals survived the Committee stage largely intact.

Although this debate of 2 June was a lack-lustre affair it did nevertheless give rise to many important expressions of opinion about the Company's executive, administrative, and judicial affairs in Bengal. North concentrated upon the need to draw a very distinct line between British civil and commercial responsibilities. He again described his Bill as an experiment, this time on the grounds that 'military and civil commands should be separate from the commercial'. In order to do this, and to discourage those in positions of executive authority from indulging in private trading activities, he announced the payment of handsome salaries to high officeholders: £25,000 to the Governor-General, £10,000 to the councillors, £6,000 to the Chief Justice, and £5,000 to the other officers, including judges.[52] This initiative was applauded by Clive, who declared that appointments under such terms would endow individuals with 'stronger ideas of doing their duty'.[53] However, a number of stockholding MPs again argued that North's measures would throw the Company into the hands of the Crown and the ministry.

George Johnstone made a long speech on the subject, and he declared that the ministry's entire position was based upon a fundamental misunderstanding of the Company's role in Bengal. He argued that a line could not, and should not, be drawn between the commercial interests of the Company and its political and military activities.[54] Laurence Sulivan developed this theme and declared that as the native population 'never part with their money but by compulsion' it would be impossible for the Company to pursue its activities without the executive authority 'vested in its own hand'.[55]

The debate drifted on in this vein for some time, but it was clear that general discussion of the Company's operating practices would not hinder the progress of the Bill for very long. This proved to be the case when the question was finally put, that the Governor-General and

---

[50] This was after the loan of £1,400,000 from state to Company had been agreed to by the House on 29 May, and after it had been ordered that the measure be drafted into a Bill.
[51] Soame Jenyns to Lord Hardwicke, 3 June 1773, BL, Add. MSS 35631, f. 170.
[52] BL, Eg. MSS 249, pp. 126–31.   [53] Ibid., 249, p. 132.
[54] Ibid., 249, pp. 136–51.   [55] Ibid., 249, p. 168.

Council be appointed by the Crown, and the motion was passed by 161 votes to 60.[56] Once more the opposition had raised important theoretical objections which were swept aside by the ministry's numbers: the attempt to focus debate on consideration of how reform would affect the Company's operational status and responsibilities in India was a failure. The ministry could not afford a diversion at a time when thoughts of the summer recess were uppermost in the minds of most uncommitted MPs, and hence North had few qualms about pressing on with the business as fast as possible. He could not at this point allow lengthy debate about the detailed mechanics of British imperial activity on the subcontinent.

The Committee completed its business the following day, 3 June, when the few remaining clauses were discussed. With the main principles of the Bill firmly established all that remained was the addition of some of the outstanding details. North had steered the Bill this far without encountering too many problems. Although it had been a protracted and often tedious business, this was a consequence of the detailed nature of the Bill rather than opposition to it during the Committee stage. In fact the Committee had been characterized by a notable lack of sustained opposition to the ministry. The various division results had demonstrated the strength of the ministry's position, and this indicated that North would have few problems in bringing the business to a swift and satisfactory conclusion.

The printed Bill was read to the House on 8 June and, after receiving two petitions of protest from the Company,[57] the House began to vote on each clause of the measure. Only one important addition was made at this stage. Rose Fuller suggested that a system of proportional voting might be incorporated in the Bill and, because North admitted that he agreed with this important amendment, it was added at the very last moment. From 1 October 1773 owners of £1,000 Company stock would be entitled to one vote at the General Court; those owning £3,000 would have two votes; £6,000 would bring three votes; and £10,000 would allow four votes to be cast.[58] There had been discussion of such a measure a few weeks earlier, but Fuller had bided his time and waited until it was likely that his proposal would be accepted; that is, when the main battles over the Bill had been won and lost.[59] The only difficulties

[56] *Ibid.*, 249, p. 207. Parliament would only name the Governor-General and Council in the first instance. Thereafter, any vacancies would be filled by the directors.

[57] Both petitions complained about the violation of the Company's chartered rights. One was from Alexander Dalrymple, who was later to become the Company's Hydrographer; while the other, presented by Henry Crabb Boulton, was from a group of disaffected and soon to be disfranchised £500 stockholders: *CJ*, XXXIV, 362.

[58] For these, and other minor amendments, see *ibid.*, XXXIV, 363.

[59] *London Evening Post*, 29 May 1773; Cobbett, *Parl. Hist.*, XVII, 891. Fuller had raised the matter at the Committee stage, but had then withdrawn the measure. Had his

that were encountered came when the time came to fill in the blanks in the Bill related to the appointment of the Governor-General and his four-man Council.

North had recommended Warren Hastings as Governor-General as early as 3 May, and his appointment was now confirmed without any debate or opposition.[60] However, difficulties arose over the appointment of the Council members when North recommended that General Sir John Clavering, George Monson, Richard Barwell, and Philip Francis be nominated.[61] Thomas Townshend junior moved the previous question on Clavering's name and proposed that General Robert Monckton be named in his place. Earlier in the day Townshend had presented a petition to the House on Monckton's behalf. In the petition the General had established his distinguished military credentials, and reminded MPs that the previous year the Company had appointed him as one of their commissioners or supervisors. He asked that as another appointment 'under another name' was now being made he should not be overlooked. If he was, it would leave a 'disgraceful mark' against his character and good name.[62]

This placed the ministry in an embarrassing position for they would now have to make a direct choice between Monckton and Clavering.[63] Indeed, the King, also the recipient of a petition from Monckton, had become embroiled in the dispute. He had suggested that by way of compensation Monckton could be offered command of the army in North America at the first vacancy but, when the General turned this idea down, the King came to the conclusion that he was being used by Company proprietors to embarrass the ministry and he recommended that the petition be rejected.[64] North thus entered the debate on 8 June with this in mind. The proceedings were punctuated with lavish praise for both men and many speakers argued that Monckton could not be discarded by the ministry as the Company were already considering appointing him to their military command. Again, however, the weight of ministerial numbers was the decisive factor and, when the main question was put, it was agreed that Clavering's name should stand as a member of the Council together with those of the other appointees. The dispute over the rival claims of Monckton and Clavering represented the very last stage of the debate on the content of the Regulating Bill,

amendment been formally overruled as Sutherland suggests (*East India Company*, p. 263), it could not have been reintroduced at the report stage because that would have contravened parliamentary practice.   [60] Cobbett, *Parl. Hist.*, XVII, 896.

[61] BL, Eg. MSS 250, pp. 63–6.   [62] *CJ*, XXXIV, 361–2.

[63] Clavering (1722–77) had led the attack on Guadeloupe in 1759, although the operation had been nominally under the command of Lord Barrington. For Monckton see above p. 137, n. 20.

[64] George III to North, 4 and 8 June 1773, *George III Corr.*, II, nos. 1262, 1265.

because at the end of the proceedings on 8 June it was resolved that the final reading of the Bill would take place two days later.

Within the Company Clavering's appointment to the new Council was identified as an issue upon which further opposition could be mounted against the ministry. This opposition was heightened when North met with the directors on 9 June and asked that Clavering be appointed as Commander-in-Chief of the Company's forces. The directors declared that acceptance of a ministerial nominee would provoke considerable resentment in the General Court, but they resolved to continue discussion of the matter a week later.[65] However, events in the General Court on 11 June pre-empted any action by the directors when, at the prompting of the Duke of Richmond, the proprietors threw out a direct challenge to the ministry by appointing Monckton as Commander-in-Chief.[66] The King suggested to North the following day that he speak to the General so that 'after the former kindness expressed towards him [he] will...I trust decline nomination'.[67] Such a crude attempt to influence Monckton proved to be unnecessary, however, for the General had already declined the post, thus offering the ministry an escape from a tight political corner.[68]

Of more immediate concern to the ministry was a resolution passed by the General Court on 11 June to withdraw its formal application to the ministry for a loan. This decision was based on the grounds that the terms of the Loan Bill were 'disadvantageous and unreasonable', and that the terms of the Regulating Bill were 'subversive of the rights of the Company'.[69] This defiant opposition had been prompted by events in the House of Commons the previous day, when the Loan Bill had passed its first reading and the Regulating Bill had received its third and final reading. When the Loan Bill was introduced there was a protracted debate over whether the Company was obliged to accept the terms of the financial settlement. In particular, Charles Cornwall made a strong case against forcing the loan upon the Company without its consent. Nevertheless, North assured the House that, whether or not the Company accepted the loan, the Bill secured the Company's many creditors. In spite of strong protests from George Dempster, North declared that it was not necessary for the House to await the sentiments of the Company, and it was ordered that the Bill be read a second time.[70]

Opposition to the Regulating Bill had centred upon two long speeches

[65] IOR, B/89, pp. 203–5.   [66] Ibid., B/89, p. 213.
[67] George III to North, 12 June 1773, George III Corr., II, no. 1274. As compensation for his failure to gain a place on the Council, Monckton was granted land on the West Indian island of St Vincent. This was done on the pretext that it was being given in recognition of the part he had played in the capture of Martinique in 1762.
[68] IOR, B/89, p. 238.   [69] Ibid., B/89, p. 213.
[70] BL, Eg. MSS 250, pp. 109, 111, 117.

from William Dowdeswell and Edmund Burke, the latter of whom was breaking his silence on the ministry's East India legislation. Both men rather predictably returned to well-worn themes: the abrogation of chartered rights, and the unjustifiable increase in Crown patronage.[71] The Bengal dimension received little attention. The battle-weary opposition was now fighting a lost cause, and the debate excited very little interest. The concluding remarks were made by North who conceded that, despite many useful amendments, the Bill was still far from perfect. However, he maintained that a sound start, but only a start, had been made in the ministry's attempt to regulate British activity in India. The Company's management had been placed on a firm footing at home, and this could only lead to better decision-making and greater stability in future.[72] The Bill was then approved by 131 to 21. The King was delighted at this outcome, but he too believed that this was only the first step in an ongoing review of Company affairs. The measures, he declared to North on 11 June, 'lay the foundation for a constant inspection from Parliament into the affairs of the Company which must require a succession of regulations every year; for new abuses will naturally come to light, which in the end Parliament alone can in any degree check'.[73]

A start had indeed been made, but the administrative guidelines established by the Act would have to be the subject of constant and thorough examination, certainly in 1780 when the charter expired. It was assumed that a significant amount of parliamentary time each year would be devoted to this monitoring of Indian affairs but, of course, this presupposed that politicians were not preoccupied with other affairs. In the event, the crisis in the American colonies undermined North's East Indian strategy. Ministers and parliamentarians had little time to consider events in the East during the late 1770s as they struggled to come to terms with problems in the West and, because of this, India did not again adopt a central position in British politics until the 1780s, when the Company's affairs were once more plunged into crisis.

With the passage of the Regulating Bill safely negotiated, attention turned to the Loan Bill. George III evidently believed that the business would soon be complete, for he informed North that he intended to prorogue Parliament on 26 June.[74] But there was still the last stubborn resistance of the Company to overcome. This manifested itself on 15 June, when a petition asking for the withdrawal of the Company's previous requests for assistance was presented in the Commons by Henry Crabb Boulton.[75] The petition was not well received, and the fact that it had not been balloted for in the customary Company fashion

---

[71] Ibid., 250, pp. 119–60, 181–223.   [72] Ibid., 250, pp. 241–50.
[73] George III Corr., II, no. 1271.   [74] Ibid.   [75] CJ, XXXIV, 374–5.

served to anger many Members.[76] One government supporter, Jeremiah Dyson, made much of this point and he reminded the House that the General Court had overwhelmingly endorsed the original application for a loan from the state.[77] Even members of the opposition were annoyed and frustrated by the Company's *volte face*, and Charles Cornwall, who only a few days earlier had defended the Company's right to refuse assistance, advanced the opinion that the application of the loan to the Company's debts should now be made compulsory.[78] The House agreed with these sentiments and voted that the withdrawal of the request for assistance should not be granted.

The Committee on the Loan Bill met again on 17 June, and North reported that as acceptance of the Bill had now been made obligatory a number of amendments had been made. This had been done so as to sugar the bitter pill of reform for the Company, and thereby to put an end to resistance from the General Court. The immediate claim of the public to a share of the territorial revenues was suspended, although the state's right to the acquisitions was again asserted. With regard to the dividend, payments were restricted to 6 per cent until the loan was repaid, and to 7 per cent until the bond debt was reduced to £1,500,000. Thereafter the composite surplus accruing from the territorial revenues and commercial profits would remain with the Company alone. The previously mentioned term of six years was deleted, and the state effectively gave up its claim to a share of the revenues. This important last-minute reshaping of the Bill was unanimously endorsed by a House that was now eager to complete the business.[79]

The proceedings were still not at an end, for two further amendments were proposed. First, Secretary to the Treasury Grey Cooper proposed that the Company should in future be obliged to export annually to India British manufactures worth £387,000. This was opposed by Boulton and Sulivan, and North declared that it was a matter of 'too much delicacy' to be entered into at this late stage. However, the minister then gave notice that he would himself propose an amendment which would limit the Company's future acceptance of bills of exchange to £300,000.[80] This he never did, but the debate continued in the Committee the following day when Cooper's amendment was discussed again. The directors, who had resolved to draw attention to the 'injurious nature' of the exportation clause, informed the House that British manufactures to the value of £407,130 already lay unsold in the Company's Indian warehouses, and that goods worth £292,815 had

---

[76] The difficulties of the situation, not least of which was the lack of available time, had meant that it had been impossible to submit the petition to the proprietors for approval.
[77] Cobbett, *Parl. Hist.*, XVII, 926.   [78] *Ibid.*, XVII, 923–4. Cf. above p. 182.
[79] BL, Eg. MSS 250, pp. 327–32.   [80] *Parl. Hist.*, XVII, 929.

been sent out in the previous season.[81] It was reported that the ministry 'relaxed' after the presentation of these statistics and, at length, upon an amendment from George Johnstone, the House voted that the Company should be obliged to export only £287,000 worth of manufactures each year.[82] The following day, 19 June, the Bill passed its final reading.

In order to ease the passage of his legislation through the House at the end of a long session, North had made rather more concessions than he perhaps would have wished at the outset. Indeed, the Company had secured almost everything that it had asked for and, to this extent, the campaign of resistance fought by directors and proprietors had been a successful one. The only remaining major area of concern was that the ministry would be able to interfere much more easily in the Company's affairs both at home and abroad. Nevertheless, the legislative framework established by North at a very early stage of the proceedings had survived largely intact. But, in view of the attention he had devoted to the subject, the most surprising development had been the last-minute suspension of the state's claim to a share of the Bengal revenues. The principle that had underpinned the agreements of 1767 and 1769 was abandoned as a consequence of the Company's complete inability to meet its financial obligations. However, suspension of the claim had enabled the ministry to wring important concessions from the Company; namely the acceptance of the loan and its intended application. As far as North was concerned, like other aspects of his policy, the whole question of the territorial revenues would be reviewed in 1780.

With the business in the House of Commons now complete, attention turned to the House of Lords where the opposition and, in particular, the Rockinghamites, promised and again delivered a vigorous challenge to the ministry. But the Lords had waited a long time for the legislation to arrive from the Commons. The delays meant that there was little important business for peers to attend to and daily attendance in the House was very low. Thus, while there were more meetings of the Lords in the session of 1772–3 than in any other between 1760 and 1775, the average daily attendance was far lower than at any other time.[83] The East Indian legislation was contested by the Rockinghams in a thinly attended House but, even then, their weakness in numbers was such that they could do little to prevent the measures entering the statute book. In debate the Rockinghamite peers led by the Duke of Richmond adopted the same arguments that had been used by Burke and Dowdeswell in the Commons, but speeches made little impression in a House with a large

---

[81] IOR, B/89, pp. 224–5.   [82] *Parl. Hist.*, XVII, cols. 930–1.

[83] There were 106 meetings in the session of 1772–3, with an average daily attendance of 24 peers; W.C. Lowe, 'Politics in the House of Lords, 1760–1775', unpublished Ph.D thesis, Emory University, 1975, p. 943.

ministerial majority. Instead, the most effective weapon they used was the employment of a number of delaying procedural tactics in an attempt to disrupt the ministry's legislative timetable. They asked for a conference with the Commons; they requested that the Secret Committee reports be read in the Lords; and they entered *Protests* against the ministry's handling of the business.[84] But this was to no avail.

During the third week of June the Regulating Bill was voted on clause by clause, but at no time did the opposition threaten the ministry's majority. The end came on 19 June when the Regulating Bill was passed by 47 votes to 15. Following a call for proxies, the figures were amended to read 74 in favour of the Bill and only 17 against, and the Rockinghams had to content themselves with entering yet another *Protest* on the record of the day's proceedings.[85] This gesture was made by thirteen peers, but it was no more than a defiant act from a thoroughly dispirited and downhearted opposition. The long passage of the Regulating Bill was complete but, as the Rockinghams had complained in their *Protest*, it had taken eight weeks for the Bill to pass through the Commons and only eight days to pass through the Lords. Three days later, on 22 June, the King was able to set out to inspect the fleet at Portsmouth as planned, and a week later the Loan Bill, having enjoyed an uncontested passage through the House, was approved by the Lords.[86] Royal Assent was given to the Regulating Act on 21 June, and to the Loan Act on 1 July, and they entered the statute book as 13 Geo. III, c. 63 and c. 64 respectively.

[84] See, for example, *LJ*, XXXIII, 670–1.   [85] *Ibid.*, XXXIII, 680–1.
[86] Walpole, *Last Journals*, I, 239.

Conclusion

The parliamentary session of 1772–3 represented a watershed in the development of the relationship between the state and the East India Company. The statutory arrangements formulated by North and his colleagues were no more, and intended to be no more, than temporary measures, but they did serve to extend government control over the Company at home. However, it remained to be seen whether or not reforms generated in Britain by ministers and politicians could solve the Company's economic and administrative problems in Bengal. Whatever the outcome, and examination of that matter lies beyond the scope of this study, North, unlike his predecessors, had made a very real attempt to come to terms with the responsibilities that went hand in hand with the extension of the Company's commercial and political activities. He fully recognized that a permanent solution to the questions related to the Bengal territorial revenues had not been found, but that had not been his overriding concern. Necessity, the collapse of the East India Company, had demanded that he look well beyond the extraction of a simple financial return from British activity in Bengal. Reform had replaced revenue in the ministerial order of priorities, and it was now accepted in government circles that without quite fundamental change Bengal would remain little more than a very fragile British asset.

It is worth stressing that the gradual transformation in ministerial attitudes towards the Indian problem may partly be explained by placing Indian issues in a wider imperial context. While it is difficult to discern any direct connexion between American and Indian policy, it is nevertheless possible to see ministers attempting to exert a much stronger general degree of control over British overseas affairs during the 1760s and 1770s. In particular, the hitherto unchecked and unregulated development of British activity in the Southern Hemisphere was closely monitored by ministers during the late 1760s in a way that bears a striking similarity to attempts to control, if not prohibit, expansion into the American interior.[1] In most metropolitan quarters (speculators apart) possession of new territory, be it in Awadh, Borneo, or the American wilderness, was now seen as being dangerous and expensive. It was for this reason that many politicians increasingly sought a direct financial return from the nation's overseas territories. Of course, trade profit was still important in its own right, but this alone could not pay for the deployment of the Crown armed forces, naval squadrons, and administrators that were necessary for the protection of British interests. In an Indian context, this concern manifested itself in Chatham's clumsy attempt to direct some of the Company's revenue profit away from private pockets and into the Treasury's coffers. Different solutions to essentially the same problem were to be found in ministerial schemes such as the Stamp Act and the Townshend Duties Act, which were designed to make North American colonists contribute towards the cost of governing and defending British North America. These financial issues formed the cornerstone of political involvement and interest in imperial affairs, as ministers from George Grenville to Lord North sought to balance the imperial books in an attempt to ensure that the cost of maintaining a large and growing empire did not outstrip the nation's ability to pay for it.[2]

At first few ministers saw beyond this narrowly defined problem. Thus, while in the thirteen colonies the increase in duty payments did not produce by way of compensation any redefinition of the British–American political relationship, in an Indian context the state stood back from accepting any responsibility for ensuring that the East India Company performed its functions properly and in keeping with national interests. Chatham in 1767, Grafton in 1769, and, indeed, North in 1770–1 were not prepared to involve themselves in any reassessment of the nature and purpose of British activity on the Indian subcontinent. Moreover, they steadfastly ignored the Company's pleas for legislative assistance. The opportunity for the creation of a state–Company partnership of equals was lost, and when reform did eventually come it was formulated in an atmosphere of crisis, acrimony, and hostility. This did not bode well for future good relations between ministers and the Company. Many felt, both inside and outside India House, that reform had been forced upon the Company in return for the state's financial help.

[1] British policy towards the American interior is discussed in Thomas, *Townshend Duties Crisis*, pp. 51–75. Of course, ministers took a much more active role in developing policy for America, but the comparison is still a valid one.
[2] Some of these issues are discussed in their broadest context in C.A. Bayly, *Imperial Meridian: The British Empire and the World 1780–1830* (1989), pp. 89–99. See also P.J. Marshall, 'Empire and authority in the later eighteenth century', *Journal of Imperial and Commonwealth History*, XV (1987), 105–22.

In many ways the legislative arrangements of 1773 do suggest a simple connexion between ministerial regulation of the Company's affairs and the reflation of corporate finances, but the Company did in fact obtain from Lord North many of the measures it had been requesting for years. Informed observers of British Indian affairs, such as Clive and Laurence Sulivan, accepted North's reforms as essential for the maintenance and future development of the Company's position in Bengal. In theory, private trade was prohibited by statute; large salaries were paid to senior Company servants; the administration of justice was improved; continuity in decision-making became easier; overall control of British activity in India was placed in the hands of a Governor-General and small executive council; and parliamentary and ministerial supervision of the Company's affairs was now to be conducted on a regular basis. Indeed, this comprehensive series of reforms prompted Sulivan to declare that North 'was the boldest minister this realm has been blest with since the days of Oliver Cromwell'.[3]

Yet, bold as he undoubtedly was in some areas, North, like most others, had failed to perceive the full scope of the Indian problem. No attempt had been made to establish a coherent economic policy for Bengal. This, many would have argued, was still the sole responsibility of the East India Company, but surprisingly little attention was devoted by those in government to the question of what part, if any, the Company could play in regenerating the Bengal economy. British economic interests in India were still dependent on flourishing indigenous agriculture, trade, and commerce, but many seemed resigned to the fact that Bengal had already been squeezed dry. After almost a decade of British control in the province, Bengal's economy was locked in a deep recession, the East India Company's finances were in disarray, and the state was forced into underwriting future operations. No-one, least of all the native population, had benefited from the Company's acquisition of the *Diwani*, and this was unlikely to change in the immediate future. All parties concerned would have been much better served if reform had preceded rather than followed the extraction of revenue from Bengal. As it was, the Indian problem was not solved, and its full extent was only gradually being realized.

[3] Quoted in Marshall, *Problems of Empire*, p. 34.

Select bibliography

PRIMARY SOURCES

A. MANUSCRIPTS

1. British Library

Additional MSS 18469: Evidence presented to the House of Commons Committee, 27 Mar.–13 Apr. 1767.
Add. MSS 29133–4: Hastings Papers.
Add. MSS 32976–82: Newcastle Papers.
Add. MSS 35349–36278: Hardwicke Papers.
Add. MSS 38397–8: Liverpool Papers.
Add. MSS 42084–7: Grenville Papers.
Add. MSS 57187A–B: Supplementary Grenville Papers.
Egerton MSS 215–63, 3711: Parliamentary Diary of Henry Cavendish (1768–74).

2. India Office Library

MSS Eur. G. 37: Clive Collection.
MSS Eur. F. 128: Sutton Court Collection.

3. India Office Records

B/82–9: Court Minutes (1766–73).
B/255–8: General Court Minutes (1702–73).
HMS vols. 100 and 101: Home Miscellaneous Series.

4. Public Record Office

30/8: Chatham Papers.
30/29: Granville Papers.
CO 77, vols. 21–2: Colonial Office Papers.
WO 1/679–82: War Office Papers.

5. Other Repositories

Bodleian Library, Oxford
MS. Eng. hist. b. 190–1, 237, c. 269–71: Laurence Sulivan Papers.
Central Library, Sheffield

Wentworth Woodhouse Muniments: Papers of the 2nd Marquess of Rocking-
   ham.
Mount Stuart, Isle of Bute
Loudoun Papers.
National Library of Wales, Aberystwyth
Clive Papers.
William L. Clements Library, Ann Arbor, Michigan
Lansdowne MSS: Papers of the 2nd Earl of Shelburne.
Suffolk Record Office, Ipswich
Papers of the 2nd Viscount Barrington.

B. PRINTED SOURCES

1. Official and Parliamentary Sources

Calendar of Home Office Papers ... 1760 to 1775 (4 vols., 1878–99).
House of Commons Sessional Papers of the Eighteenth Century, ed. S. Lambert
   (147 vols., Wilmington, Delaware, 1975).
Journals of the House of Commons.
Journals of the House of Lords.
*Ninth Report of the Select Committee of the House of Commons on East India
   Company Affairs* (1783).
Parliamentary Papers, VIII (1812–13), LII (1898).
Reports from Committees of the House of Commons, 1715–1801 (15 vols., 1803),
   III (Five reports from the Select Committee on East India Company
   Affairs, 1772–3), and IV (Nine reports from the Secret Committee on East
   India Company Affairs, 1772–3).
Statutes at Large, 1225–1800 (10 vols., 1811).
W. Cobbett, *Parliamentary History of England from ... 1066 to ... 1803* (36 vols.,
   1806–20).
R.C. Simmons and P.D.G. Thomas (eds.), *Proceedings and Debates of the British
   Parliaments Respecting North America 1754–1783* (6 vols., New York,
   1982 to date).
P.D.G. Thomas (ed.), 'The parliamentary diaries of Nathaniel Ryder 1764–7',
   Camden Miscellany, XXIII, Royal Historical Society, Camden Fourth
   Series, vol. VII (1969).

2. East India Company Records

*Fort William – India House Correspondence and Other Contemporary Papers
   Relating Thereto (Public Series)*, vol. IV: 1764–1766, ed. C.S. Srinivasachari
   (New Delhi, 1962); vol. V: 1767–9, ed. N.K. Sinha (New Delhi, 1949);
   (Select and Secret) vol. VI: 1770–2, ed. B. Prasad (New Delhi, 1960);
   (Secret and Select Committee), vol. XIV: 1752–1781, ed. A. Prasad (New
   Delhi, 1985).

3. Historical Manuscripts Commission Reports

Fourteenth Report, Appendix Part IV: Kenyon MSS (1894).
Report on the Palk MSS (1922).

4. Contemporary Correspondence, Memoirs, and Printed Books

The Correspondence of Edmund Burke, I: ed. T.W. Copeland (Cambridge, 1958), II: ed. L.S. Sutherland (Cambridge, 1960).

The Writings and Speeches of Edmund Burke, I: ed. P. Langford (Oxford, 1981).

William Bolts, *Consideration on Indian Affairs; Particularly Respecting the Present State of Bengal and its Dependencies* (1772).

The Correspondence of William Pitt, Earl of Chatham, ed. W.S. Taylor and J.H. Pringle (4 vols., 1838–40).

Sir George Colebrooke, *Retrospection: or Reminiscences Addressed to My Son Henry Thomas Colebrooke Esq.* (2 vols., 1898–9).

Alexander Dow, *The History of Hindostan* (3 vols., 1768–72).

The Correspondence of George III from 1760 to 1783, ed. Sir J. Fortescue (6 vols., 1927).

The Letters of Edward Gibbon, ed. J.E. Norton (3 vols., 1956).

The Autobiographical and Political Correspondence of Augustus Henry 3rd Duke of Grafton, ed. Sir William Anson (1898).

Memoirs of the Life of the Right Honourable Warren Hastings, ed. Rev. G.R. Gleig (3 vols., 1841).

J.Z. Holwell, *Important Facts Regarding the East India Company's Affairs in Bengal from the Year 1752 to 1760* (1764).

Thomas Mortimer, *The Elements of Commerce, Politics, and Finance in Three Treatises on Those Important Subjects* (1780, reprinted from the 1772 edition).

Thomas Pownall, *The Administration of the Colonies* (4th Edition, 1768).

The Correspondence of Adam Smith, eds. E.C. Mossner and I.S. Ross (Oxford, 1977).

Adam Smith, *An Inquiry into the Nature and Causes of the Wealth of Nations* (1776), eds R.H. Campbell, A.S. Skinner, and W.B. Todd (2 vols., Oxford, 1976).

Harry Verelst, *A View of the Rise, Progress, and Present State of the English Government in Bengal; Including a Reply to the Misrepresentations of Mr Bolts and Other Writers* (1772).

The Last Journals of Horace Walpole during the Reign of George III from 1771 to 1783, ed. A. Francis Steuart (2 vols., 1910).

Horace Walpole, *Memoirs of the Reign of King George the Third*, ed. G.F. Russell Barker, (4 vols., 1894).

The Yale Edition of Horace Walpole's Correspondence, ed. W.S. Lewis (48 vols., Oxford, 1939–84).

5. Contemporary Pamphlets and Tracts

Arranged alphabetically by author or by title where author is unknown.

An Address to the Proprietors of East India Stock, Showing from the Political State of Indostan, the Necessity of Sending Commissioners to Regulate their Affairs Abroad (1769).

An Attempt to Pay Off the National Debt by Abolishing the East India Company of Merchants and Other Monopolies with Other Interesting Measures (1767).

By-Laws, Constitutions, Orders and Rules for the...Government of the United Company of Merchants Trading to the East India Company (1709).

By-Laws, Constitutions, Orders and Rules of Government of the East India Company (1774).

A. Dalrymple, *A General View of the East India Company* (1772).

An Enquiry into the Rights of the East India Company of Making War and Peace; And of Possessing Their Territorial Acquisitions Without the Participation or Inspection of the British Government (1772).

An Essay on the East India Trade and its Importance to This Kingdom; With a Comparative View of the Dutch, French, and English Companies (1770).

The Genuine Minutes of the Select Committee Appointed by the House of Commons, Assembled at Westminster in the Fifth Session of the Thirteenth Parliament of Great Britain to Enquire into East Indian Affairs (1773).

A Letter to a Late Popular Director (L—S—Esq.) Relative to Indian Affairs and the Present Contests (1769).

A Letter to the Proprietors of East India Stock, Containing a Relation of the Negotiations with Government from 1767 to the Present Time, Respecting the Company's Acquisitions in India (1769).

A List of the Names of All the Proprietors of East India Stock; Distinguishing the Principal Stock Each Proprietor Now Holds and the Time When Such Proprietors Became Possessed Thereof (9 Mar. 1773).

T. Pownall, *The Right, Duty, and Interest of Government, as Concerned in the Affairs of the East Indies* (1773).

Report from the Committee of Proprietors, Appointed 1 December 1772...to Enquire into the Present State and Condition of the Company's Affairs (1773).

Vox Populi Vox Rei: Lord Weymouth's Appeal to a General Court of Indian Proprietors Considered (1769).

6. Contemporary Newspapers and Periodicals

Annual Register
Court and City Register
Gazetteer
General Evening Post
Gentleman's Magazine
Lloyd's Evening Post
London Chronicle
London Evening Post
London Magazine
Middlesex Journal
Monthly Review
Newcastle Chronicle
Public Advertiser
Royal Kalendar

SECONDARY WORKS

1. BOOKS

B. Barui, *The Salt Industry of Bengal, 1757–1800: A Study in the Interaction of British Monopoly Control and Indigenous Culture* (Calcutta, 1985).

C.A. Bayly, *Imperial Meridian: The British Empire and the World 1780–1830* (1989).

Indian Society and the Making of the British Empire (Cambridge, 1988).

M. Bence-Jones, *Clive of India* (1974).

J. Brewer, *Party Ideology and Popular Politics at the Accession of George III* (Cambridge, 1976).

J. Brooke, *The Chatham Administration 1766–1768* (1956).

A. Broome, *A History of the Rise and Progress of the Bengal Army* (1851).

K.N. Chaudhuri, *The Trading World of Asia and the English East India Company 1660–1760* (Cambridge, 1978).

Sir J. Clapham, *The Bank of England* (2 vols., Cambridge, 1944).

S.V. Desika Char (ed.), *Readings in the Constitutional History of India, 1757–1947* (Oxford, 1983).

H.T. Dickinson, *Liberty and Property: Political Ideology in Eighteenth-Century Britain* (1977).

P.G.M. Dickson, *The Financial Revolution in England: A Study in the Development of Public Credit 1688–1756* (1967).

H. Dodwell, *Dupleix and Clive: The Beginning of Empire* (1920, reprinted 1967).

Sir G. Forrest, *The Life of Lord Clive* (2 vols., 1918).

Sir J. Fortescue, *A History of the British Army* (13 vols., 1899–1930).

N.L. Hallward, *William Bolts: A Dutch Adventurer under John Company* (Cambridge, 1920).

V.T. Harlow, *The Founding of the Second British Empire, 1763–1795* (2 vols., 1952 and 1964).

J.M. Holzman, *The Nabobs in England 1760–1815: A Study of the Returned Anglo-Indian* (New York, 1926).

J.A. Houlding, *Fit for Service: The Training of the British Army, 1715–1795* (Oxford, 1982).

J.W. Kaye, *The Administration of the East India Company: A History of Indian Progress* (1853).

A.B. Keith, *A Constitutional History of India, 1600–1935* (1936).

A.M. Khan, *The Transition in Bengal, 1756–1775: A Study of Saiyid Muhammed Reza Khan* (Cambridge, 1969).

D. Kumar (ed.), *The Cambridge Economic History of India*, vol. II c. 1757–c. 1970 (Cambridge, 1983).

B.W. Labaree, *The Boston Tea Party* (Oxford, 1964).

A. Lamb, *British India and Tibet, 1766–1810* (2nd revised edn, 1986).

P. Langford, *A Polite and Commercial People: England 1727–1783* (Oxford, 1989).

P. Lawson, *George Grenville: A Political Life* (Oxford, 1984).

D. Macpherson, *The History of the European Commerce with India* (1818).

Sir John Malcolm, *The Life of Robert, Lord Clive; Collected from the Family*

Papers Communicated by the Earl of Powis to Major-General Sir John Malcolm (3 vols., 1836).

P.J. Marshall, *Bengal: The British Bridgehead. Eastern India 1740–1828* (Cambridge, 1987).

East Indian Fortunes: The British in Bengal in the Eighteenth Century (Oxford, 1976).

The Impeachment of Warren Hastings (Oxford, 1965).

Problems of Empire: Britain and India 1757–1813 (1968).

P.J. Marshall and G. Williams, *The Great Map of Mankind: British Perceptions of the World in the Age of Enlightenment* (1982).

B.B. Misra, *The Central Administration of the East India Company 1773–1834* (Manchester, 1959).

The Judicial Administration of the East India Company, 1765–1782 (Delhi, 1961).

Sir L. Namier, *England in the Age of the American Revolution* (2nd ed., 1961).

The Structure of Politics at the Accession of George III (2nd ed., 1957).

Sir L. Namier and J. Brooke, *Charles Townshend* (1964).

Sir L. Namier and J. Brooke (eds.), *History of Parliament. The House of Commons 1754–1790* (3 vols., 1964).

P. Nightingale, *Trade and Empire in Western India, 1784–1806* (Cambridge, 1970).

F. O'Gorman, *The Rise of Party: The Rockingham Whigs 1760–1782* (1975).

M. Peters, *Pitt and Popularity: The Patriot Minister and London Opinion During the Seven Years' War* (Oxford, 1980).

C.H. Philips, *The East India Company 1784–1834* (Manchester, 1940).

J.M. Sosin, *Whitehall and the Wilderness: The Middle West in British Colonial Policy 1750–1775* (Lincoln, Neb., 1965).

P. Spear, *The Nabobs: A Study of the Social Life of the English in Eighteenth-Century India* (Oxford, 1932).

F.C. Spooner, *Risks at Sea: Amsterdam Insurance and Maritime Europe 1766–1782* (Cambridge, 1983).

L.S. Sutherland, *The East India Company in Eighteenth-Century Politics* (Oxford, 1952).

Finance and Politics in the Eighteenth Century, ed. A. Newman (1984).

P.D.G. Thomas, *British Politics and the Stamp Act Crisis: The First Phase of the American Revolution, 1763–1767* (Oxford, 1975).

The House of Commons in the Eighteenth Century (Oxford, 1971).

Lord North (1976).

The Townshend Duties Crisis: The Second Phase of the American Revolution 1767–1773 (Oxford, 1987).

I.B. Watson, *Foundations for Empire: English Private Trade in India, 1659–1760* (New Delhi, 1980).

B. Williams, *The Life of William Pitt, Earl of Chatham* (2 vols., 1913).

2. ARTICLES AND OCCASIONAL PUBLICATIONS

H.V. Bowen, ' "Dipped in the traffic": East India stockholders in the House of Commons, 1768–74', *Parliamentary History*, V (1986), 39–53.

'The East India Company and military recruitment in Britain, 1763–71', *Bulletin of the Institute of Historical Research*, LIX (1986), 78–90.

'Investment and empire in the later eighteenth century: East India stockholding, 1756–1791', *Economic History Review*, 2nd ser., XLII (1989), 186–206.

'Lord Clive and speculation in East India Company stock, 1766', *Historical Journal*, XXX (1987), 905–20.

'A question of sovereignty? The Bengal land revenue issue, 1765–67', *Journal of Imperial and Commonwealth History*, XVI (1988), 155–76.

G.J. Bryant, 'Officers of the East India Company's army in the days of Clive and Hastings', *Journal of Imperial and Commonwealth History*, VI (1978), 203–27.

'Pacification in the early British Raj, 1755–85', *Journal of Imperial and Commonwealth History*, XIII (1985), 3–19.

P.J. Cain and A.G. Hopkins, 'The political economy of British expansion overseas, 1750–1914', *Economic History Review*, 2nd ser., XXXIII (1980), 463–90.

R. Davis, 'English foreign trade, 1700–1774', *Economic History Review*, 2nd ser., XV (1962–3), 285–301.

W. B. Elofson, 'The Rockingham Whigs in transition: The East India Company issue 1772–1773', *English Historical Review*, CIV (1989), 947–74.

H. Hamilton, 'The failure of the Ayr Bank, 1772', *Economic History Review*, 2nd ser., VIII (1955–6), 405–17.

E. Hughes (ed.), 'Lord North's correspondence, 1766–1783', *English Historical Review*, LXII (1957), 218–38.

P. Lawson, 'Parliament and the first East India inquiry, 1767', *Parliamentary History*, I (1982), 99–114.

B. Lenman and P. Lawson, 'Robert Clive, the "black jagir", and British politics', *Historical Journal*, XXVI (1983), 801–29.

P.J. Marshall, 'British expansion in India in the eighteenth century: a historical revision', *History*, LX (1975), 28–43.

'Empire and authority in the late eighteenth century', *Journal of Imperial and Commonwealth History*, XV (1987), 105–17.

P.E. Mirowski, 'The rise (and retreat) of a market: English joint-stock shares in the eighteenth century', *Journal of Economic History*, XLI (1981), 559–77.

C.H. Philips, 'The Secret Committee of the East India Company', *Bulletin of the School of Oriental and African Studies*, X (1940–2), 299–315, 699–716.

R.B. Sheridan, 'The British credit crisis of 1772 and the American colonies', *Journal of Economic History*, XX (1960), 161–86.

P.D.G. Thomas, 'Sources for debates of the House of Commons, 1768–1774', *Bulletin of the Institute of Historical Research*, Special Supplement no. 4 (1959).

R.P. Thomas and D.N. McCloskey, 'Overseas trade and empire, 1700–1860' in R. Floud and D.N. McCloskey (eds.), *The Economic History of Britain Since 1700. I: 1700–1860* (1981), 87–102.

N. Tracy, 'Parry of a threat to India, 1768–1774', *Mariner's Mirror*, LIX (1973), 35–48.

3. UNPUBLISHED UNIVERSITY THESES

H.V. Bowen, 'British politics and the East India Company, 1766–1773' (University of Wales Ph.D., 1986).

J.D. Gurney, 'The debts of the Nawab of Arcot, 1763–1776' (University of Oxford D.Phil., 1968).

W.C. Lowe, 'Politics in the House of Lords, 1760–1775' (Emory University Ph.D., 1975).

J.D. Nichol, 'The British in India 1740–1763: a study of imperial expansion into Bengal' (University of Cambridge Ph.D., 1976).

J.G. Parker, 'The directors of the East India Company, 1754–1790' (University of Edinburgh Ph.D., 1977).

T. Shearer, 'Crisis and change in the development of the East India Company, 1760–1773' (University of Oxford D.Phil., 1976).

J.P. Thomas, 'The British empire and the press, 1763–1774' (University of Oxford D.Phil., 1982).

F.D. Van Aalst, 'The British view of India, 1750–1785' (University of Pennsylvania Ph.D., 1970).

Index

Aberdeen, 19
Adair, James, 33, 42, 43, 149n., 154, 155, 158, 177
Afghans, 69
Agreement of 1767, details of, 65
Aldercron, Colonel, 53n.
Allahabad, 7
American Department, 26
Amherst, Sir Jeffrey, 136
Annual Register, 2, 28
Aubert, William, 106
Aurora, the, 83, 98n., 133
Awadh, 68, 188
Ayr Bank, 127

Balambangan, 69, 70, 74
Bank of England, 36, 103, 127–8
Barré, Isaac, 26, 54, 55, 57, 62n., 92n., 136, 173
Barrington, William Wildman, 2nd Viscount Barrington, 62n., 91–2, 181n.
Bath, 89
Batson, Stanlake, 158n.
Beauchamp, Lord, *see* Seymour Conway, Francis
Becher, Richard, 30, 172
Beckford, William, 19–20, 21, 51, 57, 59, 62n., 64, 144
Bedfords, 50, 142, 173
Bengal, administration of, 9–11
    British expansion in, 5–7
    economy of, 103, 104, 106–7, 108
    justice in, 93–4, 99–101
    revenue collection in, 7–9, 103–4, 113–14
    revenues of, 55–7
    settlement of 1765, 7
Bihar, 6, 8, 11, 49, 57, 69, 113
bills of exchange, 116, 119–20, 136, 184
Bishop's Castle, 17, 98n.
Blackstone, William, 63

Bolts, William, 28, 95, 96
Bombay, 10, 69, 89, 120
Borneo, 69, 70n., 188
Boston, 122
Boston Tea Party, 164
Boulton, Henry Crabb, 33, 38, 42, 126, 165, 177, 180n., 183, 184
Bristol, 19
bullion, exports by Company, 110–11, 112
Bulwant Singh, 68
Burdwan, 8, 103, 113
Burgoyne, John, 33, 92n., 97, 134, 135, 136
    attack on Clive by, 169–73
    and re-establishment of Select Committee, 145–6
Burke, Edmund, 23, 24, 31, 33, 35, 43, 55, 60, 62, 97, 100, 129, 131, 136, 137, 142, 144, 146, 149, 150, 151, 172, 185
    attacks North ministry, 160, 161, 163
    criticizes Regulating Bill, 181–2
    views on East India Company, 140–1
Burke, William, 33, 42
Burrell, William, 131, 144, 146
Bute, Lord, *see* Stuart, John
Buxar, battle of, 5

Caillaud, John, 42, 43, 88, 166
Calcutta, 8, 10, 85, 93, 114, 117, 118, 136
Camden, Lord, *see* Pratt, Charles
Campbell, Lord Frederick, 146n.
Canton, 108, 122, 125
Cape of Good Hope, 133
Caribbean, 17
Carmanassa, River, 69
Carnac, John, 32
Carnatic, 23, 69
Cartier, John, 120n.
Catherlough, Lord, 62n.
Cavendish, Lord John, 148

Printed in the United Kingdom
by Lightning Source UK Ltd.
101427UKS00003BB/205-207